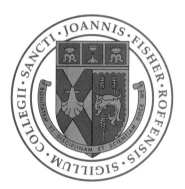

Shortcuts
for
Smart Managers

Shortcuts
for
Smart Managers

Checklists, Worksheets, and Action Plans for Managers With No Time to Waste

Lisa Davis

AMACOM

American Management Association

New York • Atlanta • Boston • Chicago • Kansas City • San Francisco • Washington, D.C.
Brussels • Mexico City • Tokyo • Toronto

This book is available at a special
discount when ordered in bulk quantities.
For information, contact Special Sales Department,
AMACOM, a division of American Management Association,
1601 Broadway, New York, NY 10019.

*This publication is designed to provide accurate and authoritative
information in regard to the subject matter covered. It is sold with the
understanding that the publisher is not engaged in rendering legal,
accounting, or other professional service. If legal advice or other expert
assistance is required, the services of a competent professional person
should be sought.*

Library of Congress Cataloging-in-Publication Data

Davis, Lisa, 1945–
      *Shortcuts for smart managers : checklists, worksheets, and action
      plans for managers with no time to waste / Lisa Davis.*
            p.   cm.
      Includes index.
      ISBN 0-8144-0432-4
      1. Management.   I. Title.
HD31.D248   1998
658—dc21   *98-14987*
                                                                CIP

Printing number

10   9   8   7   6   5   4   3   2   1

To the memory of my parents,
Brenda and Nathan Davis

Contents

List of Organizer Sheets

Introduction

For most people, the struggle up the corporate ladder can be a little like a safari into unknown territory. Succeeding at work often involves picking a careful path through the potential minefield of interpersonal relationships, running the gauntlet of corporate meetings, and, in general, trying to keep your eye on the ball while everyone else appears to be playing a different game.

Being a manager, in any kind of organization, is never, ever easy. In part, this is because managers carry the ultimate responsibility not only for every decision that they, as individuals, make, but also for everything that *their people* do. It really is true that, for a manager, "The buck stops here." But perhaps the toughest aspect of being a manager is the isolation. A manager no longer has the safety net of sharing responsibility with the team because he or she is the team leader. A manager is expected to support, encourage, motivate subordinates, and, of course, model and demonstrate good practice day after relentless day. And while a manager is part of a management team that on the surface may appear to be working together, none of those individuals are going to want to chance losing their credibility and possibly damaging their career by admitting to failure—making a mistake, being disappointed by results, or making a poor judgment or a bad decision.

It really is tough at the top. For most managers in most organizations, every day at work is *showtime*. Managers who want to get ahead simply can't afford to say, "I don't know how to do this," "I can't cope," or "I need some help." Managers who want to get ahead smile, keep calm, stay sharp, and never, ever allow anyone at work to know what is really going inside their head.

This book is written for real people who happen to be managers. And when real people get worried and confused, they need encouragement and practical advice, and they need it *fast*.

Each chapter covers a different topic and will give you an overview of the key principles you need to be aware of and the key skills you need to utilize when you're engaged with that specific activity: appraising, delegating, mentoring, or whatever.

You'll find checklists of key actions plus organizer sheets. The organizer sheets are designed to help you in a very practical way. Use them to find the answers to your specific problems, to help you manage the specific people—coworkers, colleagues, and clients—you deal with every day, and to work out how you can take the most advantage and make the best use of the opportunities that present themselves to you in your corporation.

Whether you are a new manager starting out in your first job with high hopes and even higher adrenaline levels or whether you're an established manager who is determined to go as far as you can, this book has been written for you by someone who has been there! I've inserted formal management theory in this book where I've felt it's been necessary, but for the most part, I have dealt with the real, practical, bottom-line issues that every manager has to deal with on a day-to-day basis.

My best advice to anyone who intends to make a success of management as a career is:

- Learn to rely on yourself because, at the end of the day, in business you're the only person you can really trust.
- Don't expect anyone to behave, think, or respond as you would.
- Always expect the unexpected and plan for people to be unpredictable.
- Always prepare for the worst, and don't be surprised if it happens.
- Always have Plan B available so that when Plan A bites the dust, you know—more or less—what to do next.
- At the end of each day, review your mistakes, learn from them, and let them *go*. That way you can start each day fresh, with a little more wisdom and a touch more optimism.
- Give each day your best shot, but don't expect perfection from yourself or anyone else.

Acknowledgments

Thank you to all the people I have had the privilege to work with on the many training courses I have facilitated. I have learned so much from your hopes, fears, problems, and aspirations.

Thank you to my agents, Nicholas Smith and Andrea Pedolsky, and everyone at AMACOM Books, especially Jacquie Flynn and Ellen Kadin.

Thank you to all the very special people in my life: particularly Irene Reddish, Christopher Sell, Ann Bowen-Jones, Tom Hutchinson, Nancy Booth, Moira Southby, Phillipa Lee, Paul Johnson, Eileen Baldwin, Margaret Bell, and Cathy Lake.

My special thanks and deep appreciation to Rabbi Yehudah Black, Manny Cohen, Monty Fenton, Eli Jankelewitz, Bernard Lewis, Geoffrey Lurie, Henry Ross, Jerome Shaw, Joshua Shields, Natie Sterrie, and Bernie Shaffer.

Appraisal

Staff appraisal is the art of comparing what someone has actually done and achieved with what that same person is supposed to have accomplished, and then agreeing on how improvements can be made or how existing success can be sustained. Appraisal is also the time to reassess goals and to decide if they need to be changed for the next review period.

A meaningful appraisal is a two-way process that benefits both the employee and the manager. For employees, appraisal is the time to find out how their manager thinks they are performing in the job; what their manager wants them to continue doing in the same way, stop doing, or do differently in the future; and what new performance goals, targets, and deadlines their manager expects them to achieve over the next six or twelve months.

For managers, a formal appraisal interview is a good time to find out how employees think they are performing in the job (and, perhaps, the reasons why job performance has been less than satisfactory); how employees feel about the job itself (e.g., which aspects are easy and enjoyable and which are not, and the reasons why); and what concerns or requirements employees have with regard to training, welfare, salary, career prospects, or work relationships.

Ideally, at the end of the appraisal interview, both the manager and the employee should have laid their cards on the table, identified problems, and discussed possible solutions.

Depending on the circumstances and the people involved, the appraisal interview is likely to be a mixture of good news and bad news. Even if you feel that the bad news outweighs the good, the meeting should always be a two-way dialogue rather than a one-sided formal interview.

For appraisal to be meaningful and useful for everyone in-

1

volved, you need to plan your strategy with care and make sure that certain things happen before, during, and after the appraisal process.

Planning Your Appraisal Strategy

Before the Appraisal

Establish key task areas and performance goals.

Key question: What does this person do in his job?

Before you start comparing what has happened on the job with what should have happened, it is important to clarify for yourself exactly what it is you want someone to do and to what standard.

Your first task is to define, for each person on your team, a list of his key task areas. Each of these key task areas represents an important aspect of someone's job and can be easily worked out by looking at each person's job description.

For example, the key task areas for a sales representative could be:

1. Generating new business
2. Maintaining and increasing existing business
3. Communicating and building relationships with customers
4. Managing paperwork and administration
5. Managing after-sales follow-up and ensuring customer satisfaction

The key task areas for a secretary could be:

1. Preparing correspondence and other word-processed documentation
2. Filing
3. Managing the boss's calendar

4. Making travel arrangements
5. Screening calls

Before you start the appraisal process, use Organizer Sheet 1, Key Job Task Areas, to identify the key task areas for each job for which you have managerial responsibility. (Remember that one person can be responsible for anywhere from three to seven key task areas, depending on the job.)

Once you've defined someone's key task areas, make sure that at some point during the appraisal interview, you verify that these tasks are still relevant to the job. Jobs can change over time, and sometimes an employee takes on new responsibilities and relinquishes old ones. You need to be aware of any variations within key task areas.

Set performance goals for each key task area.

> *Key question: In each key area of a person's job, what do I want him to do, and to what standard do I want him to do it ?*

Once you are clear about the key task areas for each job, your next step is to establish performance goals for each key area. People need to know what it is they are expected to do. If they have clear performance goals to work toward, they can see for themselves how they are doing.

A performance goal is a short statement that simply and clearly describes precisely what you expect people to do in each key task area, and the standard to which you expect them to do it. Make sure that the performance goals you set are SWEET— sensible, written, easy to understand, easy to measure, and task-related.

S   *Sensible.* Sensible performance goals are challenging yet realistic and achievable. With sensible performance goals, success is possible. People quickly become stressed and demoralized if they have to face up to Mission Impossible performance goals all the time. Your people need to feel

3

Key Job Task Areas

Use this Organizer before the appraisal interview.

Date: _____

Employee: _____

Job title: _____

Key Task Areas:

1. _____

2. _____

3. _____

4. _____

5. _____

6. _____

7. _____

that, if they stretch themselves and work hard, they can successfully achieve their goals.

W   *Written.* Agree to the performance goals and write them
down. This way both you and the other person have a record of what has been agreed on. Written performance goals
mean that, later on, disputes and disagreements about what
was agreed on are unlikely to occur.

E   *Easy to understand.* Easy-to-understand performance goals
are short, clear, and straightforward. They are not complex
and they do not contain jargon or clever words. They state,
clearly and precisely, what someone is supposed to achieve.

E   *Easy to measure.* Easy-to-measure performance goals give
specific information about when people should achieve the
goal (i.e., the time frame) or how much they have to do in
order to achieve the goal (i.e., the quantity).

T   *Task-related.* Task-related performance goals describe precisely what someone is supposed to achieve in each of the
key task areas.

Here are some examples of SWEET performance goals:

1. By the end of the year, increase the number of sales made
   to existing customers by at least ten percent.
2. Establish an up-to-date database of European suppliers by
   the end of April.
3. By September, upgrade the existing computer network to
   Pentium II 200 MHz within a budget of $20,000.
4. Every month between May and October, generate four
   new customers who will each spend, on average, $100,000
   per year.

Initially, you will need to work on your own to establish performance goals for each of your people, because you have your
own goals, targets, and schedules to meet and you will need the
help of your team in order to meet them. Before the appraisal
takes place, use Organizer Sheet 2, SWEET Performance Goals, to
help with the goal-setting process. In the organizer sheet, identify
the SWEET performance goals you want each person on your
team to achieve in each key task area of the job. (The number of

SWEET Performance Goals

Use this Organizer before the appraisal interview.

S = sensible	W = written	E = easy to understand
E = easy to measure		T = task-related

Name of person: _____ Job title: _____

Key Task Area	Performance Goals
1.	1. _____ 2. _____ 3. _____
2.	1. _____ 2. _____ 3. _____
3.	1. _____ 2. _____ 3. _____
4.	1. _____ 2. _____ 3. _____
5.	1. _____ 2. _____ 3. _____
6.	1. _____ 2. _____ 3. _____
7.	1. _____ 2. _____ 3. _____

performance goals depends on the job.) You will need to complete one organizer sheet for each person on your team.

Don't just decide on the goals and then impose them. If you discuss and even negotiate performance goals, you can ensure that the employee buys in to what has been agreed on. This, in the long term, means your employees will be more committed to making things work the way they are supposed to.

Get the facts.

It is your responsibility to carry out the appraisal fairly and objectively, with the utmost professionalism. Before the appraisal interview takes place, you should be aware of every person's strengths and weaknesses so that you have a clear picture of their achievements and failures since their last appraisal. If you do not have this information, make sure that you get it before the interview. Don't rely on hearsay or office gossip. Appraisal is important—for the persons you are appraising, for you as their manager, and for your organization—so you need the facts and figures, the hard evidence about what someone has or has not achieved.

Before each appraisal interview, take a few minutes to complete a copy of Organizer Sheet 3, Specific Performance Appraisal Issues. This organizer sheet will help you to identify the specific issues you want to raise with every person during their appraisal interview.

Schedule each appraisal interview well in advance.

Don't spring appraisals on people at the last moment. You need time to prepare, and so do they.

Set aside sufficient, uninterrupted time.

People need enough time to discuss their concerns, explain their failures, and talk through their plans and hopes for the future. They also need to hear how they are doing and how they could do better. Of course you have a busy schedule, but if you really want to get the best out of your staff, then you must make

Organizer Sheet 3

Specific Performance Appraisal Issues

Use this Organizer before the appraisal interview.

Name of person to be appraised: _____
Job title: _____
Date of appraisal: _____

During the interview, I'll mention and encourage the following strengths:

During the interview, I'll examine and explore the following weaknesses:

During the interview, I'll raise the following specific issues:

time to talk things through carefully, without any sense of rushed impatience.

Think carefully about when you want to hold the appraisals. At the start of the day, both you and the employee will be fresh, but you will probably have other meetings to attend and the prospect of a busy day ahead, so time may be an issue. At the end of the day, you may be tired, but you can probably afford to let the interview take as long as it needs. The key point is that if you invest an hour or two in someone now, you'll reap the benefits of that investment over the coming months.

Schedule appraisals carefully.

Although it may be tempting to schedule eight appraisals every day for three days to get them over with, this approach won't help you or your staff. After two or three intensive discussions, one after the other, you'll need a break. If you are tired and still continue with appraisals, you won't be able to give your full attention and interest, which is not good for your organization and certainly not good for the employee.

Try to spread the appraisals out over a period of days so that you are seeing just one or two people each day. That way you will maintain your energy and enthusiasm, and you'll be able to make the process meaningful and useful for everyone. (See Time Management.)

During the Appraisal

Encourage two-way communication.

Start by asking every person you meet with how they think they have performed since their last appraisal. Ask them to identify their main successes and failures. Find out which of their key task areas are, for them, the most and the least rewarding. Invite employees' suggestions as to how they think they could improve their job performance. Give the person sitting in the other chair your full attention, and listen carefully. You will learn far more about your employees' strengths and weaknesses and how they approach the job if you listen rather than talk.

Say how you feel and explain what you want from the employee.

Key question: Am I satisfied with this person's job performance, or do I want this person to change some aspect of her actions, behavior, or attitude?

Explain your perceptions of your employees' job performance. Clearly and honestly talk about:

- The things they have done well
- The things they have not done well
- The ways in which you would like them to do things differently

Don't just smile and nod during the interview and write a damning report afterward. It is up to you to encourage two-way communication. Explain, question, listen, and clarify everything until you are sure that both you and the employee have the same understanding of what has happened in the past and what needs to happen in the future. (See Communication.)

Discuss and agree on performance goals for the future.

Explain, for each key task area, the performance goals you think are realistic and achievable. Be prepared to negotiate. For example, you may be looking for a twenty percent increase in new business or a twenty percent reduction in production downtime. Your employee may have sensible arguments, based on fact, to show how these performance goals are not possible given the current economic climate or the current state of machinery and equipment. Again, listen carefully and, if you feel it is appropriate, be prepared to compromise.

Whenever possible, agree on the performance goals and put them in writing, there and then, while the employee is with you. If you and the employee cannot reach an agreement regarding performance goals, have a short cooling-off period of one or two days, and then schedule another meeting.

Identify, discuss, and agree on any training, development, or resource issues.

Key questions: What resources does this person need to do things better in the future? Time? Training? Staff? Money? Equipment? Something else?

As a manager, one of your key responsibilities is to make sure that your people have the resources they need to do the best possible work. For example, if you are saying that someone has poor communication skills, or is not managing his time effectively, or cannot handle the new computer software, then that person must have the opportunity to learn how to do these things the way you want them to be done.

Think about how you can help this person to achieve more at work.

Key question: What would motivate this person to do better?

Although this topic may not crop up for discussion during the interview itself, consider whether there are any changes you need to make to your actions, behavior, or attitude that would make it easier for the employee to do a good job.

Record notes of the interview.

Don't rely on your memory alone. Take a few minutes at the very end of the interview to complete Organizer Sheet 4, Record of Appraisal Meeting, jotting down notes about the substance of the interview and any special agreements that were made. Make sure your notes are sufficiently detailed and legible so that, if required, after the interview you can prepare a meaningful, formal appraisal document, if required, that can be read and signed by the employee. The organizer sheet can also be copied to the employee and the original placed into his file. That way both you and the employee have a written record of what was said and agreed on.

Record of Appraisal Meeting

Use this Organizer after the appraisal interview.

Name of employee: _____

Job title: _____

Date of appraisal: _____

Key points I raised during the meeting:

Key points the employee raised during the meeting:

Performance goals to which we agreed:

Other agreements we made relating to:

☐ Actions:

☐ Behavior:

☐ Attitude:

End the interview on an upbeat note.

Many people find appraisal stressful, particularly if they know (or have been told in advance) that their job performance has been less than satisfactory. Even if it has been a bad news meeting, offer support and encouragement for the future. Give your employees some hope and let them see that, if performance improves and they meet agreed-on performance goals in the future, all will be well. If it has been a good news meeting, offer praise and congratulations. Let them know they are valued members of the team and that you recognize and appreciate their hard work.

After the Appraisal

Prepare a formal record of the interview.

Using the notes you made during the appraisal, prepare a formal document that gives an outline of everything that was said and agreed on. Give the employee time to read and sign the report, and be prepared to discuss any points of disagreement. For example, the employee may feel that your verbal comments, at the appraisal, were more enthusiastic than your written comments.

Your written report should be an honest and accurate appraisal of someone's work. You need to be sure that you can justify everything you have written. Remember that employees are entitled to file a rebuttal to a review of their work. Make sure that everything you write is based on fact and that supporting evidence is available if you are suggesting that someone's work is below the required standard.

If the employee points out a genuine inaccuracy or misunderstanding, make sure that you put it right. Appraisal documents remain on someone's file for a long time, so they need to be carefully prepared.

Monitor performance.

Key question: How often do I need to check how employees are doing their job?

Between each appraisal, it is important that you monitor your team's work performance so that, if problems crop up, you'll know about them fairly quickly. After each appraisal interview, take a few minutes to complete Organizer Sheet 5, Monitoring Performance. This organizer sheet will help you to devise a strategy for monitoring each employee's work performance on a regular basis, according to each person's individual needs.

Monitoring Performance

Use this Organizer after the appraisal interview.

Name of employee: _____

Job title: _____

I intend to monitor this person's performance every:

- ☐ Week
- ☐ Two weeks
- ☐ Month
- ☐ Three months
- ☐ Six months

I intend to monitor performance by:

- ☐ Regular, formal, face-to-face meetings
- ☐ Regular, informal, face-to-face meetings
- ☐ Examining results
- ☐ Talking to the employee's supervisor
- ☐ Talking to the employee's colleagues
- ☐ Talking to the employee's customers

Appraisal Action Checklist

Before the appraisal:

- ☐ Establish each employee's key task areas.
- ☐ Identify SWEET (sensible, written, easy to understand, easy to measure, task-related) performance goals for each key task area—but be prepared to negotiate.
- ☐ Get the facts, especially if you have to communicate bad news about someone's work performance.
- ☐ Give people sufficient advance warning so they can prepare for the meeting.
- ☐ Allocate sufficient quality time to each interview.

During the appraisal:

- ☐ Identify an individual's strengths and weaknesses, failures and successes.
- ☐ Find out how individuals feel about their jobs and their job performance.
- ☐ Communicate good and bad news about job performance.
- ☐ Offer praise and encouragement, but also be clear about what needs to improve or change with regard to actions, behavior, or attitude.
- ☐ Discuss and agree on performance goals, and be prepared to negotiate and compromise.
- ☐ Recognize that for some people appraisal interviews can be daunting and stressful. Do your best to put people at ease. A good appraisal is a discussion, not a confrontation.

After the appraisal:

- ☐ Write up your notes before you move on to the next task.
- ☐ Monitor performance and, where necessary, take action to solve problems and difficulties.
- ☐ Don't just hope things will improve before the next appraisal because, unless you get proactive, improvement is unlikely to happen.

Budgets

Setting and managing your budget usually involves a careful balancing act between the amount of money available to spend (i.e., revenue) and the bills that have to be paid (i.e., expenses). By wisely and carefully deciding how much to spend and on what, it should be possible to maintain a balance between the two. Reckless spending, of course, tips the scales in the wrong direction and leads, in the short term, to overspending and budget deficits, and to financial disaster in the long term.

Determining Types of Budgets

Key question: What type of budget-setting process will suit my purposes best?

Zero-Based Budgets for New Projects

If you are starting a new business, setting up a new department, or running a new project that doesn't have a financial history, then you won't have any figures from previous months or years to use as a starting point for setting your budget. You are, in effect, at point zero. You can only make educated guesses about revenue (i.e., the money that is likely to come into the business) and costs (i.e., the money that is likely to go out of the business). Even so, you have to start somewhere.

A good place to begin is to clarify your objectives for the project. Ask yourself, What do I want to do and how often do I want to do it? For example, I want to build an office block in six months;

I want to sell four pieces of real estate each week; I want to train twenty members of staff in two days; I want to manufacture five television sets an hour.

Once you know what you want to do, then you can start thinking about how much it is going to cost to turn your idea into reality. What kinds of expenses will you need to allow for when setting up this new venture? For example, will you need to spend money on research? On specialized staff training? On new vehicles, plant, and machinery? Or do you just need to think about staff wages, advertising, and the cost of components or raw materials? Use Organizer Sheet 6, New Project: Expenses You Can Expect, to list the kinds of expenditure you will need to allow for in your new project budget.

Talk to other people who have been successful with similar projects in the past. Find out as much as you can about their budgeting process and what worked for them. What cost less than they expected? What cost more? What, if any, mistakes did they make? If they were setting up the same project again, with the benefit of hindsight, what would they do differently? If approached in the right way, people will be happy to offer the benefit of their experience.

Zero-Based Budgets for Existing Projects

Key question: How much is everything really costing us?

Sometimes it's necessary to take a long, hard look at what is actually happening in a business. On those occasions, zero-based budgeting can be an extremely useful (although very time-consuming) tool. The process lets you see exactly how much everything actually costs, and when these costs are compared to income, you will quickly know whether or not what you are doing is profitable.

For example, let's say that, as part of your business, you run a free customer advice service on a toll-free number. You like the idea of offering the service; you expect customers to appreciate the service; you assume the service will bring you additional business.

Using zero-based budgeting, you can find out the true costs involved in providing the service—from staff wages to telephone calling costs to advertising, and so on—and then compare these

New Project: Expenses You Can Expect

Use this Organizer before you set the budget for the new project.

Start-Up Costs	Capital Costs	Fixed Costs	Variable Costs
☐ Research	☐ Plant and machinery	☐ Core staff wages	☐ Utilities (e.g., heat, light, telephone)
☐ Design	☐ Technology	☐ Insurance	☐ Stationery and postage
☐ Marketing (including brochures, videos, CD-ROMs)	☐ Vehicles	☐ Other fixed costs	☐ Transport and travel
☐ Consultancy or other professional fees	☐ Furniture, fixtures, and fittings		☐ Advertising
☐ Initial staff training	☐ Other capital costs		☐ Additional staff payments (e.g., overtime)
☐ Other start-up costs			☐ Cost of finance and other loans
			☐ Components and other raw materials
			☐ Other variable costs

costs to the business that is generated as a direct result of offering the service. You are then in a position to make a decision based on information: For example, the service is costing a fortune and we don't seem to be getting any extra business, but it's great public relations, so we'll continue. Or, the service is costing a fortune and we don't seem to be getting any extra business—we need to make economies, so the advice line has to go.

Used within an existing project, zero-based budgeting assumes that the project is brand new and has not yet incurred any expenses. The process then examines every aspect of what is happening in the project and asks some difficult questions focusing, to begin with, on activity rather than cost. You could ask:

1. What are we doing?
2. How well are we doing it?
3. Of all the things we are doing, what do we need to stop doing?
4. Of all the things we are doing, what do we need to do more of?
5. Of all the things we are doing, what do we need to do differently?
6. Of all the things we are doing, what do we need to do better?
7. In addition to the things we are doing, what else do we need to do, and how well do we need to do it?

As a practical example of how this works, here is how a hotel might look at all of its activities and come up with the following answers to key questions:

- *What are we doing?* We provide rooms, food, and conference and leisure facilities.
- *How well are we doing it?* The rooms are good, the food is excellent, the conference facilities are great, and the leisure facilities are adequate.
- *Of all the things we are doing, what do we need to stop doing?* Nothing.
- *Of all the things we are doing, what do we need to do more of?* We must expand our conference facilities because this side of the business is profitable and we have been successful so far.
- *Of all the things we are doing, what do we need to do differently or better?* We need to provide upgraded rooms and room service and to improve our leisure facilities.
- *In addition to the things we are doing, what else do we need to do?* We need to offer a weekend-break discount card to people who use the conference facilities and a stress-buster package for people who use the leisure facilities.

Once the hotel decides what needs to be done, done better, or canceled altogether, then it can examine both the cost and revenue implications of improving the business and assess what amount of money must be spent, what amount of money can be saved, and how much revenue is likely to be generated as a result of the changes.

The key point is that, using zero-based budgeting, you can, with a fresh eye, assess everything that is happening and start all over again, from scratch, as if it were a completely new project. Organizer Sheet 7, Change Versus Cost, can be used to identify the likely increases in cost that you may have to budget for, if you intend to make any changes or improvements to your current activities.

Flexible, Historically Based Budgets for Existing Projects

Key questions: How much did we spend last year, and how much will it cost us to do the same things this year? Did we overspend anywhere and by how much?

When you are setting a budget for this period (most often a year), begin by examining the budget for the last period. Where was the overspending, if any? Where was the underspending, if any? You will be able to see, fairly quickly, if the amount of money allocated to last year's budget was an accurate estimate of the money that was actually needed. Use Organizer Sheet 8, Existing Project: Historical Budget Analysis, to compare the expenditure for the last budget period with your anticipated expenditure over the next budget period.

Your next step is to gather as much information as you can about what has happened in the previous budget period and what is likely to happen in the next budget period. Specifically:

1. *Find out why overspending has occurred.* For example, have labor costs or the costs of raw materials increased? Will these increases apply to the next budget period as well? Or have certain individuals exceeded their budget allocations, while other people have managed to control their spending? If so, talk to the people involved and get the facts.

Change Versus Cost

Use this **Organizer** to estimate likely costs before you make any changes.

Activity	Change Under Consideration	Current Cost	Projected	
			Cost	Budget +/−

Existing Project: Historical Budget Analysis

Use this Organizer to analyze how much was spent in the last budget and to estimate how much more or less you are likely to spend in the next budget.

Item	Last Budget Period			Next Budget Period	
	Budget	Actual	Variance	Budget	Change

2. *Find out why underspending has occurred.* For example, have people cut quality in order to reduce spending? If so, why? Have reduced sales had a ripple effect on spending? Ask a million questions until you are satisfied you know exactly what happened and why.

3. *Find out what is likely to affect your costs in the next budget period.*

4. *Determine whether there are any external or internal factors that may affect your budget.* External factors include any upcoming elections, changes to the law, labor negotiations, or expected national economic growth. Impending internal factors include major changes within your organization, planned expansion, or downsizing that may affect your budget.

Once you study the history of the budget (i.e., what happened last time around) and you have gathered information about any factors that are likely to affect the budget next time around, the process of setting your budget is reasonably straightforward. You can, with some degree of confidence, assume that if something cost a certain amount last year, then it will either (1) cost the same this year, plus an additional amount that reflects price increases or other changes, or (2) cost the same this year, less an amount that reflects price decreases or other changes.

Estimating Your Costs

Key question: How much is it all going to cost?

When setting a first budget for a new project, be careful not to underestimate costs. It is important to avoid the temptation to keep costs unrealistically low in the hope that the people who are funding you will be more likely to accept a budget that appears reasonable or even cheap. If you underestimate right at the start, then later on, if problems occur, people will assume that (1) your budget was not properly calculated at the start, (2) you have been recklessly overspending, or (3) you have not been monitoring expenditures.

It is far better to ask for a sensible, realistic amount and then bring the project in for less than expected. If you can't get a reasonable budget in the beginning, then, unless you have absolutely no other choice, don't attempt the project.

Where you are taking over a budget from someone else, the costs will already be established, to some extent. With a brand-new budget, you will need to establish your likely costs and allocate an appropriate sum of money to each. Costs include:

- *Capital costs*. These costs are for capital items such as equipment, machinery, vehicles, furniture, and other capital assets. At the start of a new project, capital costs are usually high. With ongoing projects, unless you choose to upgrade or replace or add to your capital items, these costs can be controlled.

- *Fixed costs*. Fixed costs are the outgoing expenses over which you have absolutely no control, such as:

  1. *Rent*. Once the building lease has been signed, rent is a fixed cost for the agreed rental period and cannot be changed.
  2. *Insurance*. Premiums are also fixed costs for the life of the policies.

- *Variable costs*. These outgoing costs are, to some extent, controllable because it is possible to economize. Variable costs include expenses such as heating, lighting, car fuel, stationery, business entertaining, advertising, and even labor costs. With variable costs, it is possible to make decisions about whether to spend less. However, as with all decisions, there will be consequences. You can save money on heating by turning down the thermostat or switching the system off altogether. The consequence may be complaints from staff and customers that the building is cold. You can save money on stationery by choosing a less expensive grade of paper for your letterhead, but the consequence may be that customers perceive your business as having a less professional image. And, if you use inexpensive paper, the consequence may even be paper jams during printing that cause frustration and downtime. You can reduce the number of staff members you employ, but the consequence could be that the remaining people cannot handle the quantity of work and cut corners to save time, so quality suffers.

Work on the basis that if something can go wrong, it will go wrong. Anticipate the worst and prepare for it. Try to build into your budget an additional sum of money, perhaps five to ten percent, to cover unexpected problems. So, for example, if you expect to spend $100,000 on capital costs, ask for $110,000. If you have done your homework and spoken to other people in the same line of business as yourself, you should have a fairly good idea of what might go wrong and end up costing more than you expected.

Once you have established your likely costs and allocated an appropriate amount of money to each, the final stage in the process is to monitor spending.

Monitoring the Budget

Key questions: What method should I use to monitor spending? How often should I monitor?

Never make the assumption that once you have set the budget you can relax. Circumstances can change, and, unless you watch the budget with an eagle eye, spending can quickly get out of control.

You may think it is appropriate to check spending every day, every two days, or every week. There is no hard-and-fast rule because every company and every situation is different. But make sure that you monitor your budget as often as is appropriate for your kind of business. Make sure that you are aware of who is spending what, and whether the amounts of money going out of the budget are appropriate for the amount of money that has been allocated. You should always be able to step in and take action before overspending actually occurs. At the very least, you should know what is happening and why.

Organizer Sheet 9, Monthly Expenditure Versus Budget, will help you to monitor spending against your budget on a regular basis. At the end of each month, use this organizer to:

- Identify how much you have spent during the month.
- Compare the amount you have spent with the amount that is allocated in the budget.
- Calculate the variance (i.e., the amount of underspending or overspending) between actual expenditure and the budget allocation.

What to Do When Overspending Occurs

Key question: I underestimated spending in some areas right at the start. Where can I reasonably make some economies in other areas to compensate for the overspending?

Ideally, you will know before one of the budget allocations exceeds the budget. Once you are forewarned that overspending is likely to occur, then you can carefully think through the available options and take measured, appropriate action. Don't ever leave budget monitoring to someone else. If it is your budget, then it is your responsibility. Be sure to check expenditures on a regular basis so you know precisely what is happening.

If overspending in one area of the budget occurs, then scrutinize the entire budget to see if there is any available money that can, on paper, be transferred from another allocation. Say, for example, over a three-month period there has been an increase in sales that has resulted in a significant increase in staff overtime payments. The end result is that in that three-month period you have spent nearly all of the money allocated to cover the entire staff wage bill for a year. Or, possibly in an attempt to generate new business, you have spent in three months all of the money allocated to cover advertising for a year.

When it looks like you are in danger of overspending in one area of your budget, assess where underspending has occurred. It is possible that less money was spent on travel or business entertaining or stationery or telephones than originally estimated. Transfer some of that available money to the area where the overspending is expected to occur. In addition, cut back on spending and make economies wherever you can.

The point is, don't put your head in the sand and hope that

Monthly Expenditure Versus Budget

Use this Organizer to analyze your monthly expenditures.

Month	Cost	Budget	Actual	Variance	Corrective Action
January	Capital				
	Fixed				
	Variable				
February	Capital				
	Fixed				
	Variable				
March	Capital				
	Fixed				
	Variable				
April	Capital				
	Fixed				
	Variable				
May	Capital				
	Fixed				
	Variable				
June	Capital				
	Fixed				
	Variable				
July	Capital				
	Fixed				
	Variable				
August	Capital				
	Fixed				
	Variable				
September	Capital				
	Fixed				
	Variable				
October	Capital				
	Fixed				
	Variable				
November	Capital				
	Fixed				
	Variable				
December	Capital				
	Fixed				
	Variable				

things will work out. Take immediate action, transfer funds from one area to another, and curb all spending until you are sure that the budget is running smoothly again. Use Organizer Sheet 10, Planning Ahead, for planning ahead to anticipate future spending. Write down, on the organizer, those areas where you may reasonably be able to make economies and cutbacks if overspending occurs in another area of the budget. By planning ahead in this way, you are able to swing into action, promptly and efficiently, if overspending does occur.

Always tell your staff what you are doing and why. If they know the reasons why economies are being made, they are more likely to offer cooperation and support. If you impose unpopular cutbacks without explanation, then confusion, misunderstandings, and bad feeling can erupt.

Looking at the Big Picture

Key question: Who else within the organization is likely to be bidding for the money I need for my budget, and what can I do about it?

Finally, remember that your budget for your project or department must fit into your organization's master budget. You may be asking for money out of the same pool that other people in the company are bidding for, too. You may need to use your influencing skills to convince people that your budget is realistic, carefully considered, and necessary.

Planning Ahead

Use this Organizer at the start of your budget period.

Cost Savings Opportunity	Required Action	Likely Savings	Consequences of Action
		$	
		$	
		$	
		$	
		$	
		$	
		$	
		$	
		$	
		$	
		$	
		$	
		$	
		$	
		$	
		$	
		$	
		$	
		$	
		$	
		$	

Budgets Action Checklist

- [ ] Before you start setting the budget, gather as much information as you can and always learn from how other people, in similar situations, have managed their budget.
- [ ] Expect everything to cost more than you originally anticipated. Build in a five to ten percent buffer zone for each element of expenditure, whether capital, fixed, or variable.
- [ ] Monitor spending against allocations, ruthlessly and regularly.
- [ ] Take action before problems occur.
- [ ] If economies become necessary, tell your people the reasons why.
- [ ] Expect problems and plan ahead for them.
- [ ] Always remember that if it is your budget, then it is your responsibility.

Business Ethics

In business there are many different ways of doing things. You can take the route that is most expedient, profitable, competitive, or productive. Or, if you choose, you can go down the road that is ethical and right.

The choice isn't always easy and straightforward. What choice do you make if, say, your organization unleashes millions of gallons of toxic material into the atmosphere? Or if insider trading within your company hits the headlines? Or if your business is offered precisely the resources needed at exactly the right price . . . provided no one asks too many questions about where the computers or the air-conditioning units or raw materials came from in the first place?

In each of these scenarios, many people may be tempted to take the easy, the expedient, or the profitable route. In each case, it would be tougher to do the right and ethical thing. Yet consumers expect businesses to know the difference between what is right and what is wrong. Organizations that fail to understand the impact of public opinion risk losing their market share, along with their reputation.

For some managers, in some organizations, there is little choice. They either toe the company line and base their decisions on what is in the best interests of the business, or they leave. For some managers, the options are less stark. Either their organizations are already actively encouraging ethical standards and behavior throughout the company, top-down, or they are working on bringing ethical behavior to the top of the agenda.

Business ethics do not suddenly spring up overnight, like mushrooms after a cloudburst. They must be nurtured and disseminated throughout the company. They have to be explained, described, and demonstrated to the labor force until, ultimately, over a period of time they take root and become embedded in the culture.

What Are Business Ethics?

Business ethics are simply the values and principles that direct people to do things in business in a way that can best be described as decent, honest, fair, and respectful toward other people and the environment. Ethical behavior is, for example, doing honest accounting and tax calculation; treating staff fairly and paying a reasonable rate for the job; paying suppliers on time; providing quality goods and services; conserving natural resources and protecting the environment.

Unethical behavior is using insider knowledge or confidential information for personal gain; loading expense accounts to provide a personal surplus; buying shoddy resources because there is a personal payoff; expecting people to work in an unsafe or unhealthy environment because it saves money; deliberately miscalculating invoices and hoping customers won't notice; providing misleading information to win contracts; making false claims about products or services; paying the lowest rate for the job and charging the highest prices. The list can go on and on.

If you are committed to making sure that your organization consistently demonstrates ethical behavior, then you'll need to develop a strategy so that the whole concept of business ethics cascades throughout the company, involving everyone who works there.

Developing a Business Ethics Strategy for the Organization

If you are serious about business ethics, then, first of all, check out what is happening at the top of the organization. Is senior management serious about taking ethics onboard? If the answer is no, then forget it. Without the commitment and lead of your top people, the strategy will fail. If the answer is yes—maybe because you are at the top or you've been delegated the job of bringing an awareness of ethical behavior into the business—then you'll need to plan a careful campaign that communicates your message loud and clear throughout the company.

Step 1: Tell Your Staff About Business Ethics

Key question: How can we spread the word so that everyone in the business understands what business ethics are and why they are important to this organization?

If people understand what ethical behavior is and why it is important, then it will be easier for them to make ethical decisions. Once people recognize that business ethics aren't just another management flavor-of-the-month but provide competitive advantage, enhance business reputations, increase profitability through increased market share, and protect jobs, then they'll buy in to the concept.

To simply state that it is important to do the right thing may not have great impact. But if you explain the importance of ethical behavior in concrete terms people can understand—we stay out of the headlines, we protect the organization, and we protect our jobs—the message hits home much harder. Use Organizer Sheet 11, Business Ethics Plan, to clarify your strategy for introducing the concept of business ethics to your labor force.

Step 2: Ask Members of Your Staff to Set Their Own Standards for Ethical Behavior

Key questions: How can we make sure that the way we treat one another and our customers, clients, shareholders, suppliers, and external agencies is fair, honest, decent, and right? What can we do to make sure that all our dealings, systems, procedures, and practices are legal, and that we do whatever we can to preserve the environment?

Business Ethics Plan

Use this Organizer before you begin to introduce business ethics.

What is ethical behavior?

Why is it important?

The best way to introduce the idea of ethical business practice is to:

- ☐ Make a formal presentation to all staff.
- ☐ Conduct a discussion session with the management team.
- ☐ Make a formal presentation to the managers and ask for ideas about how to best deliver this message to the staff.

The best way to involve people in preparing guidelines for ethical behavior is to:

- ☐ Ask managers to work with their staffs in large departmental teams.
- ☐ Ask managers to select small teams from each department.
- ☐ Organize a formal in-house event.
- ☐ Ask people to work together informally to generate ideas.
- ☐ Other (explain): _____

What would be the best timetable?

- ☐ Completion of draft documents in (*circle one*)   1   2   3   6 months
- ☐ Completion of final documents in (*circle one*)   2   3   6 months

When introducing a new concept, involvement and ownership are the key factors that will make the difference between people simply going through the motions and people enthusiastically embracing an idea. Attempting to impose ethical standards will not have the desired effect. Asking people to define for themselves what is and isn't ethical will involve them in the process and give them ownership of the concept.

You may want to create small teams, each of which has responsibility for generating ideas about a different aspect of business ethics. One team can focus on working with colleagues; another can focus on working with customers or suppliers. There can also be teams dedicated to working with the environment or with the law. Some practical ways in which your organization can demonstrate its commitment to ethical behavior and decisions include, for example:

- Pegging allowable business expenses at the same level throughout the company, from the top down
- Empowering people to keep their promises to customers all the time, every time, no matter what
- Wherever possible, using recycled paper products
- Ensuring that suppliers are paid within thirty days

Write some suggestions on Organizer Sheet 12, Ethical Guidelines; you'll find that this information will be a good starting point for your staff members when they begin to think about creating ethical guidelines. Then use Organizer Sheet 13, Delegating Roles and Responsibilities, to determine which tasks should be delegated to which people as you go through the process of increasing awareness of business ethics throughout your company.

Step 3: Prepare and Draft an Ethical Guidelines Document

Ask your staff members to work together to create a business ethics guidelines document that can be used throughout the organization. The guidelines document should contain clear guidance and specific examples of both ethical and unethical business practices. The guidelines should supply sufficient information so that everyone in the business can, without difficulty or confusion, make the ethical choice.

Ethical Guidelines

Use this Organizer before you ask your staff to answer these questions. Your responses will provide a starting point of discussion for them.

The things we can do to show our commitment to ethical business practices when we are working with each other: _____

_____

_____

The things we can do to show our commitment to ethical business practices when we are working with customers: _____

_____

_____

The things we can do to show our commitment to ethical business practices when we are working with suppliers and external agencies:

_____

_____

_____

The things we can do to show our commitment to ethical business practices when we are working with the environment: _____

_____

_____

The things we can do to show our commitment to ethical business practices when we are working with the law: _____

_____

_____

Delegating Roles and Responsibilities

Use this Organizer before the business ethics program starts. Complete the chart by writing in the names of the people to whom you intend to delegate responsibility for making the strategy work.

Task	Person to Whom I'll Delegate Responsibility for This Task
Coordinating groups/teams	
Gathering draft information	
Compiling draft documents	
Gathering feedback on drafts	
Organizing meetings to discuss final drafts	
Preparing final draft	
Distributing final draft	
Setting up communication framework	
Monitoring communication framework	
Revising and updating guidelines (document when necessary)	
Reviewing the program after: ☐ Six months ☐ One year	

Step 4: Ask Your Staff to Devise a Draft Communication Framework

People will have questions and concerns. They'll need information, guidance, and advice. A system that allows communication to flow easily and smoothly through the organization, top-down and bottom-up, will help everyone. Who should staff members turn to if they can't resolve a problem? What should someone do if a coworker is not following the guidelines? Who has the final word on what is and isn't ethical? Establishing good in-house channels of communication, available to everyone, can also prevent whistle-blowing outside the organization. Organizer Sheet 14, Communication Framework, will help you to structure a communication framework that facilitates the flow of information about business ethics throughout your organization.

Step 5: Distribute the Draft Documents Throughout the Organization

Give everyone in the business the chance to look through and comment on the two draft documents—the guidelines for business ethics and the communication framework. Invite feedback and, where appropriate, act on the feedback and make changes. Pay particular attention to any criticisms regarding the clarity of the guidelines document and the simplicity of the communication framework. Everyone currently working in the business, and everyone coming into the business in the future, should be able to clearly understand what is and what is not acceptable; they should also be able to get help and guidance quickly, when they need it.

Step 6: Prepare and Distribute the Finals Drafts to Everyone

Once you are confident that the document and the communication framework are as good as you can hope to get them, distribute the information to every single person on the payroll—no matter whether they are full-time, part-time, on contract, or temporary. Everyone needs to have this information.

Communication Framework

Use this Organizer before the business ethics program starts.

If people in the organization need practical help, advice, or guidance about making a business decision that involves business ethics, what should they do?	☐ Read the guidelines. ☐ Speak to their manager. ☐ Contact someone on the senior management team. ☐ Contact the person with delegated responsibility for dealing with ethical issues. ☐ Something else (explain): —————————————
If people in the organization have reason to believe that a supplier, customer, external agency, or other person outside the business is not behaving ethically, what should they do?	☐ Read the guidelines. ☐ Speak to their manager. ☐ Contact someone in the senior management team. ☐ Contact the person with delegated responsibility for dealing with ethical issues. ☐ Something else (explain): —————————————
If people in the organization have reason to believe that a colleague inside the business is not behaving ethically, what should they do?	☐ Read the guidelines. ☐ Speak to their manager. ☐ Contact someone in the senior management team. ☐ Contact the person with delegated responsibility for dealing with ethical issues. ☐ Something else (explain): —————————————
Within the organization, if there is a dispute over business ethics, who should deal with this situation?	☐ The managers of the people involved. ☐ The senior management team. ☐ The person with delegated responsibility for dealing with ethical issues. ☐ Someone else (explain): —————————————

Step 7: Put the Communication Framework Into Effect

Delegate responsibility for establishing channels of communication and brief people thoroughly. Everyone in the organization should be able either to make an ethical choice and know the decision will be supported or to obtain information and guidance to help them make the ethical choice.

Step 8: Make It Real

You'll have to work hard to show people that you mean it when you say that you expect everyone to conduct ethical business. You'll have to take the lead and make sure that your own behavior is impeccable. You'll have to constantly remind members of the senior management team that they are role models for everyone else in the organization. You'll have to incorporate business ethics into your organization's orientation program and ongoing staff development. You may even have to forgo profitability or productivity.

The payoff is knowing that your company isn't going to make headlines with negative press; that other businesses that are incorporating ethics into their culture will want to be associated with your business; and that your customers, clients, and shareholders will remain loyal and be proud to spend their hard-earned dollars with you.

Step 9: Monitor and Review Progress

You will need to keep your finger on the pulse of activities in the organization and make sure you know what's happening. You should meet regularly with the people who are responsible for dealing with the concerns, queries, and issues that will almost certainly crop up. Find out what is working, what isn't, and what changes would make things work better. Six months after you've distributed the final drafts, talk to your labor force to find out what they think about things. Are they having difficulties? If so, what are the problems? How do they think problems can be resolved?

Step 10: Keep Going

If you're making radical changes to the way people do things on the job, and if you're dealing with a cynical labor force and a reluctant senior management team, it won't be an easy ride. Even if you're dealing with people who are committed to and willing to change, it still won't be an easy ride. The key thing to remember is that if you want to make it work, you have to persist. Bang the cymbals and beat the drum. Constantly remind people that ethics in business are a key issue that, in one way or another, affects everyone in the organization. Keep going because, eventually, doing the right thing will become part of the culture, and you'll have a significant and lasting change.

Six to nine months after you've introduced the concept of business ethics, use Organizer Sheet 15, Reviewing Progress, to evaluate what's happened to date, determine how you can build on current successes and achievements, and assess where changes or improvements are necessary.

Reviewing Progress

Use this Organizer six to nine months after the start of your business ethics program.

Working with	My Evaluation of What Has Happened to Date	Suggestions for Improvement
Colleagues	☐ Excellent progress ☐ Good progress ☐ Reasonable progress ☐ Little or no progress	
Customers	☐ Excellent progress ☐ Good progress ☐ Reasonable progress ☐ Little or no progress	
Suppliers and External Agencies	☐ Excellent progress ☐ Good progress ☐ Reasonable progress ☐ Little or no progress	
The Environment	☐ Excellent progress ☐ Good progress ☐ Reasonable progress ☐ Little or no progress	
The Law	☐ Excellent progress ☐ Good progress ☐ Reasonable progress ☐ Little or no progress	

Business Ethics Action Checklist

- ☐ Tell your staff what business ethics are and why they're important. Spell out the difference between ethical and unethical behavior.
- ☐ Ask people to work in teams to create:
  1. Draft guidelines that will help them understand what is and isn't ethical in your business and that will help them to make ethical choices.
  2. A draft document that describes a straightforward communication framework that people can use if they have queries or concerns about what is and what is not ethical.
- ☐ Distribute the draft documents, ask for feedback, then incorporate sensible suggestions into the final drafts. By involving people, you'll gain their commitment.
- ☐ Prepare and distribute the final draft documents that explain:
  1. The ethical guidelines that everyone in the business should follow.
  2. The communication framework that everyone can use to get help and advice.
- ☐ Brief the people who are responsible for the communication framework and make sure they know how to handle the issues that are sure to arise.
- ☐ Review the situation on a regular basis, and don't be afraid to improve and build on what you've achieved so far.
- ☐ Show your personal commitment to business ethics by ''walking the talk'' and leading by example.

Change Management

Change—at work and at home—is a major cause of stress in people's lives. Change brings the unknown, and it is the unknown that causes the problems. For most people at work, as long as they know where they stand, what to do, how to do it, and what is expected of them, they can get by.

Even if people feel overwhelmed when they first start a new job, over time they develop a range of skills and strategies that enable them to cope. As people settle in and become familiar with their environment, their colleagues, the organization's culture, and the demands of their job, they begin to relax and get comfortable. They say to themselves, "I can do this . . . I can survive here." But as soon as change looms on the horizon—usually gift-wrapped and presented as reengineering, delayering, restructuring, or even evaluating the future direction of the organization—the old fears about not being able to cope rise up again, and people get stressed. They may move from a comfortable "I can do this" position to a very uncomfortable one, thinking, "I don't know if I can do this. What if I fall on my face?"

As a manager, your problems are amplified because your job demands that you present upcoming change in a positive light to your staff and help them to overcome their resistance. You also have to deal with your own fears and resistance to doing new things in new ways.

Helping People to Cope With Change

The change you have to implement could be anything from establishing an appraisal system to introducing multidisciplinary teams;

from introducing an early retirement program to changing work processes and systems. No matter how seemingly insignificant or how radical and necessary these changes may be, they will, in one way or another, affect every member of your team. The people who are directly affected and who are expected to participate in the change program may become anxious and fretful. Even the people who are not directly affected by the change will be aware of the plans for change, and they, too, can easily become unsettled and anxious. "What's really going to happen? I bet this change will affect me in one way or another." And, if people have been subjected to many change programs, they are likely to become cynical and disenchanted. "It's just another flavor-of-the-month and, like last time, it just isn't going to work."

Why People Resist Change

Key question: Who's going to be affected?

People resist change for several reasons. Often it is because they are familiar with the way they do things now and frightened they may not be able to learn new ways of doing things. Sometimes it is because they feel reasonably secure about the future and worry that the planned change will affect their job security, career path, lifestyle, income, or retirement. Sometimes people resist change at work because they're comfortable with their work relationships and the level of control and influence they enjoy. They become anxious that change may mean they'll lose access to the senior people with whom they currently work well and, to some extent, are able to influence. Many people are proud of their status at work, which they have worked hard to achieve. Their status may be wrapped up in having their job title, or being the only person on the team with specialized knowledge, or maybe being the person who gets to travel overseas on business trips.

In these cases, people become fearful that the changes will affect not only their status but also the way in which other people perceive them. Many people are territorial about the external trappings that signify their status and role in the organization—the window office, the reserved parking space, first-class travel, and so on. They may worry that, in the changeover to new and better things, they may lose these privileges.

In most instances, people will not be explicit about their reasons for resisting change. Rather than saying, "I'm worried about losing status in the eyes of my colleagues," or "I'm not happy about having to travel economy class," an employee may say, "I just don't think it's going to work," or "People aren't going to buy into this idea; it's been tried before and it didn't work."

It's important for you to understand why people resist change. Generally, they are not being difficult just to make your life hell; they're scared and worried about the future. It's up to you to do whatever it takes to reassure them that they will be able to cope and that the future is fairly sunny and not, as they fear, filled with storm clouds. Use Organizer Sheet 16, Resistance to Change, to evaluate every person on your team, identify their most likely reasons for resisting change, and work out a strategy for reassuring and supporting them through the change program.

Techniques to Overcome Resistance to Change

During times of change, your staff needs you to SHINE. That is, you need to be supportive, honest, informative, no-nonsense, and enthusiastic.

S   *Supportive.* You can support your staff by demonstrating, by what you do and say, that you recognize their concerns and that you will do everything within your power to make sure they have the training, resources, and time to come to terms with the upcoming change. Acknowledge people's existing skills and show them how these skills will be used after the planned change. Make people feel valued, and show them that their views and opinions and contribution to the team are important.

H   *Honest.* No matter how appealing it may be from your point of view, resist the urge to sugarcoat the situation. Be honest about the bad news as well as the good news. If your employees discover that, at any stage during the change process, you have been less than totally honest, they will lose heart.

Resistance to Change

Use this Organizer (one for each employee) before the change program starts.

Name: _____

From what I know about this person, the reasons he/she is most likely to resist change are worries about:

☐ Failure

☐ Loss of security or career path

☐ Loss of control and influence at work

☐ Loss of status

☐ Loss of privileges

☐ Some other worry (explain): _____

_____

Ways in which I can provide support and reassurance:

☐ Arrange one-to-one meetings.

☐ Provide evidence that this kind of change program has worked well in other organizations, with similar people.

☐ Discuss plans for the future in which this person has a high profile.

☐ Take some other action (explain): _____

_____

They will assume the worst and find it hard to believe anything else you have to say.

I   *Informative.* People need to know what is going on. Even bad news is better than no news at all. When people aren't kept informed, then rumor, gossip, and wild imaginings can take hold and spread like wildfire. Arrange weekly or even daily team briefings. Keep the meetings short and to the point. Give any new information and answer questions openly and honestly. If there are rumors circulating, bring them out into the open and put them to rest.

N   *No-nonsense.* As a manager, you have to get used to the idea that it's a lonely job and tough at the top. You may not, for whatever reason, be wholeheartedly committed to the upcoming change. Even so, you have to remain calm, steady, firm, and consistent. The team takes its lead from you. Sometimes, stress causes people to behave in flighty ways or to have unrealistic expectations. Keep both feet on the ground and don't be diverted from your plan. Stick to your guns, keep your promises, and don't change your mind from moment to moment.

E   *Enthusiastic.* You have to show your enthusiasm if you want to carry the team with you. Don't let the "It isn't going to work" brigade get to you. Whatever doubts you may have, keep them private. When you are with the team, be relentless in showing your commitment and enthusiasm.

Prepare the Plan for Change

Key questions: What do we want to do? Why do we want to do it? How do we want to do it? When do we want to do it by? And how much is it all going to cost?

Many change programs fall by the wayside simply because insufficient thought is given to the plan and the problems that are likely to occur. There are always problems, and it is sensible to anticipate what they may be and how they should be tackled, rather than trying to formulate plans halfway through the project. Make sure that you give due consideration to all of the most likely problems, such as technical bugs, delays caused by suppliers, or sharp increases in financing costs, to name just a few. If you do this at the beginning, you're unlikely to be thrown off course by unexpected surprises.

Organizer Sheet 17, Anticipating Problems, will help you to anticipate and prepare for the problems that you are most likely to encounter. Use the organizer sheet to write down the most likely problems that could occur at each stage of the change program, together with the most realistic solution for dealing with each one.

Although you may have a clear idea of where you are and where you want to be in six or twelve months' time, make sure that you focus, in detail, on what must happen in the intervening period to get from here to there. Your plan should include your SWEET objectives—those sensible, written, easy-to-understand, easy-to-measure, task-related statements describing exactly what it is you intend to achieve (e.g., reduce the existing workforce by five percent; introduce "While-U-Wait" on-site diagnostic and repair service; devolve budgetary control to regional centers).

Your plan should include the start and completion dates for the entire project, as well as milestone dates for completion of each part of the project. Organizer Sheet 18, Deadlines and Milestones, will help you with this aspect of your planning. Next, define areas of responsibility so that you know who will be held accountable for each part of the change program, which resources you are going to need, and how you are going to delegate responsibility for key tasks (see Delegating). Organizer Sheet 19, Resources and Responsibilities for Change Management, will help you to map out, on paper, resources and responsibilities for change management.

Your plan should also include detailed action plans for any area that will either be affected by or make a contribution to the change. Areas include staffing, buildings, finance, equipment, training, and marketing.

Say, for example, that the change program requires three people to be eliminated from the training department (so the training area will be affected by the change). At the same time, you want the training department to deliver training to the remainder of the workforce (this area will make a contribution to the change). You must work out the answers to some serious questions, such as:

(text continues on page 54)

Anticipating Problems

Use this Organizer before the change program starts.

What Can Go Wrong?	Stage When This Can Happen	Realistic **Action** for Solving or Minimizing Problem
_____	_____	_____
_____	_____	_____
_____	_____	_____
_____	_____	_____
_____	_____	_____
_____	_____	_____
_____	_____	_____
_____	_____	_____
_____	_____	_____
_____	_____	_____
_____	_____	_____
_____	_____	_____
_____	_____	_____
_____	_____	_____

Deadlines and Milestones

Use this Organizer before the change program starts.

Date on which the change program is to start: _____

Date by which the change program is to be completed: _____

Key Stages of the Program:

1. _____ Milestone date for stage 1 to be achieved: _____

2. _____ Milestone date for stage 2 to be achieved: _____

3. _____ Milestone date for stage 3 to be achieved: _____

4. _____ Milestone date for stage 4 to be achieved: _____

5. _____ Milestone date for stage 5 to be achieved: _____

Other important dates: _____

_____

Resources and Responsibility for Change Management

Use this Organizer before the change program starts.

Change program objective: _____

_____

Resources I Need to Enable Me to Achieve This Objective	The Person to Whom I'm Going to Delegate Responsibility for Obtaining and Managing This Resource
☐ Finance	_____
☐ Buildings	_____
☐ Consultancy or other professional services	_____
☐ Machinery and equipment	_____
☐ Additional staff	_____
☐ Training	_____
☐ In-house communication	_____
☐ Another resource (explain)	_____
☐ Another resource (explain)	_____
☐ Another resource (explain)	_____

- Eliminate three people from the training department:
  —Which people?
  —When?
- Deliver training to the remainder of the workforce:
  —Which training?
  —For whom?
  —When?

Ideally, your written action plan should spell out what you want to achieve and how you are going to do it. Your plan should include information about budgets and finance, and there should be details of the communication framework you will use to inform people about what is going to happen and keep them up-to-date.

There are many ways in which you can disseminate information throughout your company. You can set up formal presentations or informal team briefings to large or small groups; you can distribute letters, brochures, e-mail, videos, or an in-house newsletter. You can organize people into small quality circles or establish large departmental teams to meet and share ideas and information. Daily, weekly, or monthly meetings can be arranged to update people and give them a forum for voicing their concerns and asking questions.

The type of communication framework you choose depends on your organization's culture. Formal presentations to large groups may work best in a formal, multilayered organization; informal team briefings may work best in a flat, informal organization.

You know what will work best in your own company, but whatever format you choose, always remember that the focus should be on presenting accurate and honest information to everyone in the company at the same time. That way, everyone is playing the same game, according to the same set of rules.

Expect the Unexpected

Key question: What can go wrong?

It's important that you also work out a reasonable alternative course of action (i.e., Plan B) that you can implement if Plan A (your original plan) does not appear to be working. Plan B should take you to the same goal as Plan A, but perhaps by a slightly different route. Once the planned change is initiated, then you must monitor and review progress to make sure that you are on target to meet your stated objectives. (See Project Planning.)

Helping Yourself to Cope With Change

Pushing change through an organization, particularly if you have a less than receptive and enthusiastic workforce, is tough. Take into account that your job will be even more demanding and stressful at these times. No matter where you are in the organizational structure, you are bound to have some concerns of your own. These may be related to the change process itself—"Can I carry out this project to a successful conclusion?"—or to the outcome of the change process—"Where am I going to fit in? Am I going to be able to cope?"

To help yourself during these turbulent times, make sure you access every available scrap of information. The more you know, the better. If you are managing just a part of the change program, don't get in a flap about what other managers are or aren't doing. Focus on fulfilling your responsibilities smoothly and efficiently. At work, keep your fears to yourself. Whatever you do, don't contribute to the rumor machine. Keep your head down and get on with the job. Recognize that this isn't an easy time for anyone, including you, and take positive action to manage your stress. (See Stress Management.)

If it seems as though you won't fit into the organization when the change program is finalized, start thinking about your other options and begin making plans. This way, any changes will be those you have chosen for youself, rather than those imposed by someone else. Finally, if you are someone who loves a challenge and relishes change, then spare a thought for your colleagues and team members for whom change represents stepping over a steep cliff into the unknown.

Change Management Action Checklist

☐ Before you begin your change program, be clear about precisely what it is you want to achieve and how you plan to achieve it.

☐ Create a detailed plan that includes:
1. Your objectives
2. Dates for starting and completing not only the entire program but also each individual element of the program
3. Persons to whom responsibility for each area of activity is to be delegated
4. Detailed action plans covering every aspect of the change program
5. Budgets
6. Communication framework

☐ Expect things to go wrong, and prepare for all eventualities.

☐ SHINE when you are managing change by being:
1. Supportive
2. Honest
3. Informative
4. No-nonsense
5. Enthusiastic

☐ Recognize that some people on your team may perceive the change program as a threat to their physical, mental, and emotional well-being.

☐ Acknowledge your own fears and concerns about the change program and take positive action to manage your own stress.

☐ Recognize that some people love change. Harness their energy and optimism to motivate the less enthusiastic people on the team.

Coaching

It's important to recognize the difference between coaching and mentoring and to know when it's appropriate to use each technique.

Mentoring is usually a partnership between two people, one of whom is often more capable, more experienced, or more expert than the other. A mentor is usually available to act as a role model, a sounding board, an advisor, and sometimes even a counselor or a surrogate parent. A mentor is likely to say, "Sure, I've been there. This is what happened to me, and this is what I learned from it. In your situation now, what I'd advise you to do would be _____."

Coaching is much more hands-on and practical. A coach is likely to say, "Okay, this is how I want you to do it." Or, "Sit in with me and watch what I do, then you can try it out for yourself."

Coaching is a key management tool. Often, the only way for people to improve their performance is for their manager to tackle the problem head-on and explain and demonstrate how something should be done. It is unrealistic to think to yourself, "Betty is going to have to take a long, hard look at the way she's handling customers," or "Someone is going to have to tell Joe about his communication skills," and then just walk away and hope that matters improve. In nine cases out of ten, they won't unless you, as a manager, take action and tell and show your employees what you want.

Because coaching is about sharing skills as well as knowledge and experience, you could find yourself coaching someone new to the corporation or someone who has been with the organization almost as long as you have. When coaching involves sitting down with employees and telling and showing them what to do, you must give detailed and specific feedback after they've done the work. Coaching can also be about providing special opportunities for someone to learn, grow, and develop.

Telling and Showing

If you're not satisfied with someone's performance at work, then it is up to you to get proactive and do something about it, rather than hoping the individual's performance will get better or assuming someone else will help the worker.

You may be thinking to yourself, "I can't find anything in this office. Sandy's filing is driving me crazy." Left alone, the situation can escalate out of control. The filing doesn't improve, but you become more irritated as each day goes by until, finally, unable to find a vital document, you snap and unleash all of your anger and frustration in one brief exchange with Sandy. To resolve the situation, what you must do is specify how you want Sandy's filing to change, then explain and demonstrate what you want. This process applies to any task where you're looking for an improvement in performance.

Be Specific

Key question: What, specifically, do I want this person to do or do differently?

Coaching is about specifics. How, precisely, do you want someone's performance to change? What exactly do you want the employee to stop doing or start doing? Answer the phone within three rings? File documents using another system so you can find something when you want it? Be more upbeat and outgoing with customers? Put the green memos in the right-hand holder, and the blue ones underneath the yellow plastic?

When you find yourself wanting things to change, use Organizer Sheet 20, Coaching Planner, to clarify the specific improvements you want someone to make. By working through this organizer on your own, before talking to the employee, you'll be able to sort out what aspect of her job performance needs to be improved and precisely what changes the individual will have to make in order to achieve those improvements.

Explain What You Want

Key question: How do I make sure that my explanations are clear and concise?

Most people like to do a good job. And most people love to get positive feedback and encouragement. Explaining how you want someone to do something is not demoralizing. It's taking employees to a position where they can do a good job and where, as a result of that, they'll receive the positive feedback and encouragement they need.

Talk through exactly what you want. Carefully explain how you want something done and why. For example, "The way it is at the moment, I can't find the letters you've processed the previous day. I think that's because you're holding back the copies so you can file them. What I'd like you to do is to print an extra copy of each document, slip it into a file, and put the file on my desk at the end of the day. That way, if someone calls me the next day, I've got a copy of what I said right in front of me. As soon as the filing is up-to-date, you can shred the extra copy."

Demonstrate the Process

Key question: How do I show this person exactly what I want him to do?

Once you've explained what you want, demonstrate what you want. That way you can be sure that someone is going to understand completely. If it's a complicated task, tell, show, and then ask the individual to show you how it's done. That way you can guide the person through the process, correcting mistakes as they occur and repeating your demonstration if necessary.

One of the best ways to learn something new is to watch an expert do it and then try it for yourself while the expert offers

Organizer Sheet 20

Coaching Planner

Use this Organizer (one for each employee) before the coaching interview.

Name of employee: _____

I want this person to make the following improvements:

☐ The way he/she currently _____

_____ needs to be improved.

He/she can improve performance in this area by: _____

_____.

☐ The way he/she currently _____

_____ needs to be improved.

He/she can improve performance in this area by: _____

_____.

☐ The way he/she currently _____

_____ needs to be improved.

He/she can improve performance in this area by: _____

_____.

advice, guidance, and how-to tips. You've probably learned a new skill this way yourself. The key point here is that if you're looking for measurable improvements in performance, you have to be prepared to commit the time and the energy to explain and show how something should be done.

Coaching Through Feedback

Key question: How can I make sure that the feedback I'm giving is clear, detailed, and encouraging?

Coaching is also about observing someone doing something and then offering specific and detailed feedback. Maybe one of your employees needs to improve negotiating skills. You start the coaching process by telling and showing the person what to do. Then you take her with you to a negotiation and, again, you demonstrate the skills involved. Finally, you sit in with the individual while she negotiates, and you watch and listen to everything that happens. Afterward, you organize a one-on-one meeting and take the person through each stage of the process, giving detailed and constructive feedback on what she did, how well it was done, and how it can be done better next time. In essence, through this process, you are offering intensive coaching in negotiating skills.

Coaching Through Challenges

Key question: Is this person ready to succeed?

The very best coaches are inspirational. They believe in their people. They push them to try more difficult, more complex, and more rewarding tasks, and because they believe that their people can come through, their people respond with energy and determination and enthusiasm.

Provided you genuinely believe someone is ready to tackle a new challenge and you are able to be there to support him (ready to catch him, just in case he falls), then you can coach someone by setting new and exciting challenges.

The key point here is that you should never set someone up to fail. If you believe the individual can do it, provided he is willing to work hard and stretch for success, then offer the opportunity. If you know in your heart that the person is not ready, then hold back and wait awhile.

Coaching is an ongoing process, and effective coaches don't just walk away and leave people to sink or swim. They love to see their people do well, and they willingly offer praise, recognition, and encouragement when they see someone is putting energy and effort into learning something new. And, especially important, they recognize that everyone makes mistakes and that much can be learned through the process of getting it wrong and then finding out how to put it right.

Organizer Sheet 21, Coaching Record, will help you to keep an ongoing record of the coaching you've done with individuals and the progress that's been achieved. After each coaching session, write down the skills you explained and demonstrated. When you next have an opportunity to observe that person in action, using the skills you've coached her in, record the results. Then, either on your own or with the employee, decide what should happen next and check the appropriate box on the organizer sheet.

The coaching record only takes a minute or two to complete, yet it can provide evidence (especially useful with difficult employees) that you have provided the right kind of assistance to help a person do a better job.

Coaching Record

Use this Organizer (one for each employee) after the coaching interview.

Name of employee: _____

Date of coaching session: _____

During the session, I explained and demonstrated:

What I told the employee was expected of him/her:

Date by which results are expected: _____

Assessment of results:

- ☐ Performance has improved to desired level. No additional coaching is necessary.
- ☐ Performance has improved, but not to desired level. Some additional coaching is needed.
- ☐ Performance has not improved. Discussions must take place with the individual to find out why there hasn't been any improvement and agree on the next course of action.

The next step:

- ☐ Repeat coaching session.
- ☐ Offer one-on-one feedback following performance.
- ☐ Ask someone else to explain and demonstrate.
- ☐ Meet with the employee for a discussion.
- ☐ Other actions (explain): _____

Coaching Action Checklist

☐ Decide how you want someone to improve, and be prepared to commit time and energy to the coaching process.

☐ Explain the changes you want people to make to their performance.

☐ Demonstrate how you want something done.

☐ Get employees to try doing something for themselves, while you watch.

☐ Provide detailed feedback on performance.

☐ Recognize that people learn just as much from mistakes as they do from getting it right the first time.

☐ When you judge someone is ready, offer the person a new and exciting challenge, but don't ever set someone up to fail.

Communication

If you want to influence, persuade, sell, explain, instruct, delegate, monitor, review, appraise, contribute at meetings, build and lead your team, and do all the other things that managers do, then you have to be able to communicate clearly and effectively.

Good and Bad Communication

Bad communication is often a one-way process that can leave you feeling that the other person hasn't understood, hasn't been interested, or hasn't made any effort to understand your point of view. Or, if you are on the receiving end of bad communication, it can make you feel as if you've been lectured, interrogated, patronized, or dismissed as being of little or no importance.

Good communication is a two-way process. It occurs when people exchange thoughts, views, ideas, requests, or information. And when people express clearly how they feel or what they want. And when people listen attentively and make a real effort to understand where the other person is coming from. Good communication leaves you feeling as if you've had every opportunity to make your point and the other person has understood, just as you've understood them. Even if you disagree, you are both clear about what has been said and agreed on and what should happen next. There are no gray areas.

Good communication involves:

- Saying what you have to say, clearly and concisely
- Listening attentively and courteously

- Encouraging mutual understanding by clarifying and summarizing
- Building rapport and encouraging the flow

All these techniques help you to build successful relationships, enhance your reputation, and get what you want out of life.

Saying What You Have to Say, Clearly and Concisely

Key question: What do I need to say?

Giving Instructions

By giving unclear or ambiguous instructions, the unwary manager can unleash an unfortunate chain of events. Here are two examples:

You think:	I must get that report typed up and delivered to Sheryl this morning.
You say:	"Louisa, will you get that report to Sheryl this morning, please? It's really urgent."
You assume:	Louisa will type up the report and deliver it, smart and neat, to Sheryl's desk.

What actually happens is that Louisa collects your sheaf of torn and scribbled notes and delivers them in their dog-eared, coffee-stained folder. As a result Sheryl, the vice president, makes several negative assumptions about you and your attitudes.

You think:	I must ask Mike to talk to Howie and find out what the delay is about—and see if we can't do something to help.
You say:	"Mike, do something for me. Will you talk to Howie and sort out the delay?"
You assume:	Mike will sit down with Howie and talk through the situation (as you would, if you were doing it) and agree on a workable plan for moving the project forward.

What actually happens is that Mike uses his own, very different approach. The next day, Howie calls you to say that he's no longer able to work on the contract and you'll have to find someone else.

Strategy for Giving Instructions

When you are giving instructions, assume nothing and leave nothing to chance. Say clearly and precisely what you want someone to do and spell out, very clearly, the outcome you're looking for. If the instructions are complex or unusual, ask questions to ensure that the other person understands what you want and is confident about being able to deliver the task on time, the way you want it. Take the time and make the effort to be pleasant. You are likely to get much more cooperation and motivation than if you use your authority to ride roughshod over people.

Explaining Ideas, Concepts, and Plans

You've done much research and a great deal of thinking, and it all makes perfect sense to you. You are comfortable and familiar with the structure and meaning of your idea, concept, or plan. You are inspired by it, and you can understand how it could work. But, no matter how straightforward or simple your cunning plan may seem to you, you must remember that your idea will be new to other people. And it usually takes people awhile to get their heads around new information.

Keep it simple. Don't go overboard with details, facts, or figures. Present your key ideas or chunks of information in a logical order. Start at the beginning, and take your listeners through your proposal in a linear fashion.

Strategy for Explaining Ideas, Concepts, or Plans

Make sure you present your information in a logical sequence. You can do this by using one of the following techniques:

1. *Time sequence.* Take your listeners through a sequence of events as they occurred, in real time. Or describe the chronological order in which you would like events to take place or things to be

67

done in the future. For example, "In January this should happen.
. . . Then at the beginning of February. . . . Then we need do
nothing until May, but in May. . . ."

2. *Place sequence.* Take your listeners through the sequence of
information from place to place. For example, "This is what happened in Paris. . . . In Zurich these events took place. . . . In Boston
we found out that. . . ." Or, for example, "When we receive an
order in the call center, this happens. . . . In the warehouse, this
happens. . . . In the accounts department, this happens. . . ."

3. *Looping sequence.* Begin with a topic that loops onto another
topic, which loops onto a third topic, and so on. An example: food;
healthy eating; vegetables; individual adult daily requirements;
nutritional value of our product. Another example: training the
senior management team; the senior management team relays information to middle management; middle managers create work-
groups and train people in the factory; our people in the factory
work together in coaching partnerships.

Whichever sequence you use to explain something, don't assume that because it is clear to you, everyone else will see it the
same way. And don't think that just because you've explained
once, you won't need to answer questions or go back over the key
points. Take it slowly, aim for clarity, and even if you cannot understand why someone doesn't understand, go through it carefully
and patiently as many times as you need to until your message gets
through.

If it is your idea, concept, or plan, then it is your responsibility
to explain it so that other people can understand. Remember, no
one is going to buy in to your proposal without being absolutely
clear about what is involved. Use Organizer Sheet 22, Key Points
Strategy, to choose the best approach for explaining your proposals to a new audience and to ensure you include all the necessary
key points.

Tough Talking

Tough talking often involves telling people something they
don't want to hear (e.g., at an appraisal or a disciplinary meeting),
asking for something you want (e.g., a pay rise or promotion or

Key Points Strategy

Use this Organizer before you need to explain a new concept, idea, proposal, or plan.

The best strategy is to explain using a:

☐ Time sequence
☐ Place sequence
☐ Loop sequence
☐ Other (explain): _____

Key points to include:

1.

2.

3.

4.

5.

6.

7.

extended vacation), or refusing a request (e.g., "No, I don't want to work in Texas for three months, even though you need me to be there," or "No, I don't want to share an office with you," or "No, I don't want to change to a different commission structure").

You may be reluctant to say how you feel, ask for what you want, or say no for many different reasons, but speaking the truth, calmly and clearly, is often the only way to go.

Strategy for Tough Talking

Key question: What's my bottom line?

If you have difficulty expressing what you think and how you feel, or asking for what you want, assess your bottom line and convert it into your core statement. Your core statement should be short and specific. It should either reflect how you think and feel or describe what you want.

Examples of core statements are: "I'm worried about the way you're handling important customers, and I want to know what's happening." " I need at least five people on the team if I'm going to bring this project in on time. I can't do it with less." "I'm not prepared to sign that document."

Creating your core statement before the tough talking starts allows you to think through and clarify your position. It will also keep you from being sidetracked. Even if the conversation strays onto other topics, by mentally hanging on to your core statement you can keep control of the discussion and steer things back on course. You may not actually verbalize your core statement during the conversation, but remember it is your bottom line and, if you keep it in mind, you won't be bullied or persuaded into taking another position.

When you are tough talking, use "I" statements (e.g., I feel that . . . I think that . . . I've noticed that . . . I'm anxious about . . .) and stay focused on what you want to say. Using "I" statements is a good way to tell someone how you feel and where you stand. You are not making value judgments or accusations; you are simply and calmly stating how you see the situation. Don't be diverted from what you have to say by someone using humor, sarcasm, anger, or any other emotion. Stick with your core statement, and use Organizer Sheet 23, Your Core Statement, to define what you want to say when you find yourself in a tough-talking situation.

Saying No

Sometimes, with some people, saying no can be easy. Other times, with other people, saying no is much more difficult. When you must say no to either someone with power over you (e.g., your boss or a key account customer) or someone you want to remain on good terms with (e.g., a coworker or a supplier), there are three key points to remember:

1. When you say no, you are refusing the request and not rejecting the person.
2. You have the right to say no.
3. It is possible to say no calmly and pleasantly, without getting angry or upset or feeling guilty.

Strategy for Saying No

- *No, and there's a good reason.* If you give a reason when you say no (e.g., No, I can't because . . .), people will know that you are not just being difficult or uncooperative.
- *No, but how about this?* You can say no and offer an alternative when you are dealing with someone who is in a position superior to you (e.g., No, I can't promise I can do that in the available time, but how would it be if I . . .).
- *No, no, no!* People may use manipulative techniques to get you to agree to do something you don't want to do. They'll make the same request in three different ways, use emotional blackmail to make you feel guilty (e.g., "I did you a favor last month. You could help me out just this once"), try to wear you down with repeated requests, or take an aggressive approach. In these situations, use the broken-record technique. Create a core statement that contains the word *no* and repeat variations based on your core statement.

For example: "No, I'm not prepared to change my plans." "I

Your Core Statement

Use this Organizer before you have a tough-talking session with someone.

What do I think? _____

_____

_____

_____

_____

How do I feel? _____

_____

_____

_____

_____

What do I want? _____

_____

_____

_____

_____

Based on this information, my core statement is: _____

_____

_____

_____

_____

understand how important it is to you, but I'm not prepared to change my plans." "No, I'm not prepared to." "I hear what you're saying, but I'm not prepared to change my plans." When you use the broken-record technique, stay calm, don't get drawn into the other person's emotional responses, stick to your core statement, and firmly and pleasantly repeat "No" until the message gets through.

Finding Out Information

Key questions: Do I just need to know the facts? Do I need to know about facts and feelings? Do I need to know about the deeper feelings and underlying issues?

A key part of the management task is finding out facts (e.g., the sales figures for this week, who's coming to sort out the computer, the number of people coming to the meeting) and finding out about feelings (e.g., the reasons two members of your team can't get along, why someone's work isn't up to standard, why a customer is refusing to settle his account). The only way to obtain the information you need is by asking the right questions in the right way.

Strategy for Asking Questions

To find out facts, use closed questions: Did you? Have you? Will you? Is there? Was there? Such questions encourage people to give you brief and factual answers.

To find out facts and feelings, use open questions: Why do you think this problem has happened? How do you think we can solve the problem? How can we put this situation right? What can we do to . . . ? What do you think would be the best way to . . . ? What would you suggest that we do? Where do you think the difficulty lies? When would be the best time for . . . ? When did the problem start?

Open questions can't be answered with a simple yes or no response, and they encourage people to give their views, opinions, ideas, and suggestions.

To find out about deeper feelings and underlying issues, use probing questions: How does that make you feel? Tell me, what do you think about that? What do you think are the main issues here? Probing questions invite people to pause and reflect on their own thoughts and feelings. Such questions are especially useful during mentoring, appraisal, or disciplinary interviews, or when you find yourself having to manage conflict situations. The answers to probing questions can usually give you insight into why someone is experiencing difficulties with customers or not achieving targets or not getting through the work. Organizer Sheet 24, Getting the Right Information, can help you clarify the closed, open, and probing questions you need to ask to obtain the information you want.

Giving Feedback on Performance

Key question: How can I say what needs to be said without damaging this relationship or demotivating this employee?

Giving feedback on performance requires an intelligent and diplomatic approach. You can, of course, be totally up-front and shoot from the hip: "I have to tell you, your presentation was diabolical. I couldn't hear what you were saying, I couldn't follow your line of thinking, and the visuals weren't worth looking at. From now on, I'm going to do the presentations myself." Although you may genuinely believe that comments such as these are an honest appraisal of someone's performance, passing them on, uncensored, would not be the most productive way to tackle the situation. Overwhelmingly negative feedback often causes genuine stress, demotivation, demoralization, and even depression, all of which can have a serious impact on how someone does his job.

Strategy for Giving Feedback on Performance

When you are giving feedback, especially feedback on poor work performance, use "I" statements, focus on the facts, be very specific, and use open questions to encourage two-way communication. For example, don't say something general such as, "You are always missing your deadlines. Things have got to improve."

Getting the Right Information

Use this Organizer before any complex or difficult discussion.

The closed questions I need to ask to get the factual information I want:

1. _____

2. _____

3. _____

The open questions I need to ask to get the facts and feelings I need to know about:

1. _____

2. _____

3. _____

4. _____

5. _____

The probing questions I need to ask to give me an insight into people's deeper feelings and underlying issues:

1. _____

2. _____

3. _____

4. _____

5. _____

6. _____

7. _____

Instead, say something specific like, "I see that you've missed two key deadlines this month, one on the ninth and one on the twentieth. What's been happening?"

Another approach is the sandwich technique. Here you focus on the facts, use "I" statements, say clearly how you want the person to change or improve, and sandwich your negative comments between positive ones. Here is an example of how the sandwich technique can be applied:

1. *Positive feedback.* "I think you handled the questions at the end of the presentation really well. You gave everyone a clear answer and just the right amount of information."

2. *Negative feedback.* "I do have some concerns about the presentation as a whole. I couldn't hear what you were saying, I couldn't follow the logic of your argument too well, and the visuals lacked color and interest."

3. *Positive feedback.* "I want you to work on these three key areas—projecting your voice, presenting the arguments in a logical, step-by-step sequence, and creating visuals that have more impact. Stay with the way you interact with the audience. That's really good."

Use Organizer Sheet 25, Sandwich Technique for Performance Feedback, before you meet with someone to give her feedback on her work performance. By creating a sandwich of positive, negative, and positive feedback, you can better express what you want someone to stop doing, do differently, start doing, or continue doing in the same way.

Listening Attentively and Courteously

Good communicators listen as much as, if not more than, they speak. They listen to show that they are interested and paying attention; they listen for both the spoken and the unspoken message; they listen because they know they'll learn more by listening than they ever will by talking. No matter whom you are dealing with— your boss, a client, a supplier, or a colleague—it is to your advantage to listen and listen hard.

What's being said? What's not being said? How is it being said?

Sandwich Technique for Performance Feedback

Use this Organizer before you have to give someone negative feedback on work performance.

Name of employee: _____

These are the specific things I want this person to stop doing:

1. _____
2. _____
3. _____

These are the specific things I want this person to do in a different way:

1. _____
2. _____
3. _____

These are the specific things I want this person to start doing:

1. _____
2. _____
3. _____

These are the specific things I want this person to continue doing:

1. _____
2. _____
3. _____

The Sandwich of Positive and Negative Comments:

☐ Positive comment: _____

☐ Negative comment: _____

☐ Positive comment: _____

How does body language match up with the words? If you are busy interrupting the speaker or drifting off into a private daydream, you'll miss out on key information that may help you to close the deal, control the negotiation, or turn a sour situation into a personal success.

Strategy for Listening Attentively and Courteously

Key question: How can I show that I'm focused, interested, and really listening?

Being heard is important to everyone, and listening to people attentively and courteously clearly shows that you are taking them seriously and that you respect and appreciate what they have to say. You can pay people a great compliment and make them feel good just by giving them your full attention.

Don't interrupt. Even if you thoroughly disagree, let them finish speaking first. Don't tune out and start formulating what you're going to say in response. Even if you are bored, or you assume you know what's coming next, listen because you could miss some important information.

Focus on what's being said, even if you've heard it all before, many times. Use positive and affirmative body language—smiling, nodding, leaning forward in your seat. From time to time, make encouraging comments (e.g., "Sure," "Right," "Yes") that confirm you are interested and are actively listening. Even though it may seem like a passive activity, effective listening is hard work.

Achieving Mutual Understanding

Key question: Do we all have the same understanding?

There is more to effective communication than just saying what you have to say and listening to the other side of the story. Because two-way communication is about two or more people making a concerted effort to understand one another, use the techniques of clarifying and summarizing to help the process along.

Encouraging Mutual Understanding by Clarifying and Summarizing

Sometimes people ramble. Or they go off on a tangent and start talking about unrelated topics. Sometimes, if they are angry or emotional, the words don't come out right, and they can get confused about what it is they are trying to say. And if they are confused, you will be, too.

Strategy for Clarifying

Key question: Do I really understand this?

Resist the temptation to pretend you understand what's been said when you don't. People will appreciate it if you take the time to ask them to clarify their comments. It shows you are listening, and it shows you are interested. If you don't understand, say so. "Can I just check this out with you? It seems like you're saying. . . ." Or, "I don't think I'm too clear on this. Can you take me through that again?" Or, "Okay, let me make sure I understand this. You're happy with the way we've laid out the campaign and think the schedule is appropriate, but you're not comfortable with the budget. Is that right?"

If you question and clarify what has been said, people will respect your determination to achieve clear, two-way communication. If you stay quiet and hope that you'll understand things better later on, you could lose the deal or wreck the relationship.

Strategy for Summarizing

Summarize arrangements, or points of agreement or disagreement, at regular intervals throughout the conversation. This technique brings everyone up to speed and ensures that everyone has the same understanding at the same time. "So we've agreed you are going to brief your team tomorrow. What we need to agree on now is how we can move the shipment out before Friday." Always summarize at the end of the meeting and don't just assume that everyone has the same understanding.

79

Building Rapport and Encouraging the Flow

Communicating With Body Talk

Key question: What am I saying without speaking?

You can communicate a great deal without actually saying a word. Your posture, facial expression, and the way you maintain eye contact all send a clear signal about the way you're feeling and how you're responding to the other person. By observing and interpreting other people's body language, you can tell whether they like what you have to say or whether they want to bring the conversation to a close.

Strategy for Using and Interpreting Body Talk

Use positive, open body talk. Maintain eye contact, but without staring. Stand tall and relaxed, to give an impression of ease and confidence. Sit still and relaxed, leaning forward to emphasize a point, leaning backward to show you are considering what has been said. Smile, don't frown. Don't fiddle with papers or doodle while someone is talking. Don't keep checking your watch or making sure your mobile phone is switched on. Don't gaze out the window or up at the ceiling.

Watch the other person for signs of hostility, boredom, or enthusiasm. Such actions as looking away, leaning away from you, folding arms over chest, fidgeting, doodling, foot tapping, sighing, frowning, and keeping a poker face are all indicators that what you have to say is not being well received.

Ask a trusted friend, colleague, or someone in your family to observe you over a period of time (maybe two or three hours or even a day) to evaluate your nonverbal communication skills. They can then use Organizer Sheet 26, Body Talk, to create a feedback form that will help you to sharpen your body language skills.

Matching and Mirroring

People tend to trust people who look and behave as they do themselves. Someone who regularly wears a business suit and

Body Talk

Use this Organizer when you want someone to give you feedback on nonverbal communication.

Eye Contact
- ☐ Stares at people.
- ☐ Maintains good eye contact. Looks people in the eye without staring. Looks away at regular intervals.
- ☐ Doesn't look people in the eye. Looks away, for example, at ceiling, at floor, or out the window, for example.
- ☐ Is open and friendly.
- ☐ Is hard and aggressive.

Eye contact could be improved by:

Posture

When standing and sitting, looks:
- ☐ Relaxed and confident
- ☐ Tense and nervous
- ☐ Intimidating and overbearing

Posture is:
- ☐ Good
- ☐ Okay

Posture could be improved by:

Mannerisms
- ☐ Shuffles and fidgets with things.
- ☐ Taps foot.
- ☐ Shifts in chair.
- ☐ Doesn't fidget or fiddle.
- ☐ Keeps mannerisms to a minimum.
- ☐ Uses a lot of distracting mannerisms.

Other comments:

drives a BMW will prefer to trust someone who also wears a business suit and drives a BMW, rather than someone who wears a leather jacket and rides a motorcycle.

In the same way, you'll find it easier to achieve rapport with people if you use the same kind of vocabulary, speak with the same speed and pitch, and match their body language. You can use matching and mirroring to indicate to people that you are like them, you are on their side, and you want to establish and maintain a good relationship.

Strategy for Matching

- *Match the vocabulary.* During conversation, if someone uses jargon and buzzwords, match him. Incorporate this vocabulary into your conversation. If someone speaks plainly and directly, match her.
- *Match the speed.* During conversation, if someone speaks quickly, speed up and match him. Conversely, if he speaks slowly, slow down and speak more slowly than you usually would so that you match him.
- *Match the level.* During conversation, if someone normally speaks quietly or very loudly, match her.
- *Match the pitch.* During conversation, if someone has a high-pitched voice, raise your voice to match. If someone has a deeper voice, lower yours to match.

By matching the way you sound to the way the other person sounds, the individual will feel more comfortable and relaxed. You'll find it easier to establish rapport and encourage the person to listen to you, and you will be able to make your points easily and smoothly. He'll respond to you because you are like him, so he'll be able to relate to you and trust you.

Strategy for Mirroring

By mirroring people's body language, you are again reinforcing the idea that you are like them and that you are eager to get along with them. When two people are engrossed in a conversation and they're enjoying each other's company, they unconsciously and spontaneously mirror one another. If one person crosses his legs, the other person will often mirror the movement by crossing her legs. If one moves forward, so will the other.

Let your clients, bosses, or colleagues know that you agree with them and that you are on their side by subtly mirroring their body movements.

Communication Action Checklist

☐ Say what you have to say, clearly and concisely.

☐ Listen attentively and courteously.

☐ Encourage mutual understanding by summarizing and clarifying.

☐ Build rapport and encourage the flow by matching and mirroring.

☐ Ask the right kinds of questions—open, closed, or probing—to get the information you need.

☐ Don't walk away from a speaker until you are absolutely clear about what has been said and agreed on.

☐ Stick with it because good communication will allow you to build relationships, enhance your reputation, and get you what you want.

Dealing With Difficult People

For most managers, the toughest part of the job is dealing with people who go out of their way to be difficult. These people, who seem to thrive on behaving badly, may cross your path as colleagues, customers, your boss, or, perhaps most troublesome of all, people on your team.

No matter who they are, how you respond to them makes a huge difference. It isn't productive or professional for you to constantly buy in to their bad behavior to appease them. This way you may keep them sweet, but you'll eventually feel powerless and inadequate. And it certainly isn't helpful for you to allow them to push your buttons because, if you lose your cool and your temper, you'll also lose credibility and respect.

Giving in or getting crazy doesn't work with difficult people. But understanding why you find them to be difficult, and recognizing why they behave the way they do, is the start of a strategy that lets you stay sane.

Recognizing the Differences Among People

Key question: Why do I find this person so hard to handle?

Do You Find Someone's Style Difficult?

If you are upbeat and outgoing, you may find it difficult to deal with someone who is basically shy and withdrawn. If you are cautious and analytical, it may be difficult for you to relate to a high-profile risk taker who loves to operate right on the edge. Recognize that you cannot change another person's style, and there is no reason for you to change your style. But, by accepting that there is a difference, you can learn to be more comfortable when you are with this person.

Is There a Conflict of Values and Beliefs?

If you are a steady, family-oriented person with fairly traditional values and beliefs, you may find it difficult to get along with someone who enjoys a free-floating, no-strings, no-commitment lifestyle. If you value life's little luxuries and count retail therapy as one of your important pastimes, you may find it hard to understand and appreciate someone who counts every dollar and lives way below his income level.

Recognizing that everyone is different and has the right to live by their own values and beliefs may help to put this difference into perspective.

Is Success the Problem?

If you have achieved recognition and success within your organization, could this be the underlying tension between you and the people you find difficult? Did they win the promotion or the pay increase that you felt was rightfully yours?

Do you drive a larger, faster, more expensive company car? Is their office more comfortable and better equipped? Remember that material success is often transitory. Nothing ever stays the same, and who knows where you'll be and what you'll be doing ten years down the road. Try to look past the trappings of success and see the person.

Do Your Goals and Objectives Conflict With Theirs?

Your objective may be to improve quality, and theirs is to increase production. Your goal may be to cut back on spending, and theirs is to invest in training. You may be looking to expand and develop new business, and they want to consolidate and keep things the way they are. Recognize that life would be hell if everyone wanted the same piece of the pie.

Do You Just Dislike Some People?

You may have a problem with some people because there is just something about them that sets your teeth on edge. Maybe it's their accent, or the ties they wear, or the color of their hair, or the way they laugh that pushes your buttons and convinces you that they are difficult to get along with. Ask yourself what the problem is, and use Organizer Sheet 27, What's the Problem?, to identify the reasons why you find someone so difficult to handle.

Sometimes just recognizing why you find someone difficult can help you to put the situation into perspective and start looking for those factors that you have in common. You may be able to honestly admit that your problem with someone is not due to a conflict of personal style, values and beliefs, success factors, goals and objectives, or even an illogical dislike of some aspect of his personality or appearance. Then you may still say, through clenched teeth, he is difficult!

Understanding Where the Other Person's Coming From

Key question: Why should someone change just because I find her difficult?

Everyone holds basic beliefs about themselves. These beliefs stem from our childhood experiences and what we learned and were told about ourselves during the first few years of life.

I'm a Winner and Most Other People Are Losers

People who hold this belief tend to adopt an aggressive approach to life and to other people. They use aggressive behavior— shouting, dominating, lying, and manipulating—to get what they want. Every time they use these tactics successfully, their belief

What's the Problem?

Use this Organizer to begin to analyze why you find some people difficult.

Name: _____

I find this person difficult to handle because of:

☐ His/her personality and personal style

☐ His/her values and benefits

☐ His/her success

☐ My success

☐ His/her goals and objectives

☐ His/her appearance

☐ Something about the way he/she speaks

☐ Something about his/her habits or mannerisms

☐ Something else (explain): _____

_____

about themselves is confirmed. Any self-doubt or guilt they may feel is swept away by their next triumph, their next big win.

Yet underneath the bravado there is usually an insecure person with low self-esteem who thinks that the only way to function is to "Do it to them before they do it to me." Specific examples of behavior from such people include saying one thing and meaning another; passing the buck and blaming others; playing the system, bending the rules, and overstepping the bounds of their own authority; saying anything to close the deal; and spreading gossip and rumor when it suits their purposes.

I'm a Loser and Most Other People Are Winners

These people genuinely believe that their feelings of inadequacy are valid. They have zero confidence in themselves and their capabilities, and they harbor a secret fear that one day people will find out that they are not bright and capable and that they can't do anything too well. They believe their every success at work has been due to luck rather than ability, and so they hope to hide their imagined shortcomings behind a smoke screen of pliable and passive behavior.

Specific examples of behavior from such people include saying yes when they long to say no; taking on more work than they can realistically handle and then acting as the martyr; and always avoiding saying what they think or giving an honest opinion in case their views conflict with yours.

Organizer Sheet 28, Behavioral Analysis and Action, is a tool to help you to analyze behavior you find difficult and to choose an appropriate response.

General Strategies for Dealing With Difficult People

Key question: Am I part of the problem?

What You Can Do

▪ *Cultivate the right beliefs about yourself.* Recognize your strengths and weaknesses, and accept that sometimes you are right and sometimes you're wrong. Be prepared to listen, argue your point of view, and say yes or no, depending on the circumstances. Understand that, in every situation, there is the potential for people to work together to find a solution that, although it may not be perfect, is acceptable all round. Accept the idea of creating win-win situations, and understand that if you allow someone to win, it doesn't mean that you have to lose.

▪ *Examine your own responses.* If someone is giving you a hard time, pause to take a deep breath, then try to decide whether peo-

Behavioral Analysis and Action

Use this Organizer before your relationship with someone hits rock-bottom.

Name: _____

What this person does that I find difficult to handle:

_____

_____

_____

_____

How I would like this person to change:

_____

_____

_____

What I can do to encourage this individual to change:

- ☐ Boost his/her self-confidence and self-esteem.
- ☐ Model the kind of behavior I would like this person to use.
- ☐ Communicate my concerns and describe the behavior changes I would like to see.
- ☐ Look for something to admire in this person.
- ☐ Other (explain): _____

ple are deliberately setting out to antagonize you or are simply unaware that they're driving you crazy. Look beneath the surface and think about why you find someone's behavior difficult to handle. Ask yourself if you are part of the problem. Honestly evaluate your behavior when you are around this person and consider whether, when dealing with this "difficult person," there is some aspect of your behavior that needs to change.

- *Look past the behavior and try to see the person.* Accept that certain behavior, such as bullying, backstabbing, procrastination, constant criticism and complaining, or a desperate need to always be right, most often stems from a person's lack of self-confidence and self-esteem.

- *Look past the behavior and try to see the other person's situation.* Recognize that personal issues that are causing real worry and concern may prompt someone's difficult behavior. Worries about money, relationships at home, or health problems may be causing the difficult behavior. Or possibly a person has more responsibility than she can handle or a heavier work load than you know about.

- *Distance yourself emotionally from the difficult behavior.* Make a commitment to yourself that, no matter what happens, you'll stay calm and keep your temper. Refuse to be drawn into other people's emotions and remember that it's their game, not yours.

- *Remember that everyone has certain rights.* When someone is behaving in a way that you find difficult, remind yourself that everybody has the right to express their opinion and say how they feel or what they want; live by their own values and beliefs; work toward achieving recognition and success; say no; make their own choices and decisions; and be themselves. Refer to Organizer Sheet 29, Bill of Rights, when you have difficulty remembering these rights with certain individuals; it will help you to decide on your strategy for the future.

- *Take action.* If someone is genuinely being difficult, to the point where the behavior is affecting your team, your productivity, or your peace of mind, then you have to do something about it. You have to communicate. Explain how you feel and describe the specific behavior that you are finding difficult. (See Communication and the section "Giving Feedback on Performance.")

What You Shouldn't Do

- Don't lose control of your emotions.
- Don't retaliate by using similar difficult behavior yourself.

Bill of Rights

Name: _____

With this person, I find it difficult to remember that I have the right to:

- ☐ Express my opinion
- ☐ Say how I feel
- ☐ Ask for what I want
- ☐ Live according to my own values and beliefs
- ☐ Work toward recognition and success for myself
- ☐ Say no
- ☐ Make my own decisions
- ☐ Be myself

How I can best deal with this situation: _____

_____

_____

_____

With this person, I find it difficult to remember that he/she has the right to:

- ☐ Express an opinion
- ☐ Say how he/she feels
- ☐ Ask for what he/she wants
- ☐ Live according to his/her own values and beliefs
- ☐ Work toward personal recognition and success
- ☐ Say no
- ☐ Make his/her own decisions
- ☐ Be himself/herself

How I can best deal with this situation: _____

_____

_____

_____

- Don't make dramatic gestures or pointless threats.
- Don't ask or expect other people to take sides. You must deal with the situation yourself.

Specific Strategies for Dealing With Difficult People

People Who Won't Communicate

Even if it sometimes seems as if you are trying to get blood out of a stone, you must keep asking open questions. And when you have asked something, sit tight and wait. Resist the temptation to jump in and provide your own answer.

People Who Won't Listen

Summarize everything and check that the other person's understanding is the same as yours. If you think it's necessary, put it in writing.

People Who Won't Say No

Tell them and show them that their inability to say no is causing difficulties for you, the team, and the organization. Sit down with these people and work out a schedule or a plan that they can stick to and that gives them the confidence to refuse future requests from other people.

People Who Try to Make You Feel Guilty

Objectively consider the issues and decide if it is your problem or their problem. If it is your problem, do something about it. If it is their problem, don't buy into it—you have probably got sufficient problems of your own.

People Who Try to Dominate, Control, or Condescend

When you are with these people, stay cool, calm, and in control (you can scream later, when you get home). The key point to remember is that it is their lack of confidence and self-esteem that is driving their behavior.

People Who Say One Thing and Mean Another

Get it in writing!

People Who Do It Their Way or Not At All

If some people on your team are operating in ways you don't like, then you have to get tough. Explain what you want them to do and how you want them to do it. Monitor the situation carefully. If your clear instructions are ignored, then it is time for them to be made aware that other, possibly more suitable, job opportunities await them in other organizations.

People Who Know Everything About Everything

If at all possible, try to sideline these people into a specialist area where they can build genuine expertise with which to dazzle their unfortunate colleagues. If it is a key account client who is the difficult person, then you will just to have grit your teeth and smile nicely.

Dealing With Difficult People Action Checklist

- ☐ Think seriously about the reason you find some people difficult to deal with.
- ☐ Be open to the idea that their behavior, no matter how unreasonable, may be due to personal or work-related problems about which you know nothing.
- ☐ View the situation objectively and do your utmost to stay cool, calm, and objective. Aim to focus on one aspect of their personality or behavior that you really admire.
- ☐ Don't rush headlong into a confrontational situation, but do make an opportunity to discuss your concerns. Open up two-way communication, stating how you feel and which aspects of their behavior you find difficult and would like them to change.
- ☐ Don't take ownership of other people's problems. If they can't say no, manage their workload, make a decision, or whatever, there's no reason for you to feel guilty or inadequate.
- ☐ Hang on to the thought that no one can take your confidence away unless you give it to them.
- ☐ Be realistic. You cannot expect to get along with everyone all of the time.

Decision Making

You may be one of those people who just loves to make decisions. And then again, you may find decision making difficult and sometimes even painful. Either way, as a manager you simply cannot get from away the fact that decision making is part of your job.

The decisions you make for yourself, in your personal life, are very different in scope and impact from the decisions you make at work. Personal decisions will probably affect you, your family, and your friends. Decisions you make at work may affect your organization's productivity and profitability in the long term and the short term, as well as the income and job stability of everyone who works there. Your decisions also affect the people who supply your company and those who deal with the organization daily. You have to get it right.

Decision making always involves choosing between one or more options. No matter which option you choose, there are always consequences. Sometimes the consequences will be minor and fairly unimportant. Sometimes they'll be major, surprising, or even downright unpleasant.

For your own peace of mind, and for the benefit of your organization, make sure you plan your strategy carefully. Define the situation and clarify the decision. List the key factors that will influence your decision. Prioritize the key factors in order of importance. Gather information on possible options. Consider all the available options and weigh all the possible consequences, and then (and not before) make the decision that you believe, on balance, will produce the best possible outcome.

Decision-Making Strategy

Define the Situation and Clarify the Decision

Key question: What, precisely, is the decision I need to make?

Start by defining the situation. For example, your offices are flooded and the telephone lines are down. The situation can be defined in terms of its impact on the business: Clients can't contact us. We could be losing business. We need to get up and running as soon as possible.

Next, clarify the decision. In these circumstances, the decision may be to consider relocating. Where do we relocate the business until our offices are habitable again?

List the Key Factors That Influence Your Decision

Whenever you make a decision, there are always certain key factors that you'll have to take into consideration. In the example of the flooded office, your list of key decision factors for relocating include finding a site that meets these requirements:

1. Within one hour's drive from home
2. Parking space availability
3. At least two rooms with space for four desks
4. Utilities (telephone, electricity) already installed
5. Security system
6. A flexible lease allowing us an option to move after three months
7. Rent that is not more than $1,000 a week

Use Organizer Sheet 30, Key Factors in Decision Making, to list all the key factors you need to take into account during decision making.

Prioritize the Key Factors in Order of Importance

Key question: What's really important here?

Key Factors in Decision Making

Use this Organizer at the start of the decision-making process.

Key Factors	Level of Importance			
	Number-One Priority	Important	Reasonably Important	Less Important
Cost				
Credit				
Time				
Space				
Security				
Staffing				

The next step is to list the key factors in order of importance. If cost containment is an issue for you, then item 7 in the previous list—rent not more than $1,000 a week—would become your most important key factor and would have the most influence on your decision. Or possibly because of the type of business you are in, security is vital. Then item 5—the security system—would be placed at the top of your list.

By prioritizing your key factors, you are able to see, at a glance, which options are worth considering and which are not. Use the key factors information from Organizer Sheet 30 to fill out Organizer Sheet 31, Prioritizing Key Factors. This will help you to put your key decision factors in their order of importance and create a master priority list.

Gather Information on All the Possible Options

Key question: Do I know anyone who has made a similar decision in the past, and how did it work out?

Good information is at the heart of the decision-making process. Gather as much data as you possibly can. Get brochures, leaflets, fact sheets, and specifications. Talk to as many people as possible. From their point of view, what were the advantages and the drawbacks of their decision to do something? Would they make the same decision again, or would they do something different?

Organizer Sheet 32, Gathering Information, will help you to identify the types of information you'll need when making a decision, as well as the places where you are most likely to locate this information.

Compare the Options Against Your Key Factors

Key question: Which option comes closest to my ideal solution?

Some of the options you'll discard immediately because they won't match up to any of your key factors. For example, returning to the flooded-office scenario:

Prioritizing Key Factors

Use this Organizer before you make a decision to compare how each option matches up to your list of important key factors.

This is my priority list of key factors:

Key factor priority 1: _____

Key factor priority 2: _____

Key factor priority 3: _____

Key factor priority 4: _____

Key factor priority 5: _____

Key factor priority 6: _____

Key factor priority 7: _____

Key factor priority 8: _____

Key factor priority 9: _____

Key factor priority 10: _____

Gathering Information

Use this Organizer before you make your decision.

The Information I Need	Source of Information (Place or Person)	Date by Which I Must Have Information
What's available?		
How much does it cost?		
When can I have it delivered, installed, or put into use?		
Are there any legal issues?		
Are there any training issues?		
Are there any health and safety issues?		
Are there any staffing issues?		
Are there any ethical issues?		
Are there any security issues?		
Am I going to need additional resources? If so, what are they?		
Do I know anyone who has made this kind of decision before? What can I learn from them? What mistakes should I avoid?		
Is there anything else I should know about? What?		

Prioritized List of Key Factors	Specification for Accommodation at 271 Second Avenue
1. A flexible lease allowing us an option to move after three months	Fixed lease for twelve-month period
2. Security system	No security
3. Utilities (telephone, electricity) already installed*	Utilities installed*
4. At least two rooms with space for four desks	One room with space for three desks
5. Within one hour's drive from home	Two hours' drive from home
6. Parking space availability	No nearby parking
7. Rent that is not more than $1,000 weekly	$1,250 weekly rental

Only one of the key factors—utilities (marked with the asterisk)—matches with the accommodation. So, realistically, this property is not an option worth considering.

After you have compared all the available information with your listed key factors, you will find that you can narrow the field to just three or four possible options.

Weigh the Possible Consequences of Each Option

Key question: If this is the wrong decision, what is the worst-case scenario?

Your next task is to look at the possible consequences that could result from each of the options available to you. For example, an option you are considering may meet all your required key factors except cost. The consequence of the additional cost may be that you must reexamine the budget. How will your manager view this decision? How will it impact on your reputation? If redoing the budget in your organization is not an insurmountable obstacle, and if this option matches all the other key factors and you have prioritized cost way down on your list, then this choice could be a serious contender.

Use Organizer Sheet 33, Benefits Versus Consequences, to list and evaluate the advantages and disadvantages of any decision you have to make.

Make Your Decision

Key question: If it is the wrong decision, what can I do to put it right?

Your final decision should match the key factors you've listed, have few disadvantages, and, if things go wrong, produce consequences that will have the minimum negative impact on you and your organization. You can only decide which option will give you these outcomes when you have been through the entire process outlined previously—define, clarify, list, prioritize, gather information, compare, and weigh the consequences of your choices.

Sometimes, of course, you must compromise. You may not be able to find a solution that meets all of the criteria in your key factors list. Or, perhaps, the consequences of your decision will be harder to live with than you'd like. At the very least, if you work through this process in a systematic and logical way, you will know that you've made the best possible decision under the circumstances.

Sometimes you'll make the wrong decision—nobody's perfect. So it is important to watch the situation carefully and to plan ahead. Recognize what can go wrong, and have an alternative plan ready. Work on the basis that, having done all the planning and preparation, you've made the right decision. But because life is generally unpredictable, if you make a wrong decision, by planning ahead, you'll know what to do to put it right.

Benefits Versus Consequences

Use this Organizer before you make your decision.

Option 1	The benefits of choosing this option (possible + factors)	The consequences of choosing this option (possible − factors)
	1.	1.
	2.	2.
	3.	3.
	4.	4.
	5.	5.

Option 2	The benefits of choosing this option (+ factors)	The consequences of choosing this option (− factors)
	1.	1.
	2.	2.
	3.	3.
	4.	4.
	5.	5.

Option 3	The benefits of choosing this option (+ factors)	The consequences of choosing this option (− factors)
	1.	1.
	2.	2.
	3.	3.
	4.	4.
	5.	5.

Decision-Making Action Checklist

- ☐ Define the situation and clarify the decision.
- ☐ List the key factors that will influence your decision.
- ☐ Prioritize the key factors in order of importance.
- ☐ Gather all the available information to help you make the right choice. Remember, every decision has both benefits and consequences.
- ☐ Compare the available options against your prioritized list of key factors.
- ☐ Weigh the possible consequences of each choice and aim to maximize the benefits and minimize the consequences.
- ☐ Make your decision, but prepare a fallback position so that if it appears that you've made the wrong decision, you know what to do next to rectify the situation.

Delegating

Unwise delegation, decided on the run without much thought for what you hope to achieve, can turn out to be disappointing or even disastrous. But thoughtful delegation, which is carefully planned to achieve real results, will enhance your reputation as a manager, help you to build a more productive and creative team, and ultimately save you time and energy.

Like many managers, if you've had a bad experience in the past, you may be reluctant to delegate work on the basis that "It only gets done right if I do it myself." Don't fall into the trap of holding on tight to all your tasks and projects because you're frightened to let go. That way you run the risk of carrying a heavy workload, and perhaps most important, you won't have time for new ideas or projects.

What you delegate and to whom are key issues. If you choose the right people for the job, brief them thoroughly, and monitor the situation regularly, you'll be able to delegate a wide range of tasks with confidence, knowing that they will be carried out the way you want them, and on time. The amount of time you invest in preparing a delegation strategy will be repaid over and over again as your staff grows in competence and confidence, and you begin to feel more relaxed about the delegation process.

Creating a Delegation Strategy

Which Tasks Are You Willing to Delegate?

Key question: What am I prepared to trust to someone else?

First of all, you need to determine which tasks you are prepared to delegate and which you want to keep for yourself. The tasks you are willing to delegate could be work that is tedious and time-consuming, requires specialized knowledge that someone on the team can contribute, or provides a member of your team with a challenging and meaningful development opportunity.

The tasks you may not be prepared to delegate might include: those that you particularly enjoy or that need your specialized knowledge and experience; those that are creative and open ended; those that give you access to the people or resources you need to further your long-term goals and ambitions; those that are confidential or that have been delegated to you for your personal attention. Organizer Sheet 34, Letting Go Versus Holding Tight, will help you to clarify which tasks you are prepared to delegate and which tasks you intend to keep for yourself.

Who's on the Team?

The next step is to take a long, hard look at your team. These are the people to whom you will be delegating. What are their strengths and weaknesses? Who is good with paperwork and detail? Who likes to organize things and establish systems and pro-cedures? Who is the "people person," the one who shines at net-working, influencing, persuading? Use your knowledge of people's special skills and abilities to match them to the tasks they'll be able to achieve successfully. Don't fall into the trap of thinking that if team members do well they'll outshine you. A successful team is a reflection of your skills and abilities as a manager.

Think about the levels of experience on the team. Whom do you respect and trust? Who is experienced, bright, highly moti-vated, and ambitious? These people will respond best if you give them a detailed briefing and then allow them to get on with the job, using their own initiative and creativity.

Which people are competent and enthusiastic but still a little unsure of themselves? These people need plenty of encourage-ment and support, and they need to know they can turn to you, at any time, for help and advice if the going gets tough.

Who is reasonably competent in some areas, but still learning the ropes and gaining experience on a daily basis? These people

Letting Go Versus Holding Tight

Use this Organizer before you start delegating.

Task: _____

This task is:

- ☐ Routine
- ☐ Time-consuming
- ☐ Requires specialized knowledge
- ☐ Connected to my long-term goals and ambitions
- ☐ Enjoyable
- ☐ Has been delegated to me
- ☐ Confidential or otherwise sensitive

- ☐ Yes, I am prepared to delegate this task.
- ☐ No, I am not prepared to delegate this task.

will appreciate regular one-on-one meetings and specific help when they are using new systems or approaches.

Who is new to the job and needs detailed explanations and careful supervision? These people will appreciate being told what to do, when to do it, and how to do it. And they need fast feedback from you about whether they are right or wrong.

Although this may seem like a lot of work, there is a payoff for you. If you are willing to take the time and trouble to delegate different kinds of work in different ways, your people will consistently be able to successfully complete their delegated tasks. Their success will motivate them to do more and better work. And their success will confirm your ability to lead your team, achieve your objectives, reach your targets, and bring projects in on time. One of the keys to successful delegation is making sure that you delegate the right kind of work to the right person. Use Organizer Sheet 35, Who's on the Team, to analyze each person on your team, identifying the delegation style that will work best with each individual, given each person's skills, strengths, and weaknesses.

Preparing the Brief

Key question: If I were doing this task myself, what information and resources would I need so I could do it right?

Once you know what you are prepared to delegate and to whom, the next step is to come up with the answers to these key questions:

- What do I want this person to do, and why?
- To what standards do I want the work performed?
- When do I want it done by?
- Is there any important information I need to share to help this person do the job right?
- Will the person doing the work need any additional resources?

What do I want this person to do, and why?

People need to know precisely what you want. If they don't know, they'll guess, and if they guess, they'll probably get it wrong. They also need to know why you want them to do it.

Understanding the reasons why they are doing something helps people to put the task into a broader context and make reasonable decisions about the work they are doing. It's the difference between saying, "I want you to make a presentation next week" and "I want you to make a presentation next week because there's a lot of data to get through, and I know that you can present figures clearly and accurately." Or, "I want you to update our client list" and "I want you to update our client list because we're running a mailing next month and we need it to be as accurate and current as possible."

To what standards do I want the work performed?

By explaining the standards, you are helping people to do the job right and to be successful. The standards you set can relate to

Who's on the Team?

Use this Organizer before you start delegating.

Name: _____

This person's key skills are:

1. _____

2. _____

This person's main strengths are:

1. _____

2. _____

This person's possible weaknesses are:

1. _____

2. _____

The method of delegating that will work best with this person is:

☐ Minimum control and maximum freedom
☐ Open-door policy to provide support when needed
☐ Regular one-on-one meetings
☐ Direction, supervision, and fast feedback

time (e.g., you'll have 20 minutes to make the presentation), cost (e.g., don't spend more than $5,000), quantity (e.g., five quotes, maximum), quality (e.g., focus on top-of-the-line, state-of the-art), or security or confidentiality (e.g., these files must not leave the building). Standards provide clear guidelines for people and give them confidence.

When do I want it done by?

You're delegating the work, so it is up to you to set the deadline. Be prepared, whenever possible, to discuss the deadline and to compromise. It may take you a week to do something, but it could take a less experienced person a few days longer.

Is there any important information I need to share to help this person do the job right?

This question deserves careful consideration. Often, when work is delegated, a small but vital piece of information is withheld, usually for no good reason other than the person who was delegating forgot to mention it. People need to know, for example, that the report they are preparing is to be copied to the unions or that the client to whom they are making a presentation has a hearing problem.

Will the person doing the work need any additional resources?

Probably the best way to answer this question is to imagine that you are going to do the job yourself and list everything you would need. Remember that authority is a resource, and it is important to make sure that whoever is doing the job won't be tied up with red tape or subjected to delays caused by coworkers who aren't aware that this person has taken on additional responsibilities. A delegation briefing can easily be prepared by answering such questions; Organizer Sheet 36, Preparing a Brief, will quickly take you through the process.

Preparing a Brief

Use this Organizer (one for each employee) before you start delegating.

Name: _____

1. What do I want this person to do?

   _____

2. Why do I want him/her to do it?

Why am I delegating the task?
Why am I delegating the task to this person?

   _____

3. To what standards do I want the job performed?

Does this person have to take into account:
   ☐ Time?
   ☐ Cost?
   ☐ Quantity?
   ☐ Quality?
   ☐ Security or confidentiality?

   _____

4. When do I want it done by?

   _____

5. What does this person need to know to do the work right?

   _____

6. What extra resources or authority is the person going to need?

   _____

7. Additional information?

   _____

Arranging a Meeting

The watercooler is not the best place to meet for the purpose of delegating responsibility. Set some time aside for a one-on-one meeting in a quiet meeting room where you will be free from interruptions. Go through everything in detail and make sure that the other person understands what is required. Give the individual ample opportunity to ask questions and discuss any points that need to be clarified. If you think it is appropriate—if, for example, the task is extremely important and urgent or you've had problems delegating to this person in the past—write down the key points. Give one copy to the other person and keep a copy for yourself. That way there can be no misunderstandings or disagreements later on.

Set a date for a review meeting as well, when the two of you can get together to discuss progress and iron out any problems. Make it clear that although you are delegating the task, as the manager, the ultimate responsibility rests with you. You'll be available to offer support, advice, and guidance if needed, and you must be kept informed and be told if there are problems.

Monitoring Progress

Once you have delegated work to someone else, you must stand back and let them get on with it. You know from your own experience that there is nothing more demoralizing than trying to do something with someone breathing down your neck. If you trust someone enough to give her the task in the first place, then you have to trust her to do the job.

Of course you need to monitor progress, but not every hour of every day. At your initial meeting, set up a schedule of follow-up meetings to review what's happening. Depending on the task and on the person, these meetings may take place every week, every fortnight, or even every month. Agree on the schedule and stick to it. Organizer Sheet 37, Delegated Tasks and Key Dates, will help you to identify your milestone dates and record progress as the delegated project moves along.

Delegated Tasks and Key Dates

Use this Organizer after you have delegated.

Name: _____

The task you're delegating: _____

_____

Deadline for completion: _____

Date, time, and place of initial briefing meeting: _____

_____

Key issues discussed: _____

_____

Schedule for Monitoring Progress

Date, time, and place of first meeting: _____

Progress achieved: _____

_____

Date, time, and place of second meeting: _____

Progress achieved: _____

_____

Date when task satisfactorily completed:

_____

Intervening in Time to Avert Disaster

When you delegate work to other people, they will, ultimately, do it their own way. And their way will almost certainly not be your way. Even so, as long as they achieve the outcome you want, you need to let them get on with the job.

Most times you can expect difficulties because they'll almost certainly occur. Be prepared to give people the time and the opportunity to fix things themselves. However, if you see that someone is seriously off course and that disaster is waiting around the corner, then it is your responsibility to intervene.

The best way to do this is to call an emergency meeting, put your cards on the table, ask questions, and listen to what the individual has to say. Provide clear guidance and assistance, encouragement and support. Steer the person back on course and then—and this is the hard part—step back and let the person continue. Unless the problem is really serious, resist the temptation to take the project away from the individual and do it yourself. If you step in and take over when there are minor but fixable difficulties, you run the risk of undermining the other person's confidence and self-esteem, losing confidence in your own ability to delegate, damaging a work relationship, and adding to your own workload.

At the very start of the project, define at what point you should intervene by completing Organizer Sheet 38, Damage Control. Hopefully you won't need to refer to this document, but if things should go wrong with the delegation, you'll know what to do and when to do it.

Damage Control

Use this **Organizer** soon after you have delegated.

Name: _____

Task: _____

If things go wrong, the very worst that can happen is: _____

_____

_____

_____

_____

I'll know that things are on a downhill slide when: _____

_____

_____

_____

_____

I will intervene when: _____

_____

_____

_____

_____

I will take control of the situation by:

- ☐ Providing advice and support and getting this person back on track
- ☐ Taking over myself
- ☐ Delegating responsibility to someone else. If so, who? _____
- ☐ Doing something else (explain): What? _____

Delegating Action Checklist

- ☐ Decide which tasks you are prepared to delegate and which tasks you want to keep.
- ☐ For the tasks you decide to delegate, set standards for performance so people know what they have to do with regard to time, cost, quantity, quality, security, or confidentiality.
- ☐ Analyze your team's strengths and weaknesses and delegate to people's strengths. This way, you are helping people to be successful.
- ☐ Adapt your delegation style to suit each individual's competence and experience. For example, offer more freedom for the more experienced people, and more help, guidance, encouragement, and support for the less experienced.
- ☐ Monitor progress—but not every hour of the day. If things go wrong, give your people a chance to put them right, by themselves.
- ☐ Provide support, encouragement, and advice, but be prepared to intervene in time to avert a disaster.
- ☐ Recognize that no one will do the job in exactly the same way as you would do it. Trust people to do their best.

Goal Setting

Goals represent our hopes and dreams. They are the signposts that lead us to more successful, more rewarding, and more contented lives. They give purpose and meaning to our work and our relationships. They are the motivators that help us to keep going, even when the going gets tough.

If goals are so important, why don't we pay more attention to setting them? People say it's because *"There just isn't the time,"* or *"Things change so quickly around here, there's no point,"* or *"If I set goals and screw up, then I'll feel like I've really failed."*

It's important to set goals, and it's even more important to ensure that they are both challenging and achievable. If we don't set goals, then we have nothing to aim for and can easily lose sight of what we want to achieve. If we set our goals too high and expect to achieve them over too short a period of time, our lack of success neatly confirms our suspicion that we're not so clever or capable, after all. But if we set meaningful and realistic goals, they will allow us to enjoy, at decent intervals along the way, a sense of achievement.

It is important, as a manager, to set goals that will drive your team forward so that your staff can achieve measurable and noticeable success. And it is important as an individual to set personal goals that lead you toward the kind of life experiences you want to have.

Your goals won't just materialize out of thin air. The goal-setting process initially requires focused thought and some time, but the payoff is that you create a road map that shows you, step by step, how to get from where you are now to where you want to be in the future.

The Goal-Setting Process

The processes for setting goals for your team and for yourself are slightly different, but both can be used to set goals that are short term (one week to three months), medium term (three months to one year), or long term (one to five years or longer).

Setting Work-Oriented Goals With Your Team

If you run performance appraisals in your company, then you know that an important aspect of the appraisal process is agreeing and setting each individual's performance goals. (See Appraisal.) But you and your staff also need team goals that will keep everyone focused on working together toward achieving the same objective.

Define the goals.

Only you and your team know the goals that will be meaningful to your department and your organization. You'll find it helpful to complete Organizer Sheet 39, What Do You Want to Achieve With Your Team?, before you meet with your staff. This organizer sheet will help you clarify the goals the team needs to focus on.

Even so, bear in mind that, as a manager, you may have a clear idea about the goals you'd like to set for the team, yet it is crucial to involve the team in the goal-setting process. Don't be tempted to call a meeting and tell everyone what you want them to achieve. If you do that, your staff members will think that you are simply imposing your goals on them and that they don't have ownership or a vested interest in the outcome.

Instead, call a meeting and begin by listing the areas in which the team needs to make improvements. These areas might be, for example, cost, quality, customer service, timeliness, creativity, innovation, technology, or something else altogether. Either explain your own priority list (e.g., "We need to cut costs first because . . .") or ask the team to prioritize the list in order of urgency and importance. (See Time Management and the section "Get Your Priorities Right.")

Select just two or three key areas to work with. For example:

What Do You Want to Achieve With Your Team?

Use this Organizer before you meet with your team to set team goals.

Key Areas: Cost, Quality, Customer Service, Timeliness, Creativity, Innovation, Technology, Administration, Communication, Productivity, Sales, Research

Key area: _____ Deadline: _____

Goal for this key area:

_____

_____

Key area: _____ Deadline: _____

Goal for this key area:

_____

_____

Key area: _____ Deadline: _____

Goal for this key area:

_____

_____

1. *Cost.* Cut the cost of packaging but retain the expensive image and appearance.
2. *Marketing.* Improve our customer brochures and related marketing material.

Then invite the team to explore all the possibilities for improvement. For example, ask, "By how much do we want to cut the cost of our packaging—five percent or ten percent or more? What makes our packaging look expensive? What can we do to maintain this image yet cut costs? When we decide how we're going to do it, and by how much, what is the target date we should set for ourselves for introducing this improvement?"

By involving the team in the process of answering such questions, you should arrive at your SWEET goals (sensible, written, easy to understand, easy to measure, task-related). For example:

1. *Cost.* Redesign the packaging so that we cut the cost by twenty percent yet retain the current quality image.
2. *Marketing.* Within a budget of $150,000, rewrite and redesign our customer brochures, price lists, and direct-mail material so they give clear, accurate, and up-to-date product information.

Organizer Sheet 40, What Does the Team Want to Achieve?, will allow you to work alongside your team to help your people identify the goals they feel are most important and that will contribute most to the team's success.

Run a SWOT analysis.

Once you and your team have defined your goals, the next step is to run a SWOT analysis. This involves defining:

S   *Strengths.* The strengths and skills that the team and the organization can bring to the process of achieving the goal. These are positive factors that will drive you forward toward success. For example:
    ▪ The team is multiskilled, highly motivated, flexible, and capable of learning new techniques and processes.

What Does the Team Want to Achieve?

Use this **Organizer** when you meet with your team to set team goals.

Key Area Where an Improvement Is Needed	Goal(s) for This Key Area	Deadline
☐ Cost		
☐ Quality		
☐ Customer service		
☐ Timeliness		
☐ Creativity		
☐ Innovation		
☐ Technology		
☐ Administration		
☐ Communication		
☐ Productivity		
☐ Sales		
☐ Research		
☐ Another key area (explain)		
☐ Another key area (explain)		

- The organization is cash-rich and eager to expand.

W *Weaknesses.* The inherent weaknesses within the team and the organization that may prevent you from achieving the goal. These are negative factors that are likely to hold you back from success. For example:

- The team is newly formed and not yet a cohesive unit used to working together.
- The team has little experience in dealing with politically sensitive issues.
- The team needs external expertise to provide input on the legal implications.
- The organization is still in the process of defining its policy and approach to this issue and wants to avoid any risk taking that might result in negative PR.

O *Opportunities.* The opportunities that are currently available or that might present themselves as the team works toward its goal. Again, these are positive factors that may assist you in achieving success. For example, "It looks like our main competitor is losing market share, so we may have the opportunity to target our product at a new type of customer. That would help us to increase sales."

T *Threats.* The threats that either currently exist or may crop up in the future. These are negative factors that may prevent you from achieving your goal. For example, "If, as we anticipate, there's a change in the law, then we'll have to rethink how we label the product," or "If the current president retires this year, the new president of the company may decide to scratch the whole campaign."

The process of defining strengths, weaknesses, opportunities, and threats allows you to see, realistically, what factors are likely to work for or against you. This information will help you when you are identifying the individual steps for achieving your goal. You can use Organizer Sheet 41, SWOT Analysis, to quickly prepare a SWOT analysis by listing:

- Strengths the team and the organization can offer that will propel you forward to success

- Weaknesses within the team and the organization that may hold you back from success
- Opportunities for the team and the organization that are currently available or likely to become available, and that may assist you in achieving success
- Threats that the team and the organization may have to face while working toward success

Identify the individual steps to success.

Until it is achieved, a goal is simply a statement about what you intend to do (e.g., increase market share by 5 percent by year-end, or install a computer network in the department by June.) To turn the statement into a reality, you and your team must do specific, practical things that will take you from "here and now" to "there and then."

With your team, determine precisely what needs to be done and who is to be responsible for each activity. (See Delegating.) This process involves breaking down the goal into small, achievable steps, each of which is assigned to one or more people and each of which has a target completion date.

The individual tasks that need to be completed to achieve the goal of "Installing a computer network in the department by June" might look something like this:

Task	Person Responsible	By When
1. Evaluate and compare Mac and PC systems.	Jodie	March 1
2. Submit report to the team.	Jodie	March 3
3. Make decision.	Team	March 4
4. Order equipment.	Mike	March 6
5. Organize staff training.	Gill	March 12
6. Install equipment.	Pip	April 1
7. Complete staff training.	Gill	April 20
8. Transfer to network.	Jodie and Pip	April 27
9. Evaluate system.	Team	June 1

SWOT Analysis

Use this Organizer (one for each goal) with your team.

Team goal we want to achieve: _____

_____

Strengths (+ factors)	Weaknesses (− factors)
1. _____	1. _____
	We can minimize this by:
2. _____	
	2. _____
3. _____	*We can minimize this by:*
4. _____	3. _____
	We can minimize this by:
5. _____	
	4. _____
6. _____	*We can minimize this by:*

Opportunities (+ factors)	Threats (− factors)
1. _____	1. _____
We can maximize this by:	*We can minimize this by:*
2. _____	2. _____
We can maximize this by:	*We can minimize this by:*
3. _____	3. _____
We can maximize this by:	*We can minimize this by:*
4. _____	4. _____
We can maximize this by:	*We can minimize this by:*

Use Organizer Sheet 42, The Route to Success, to identify the individual tasks that, when completed, will lead you to the successful achievement of your goals. This organizer will also enable you to record the name of the person to whom you have delegated responsibility for each task and the agreed on completion date.

Celebrate success.

Always celebrate success. When you and your team achieve a goal, there should be some acknowledgment that the team has done what it set out to do. You may want to organize a small celebration in the office or arrange a celebratory dinner after work. Whatever you decide and however you choose to mark the occasion, it's vital to acknowledge your people's efforts. Rewards motivate your people to do well in the future, build a strong sense of team spirit, and demonstrate to the team that you are serious about wanting success.

Setting Personal Goals

When setting personal goals, it's important not to limit yourself. If you are prepared to focus your energy, dedicate your time, and, where appropriate, make the necessary sacrifices, you can achieve almost anything.

Clarifying what you want.

By establishing goals for every area of your life (e.g., career, financial, home and family, health and fitness, leisure time and hobbies), you are in effect creating a road map to your future. To make sure you get to your destination safely, you have to know exactly where it is you're heading.

Like the goals you set at work with your team, your personal goals should be clear and precise and set within a clear time frame, so you know exactly what you are going to do and by when. Use Organizer Sheet 43, Personal Wishes, Hopes, and Dreams, to identify the key life areas where you want to make changes or improvements, then define what those changes or improvements should be.

The Route to Success

Use this Organizer once you have decided on the goals for your team.

Goal:

_____

_____

The individual tasks that, together, will lead to goal achievement:

Task 1. _____

_____

Name of person to whom I've delegated this task: _____

Agreed date of completion: _____

Task 2. _____

_____

Name of person to whom I've delegated this task: _____

Agreed date of completion: _____

Task 3. _____

_____

Name of person to whom I've delegated this task: _____

Agreed date of completion: _____

Task 4. _____

_____

Name of person to whom I've delegated this task: _____

Agreed date of completion: _____

Personal Wishes, Hopes, and Dreams

Use this Organizer before you set your personal goals.

Key life areas in need of change or improvement:

☐ Image and appearance   ☐ Career

☐ Current finances   ☐ Future financial security

☐ Relationship with children   ☐ Relationship with partner

☐ Family   ☐ Friends

☐ My home   ☐ Health

☐ Leisure and hobbies   ☐ Social life

☐ Study and personal development   ☐ Spiritual life

Specific improvements I can make to the key life areas that require attention: _____

_____

_____

_____

_____

_____

_____

_____

_____

Carrying out a risk analysis.

Achieving every goal you set will almost certainly require some measure of focused thought, energy, and time. Some goals may involve sacrifices. For example, if you want to become president of your organization within five years, you may have to dedicate all your time and energy to achieving that outcome. As a result, you may put your personal relationships with your partner, children, family, and friends at risk. It's quite common for people to reflect back on their achievements and acknowledge that the price they paid for achieving their goal was too high. Use risk analysis to help you to make an informed decision about whether to proceed along any given route. Analyze:

- The rewards you will enjoy as a result of achieving your goal
- The input from others that may help or hinder you
- The sacrifices you may have to make along the way
- The knowledge, skills, and personal strengths that you bring to the situation

Organizer Sheet 44, Risk Analysis, will help you to do a risk analysis for any goal. This analysis will let you see, on paper, the balance of rewards you might gain and sacrifices you might have to make.

Work out the individual, small steps that, together, can lead you to your goal.

Once you are clear about your goal (and satisfied that it is something you really want to achieve), you must then work out the details of what you have to do to get to where you want to be. Imagine that your goal is your final destination. How will you plan your route? As with the team process, decide on the individual, small steps that will take you from here to there. For example:

Goal: Lose fourteen pounds in a month.
Step 1: Get weighed on accurate scales.
Step 2: Join a gym and attend at least two sessions every week.

Organizer Sheet 44

Risk Analysis

Use this Organizer before you set your personal goals.

Key life area: _____

Goal: _____

Rewards (+) When I achieve this goal, what will the rewards be?	**Input (+)** While I am working toward this goal, what helpful input from others can I count on? **Input (−)** While I am working toward this goal, what unhelpful or harmful input from others is likely to cause me problems?
Sacrifices (−) What sacrifices may I have to make so that I can reach my goal?	**Knowledge, Strengths, and Skills (+)** What personal knowledge, strengths, and skills can I use to help me reach my goal?

Step 3: Walk for a half-hour each day.
Step 4: Cut sugar and fat from diet.

Use Organizer Sheet 45, Small Steps to Success, to help you to define the individual tasks you'll need to complete to take you, step by step, toward your goal.

Regularly revisit and review your goals.

Be kind to yourself. Just because you have set yourself a goal doesn't mean that it is set in stone and can't be changed. Flexibility

Small Steps to Success

Use this Organizer (one for each goal) after you have decided on your personal goals.

My Goal: _____

_____

To achieve this goal I need to:

1. _____

_____

2. _____

_____

3. _____

_____

4. _____

_____

5. _____

_____

To achieve this goal I may need help with:

☐ Information   ☐ Resources
☐ Contacts and networking
☐ Something else (explain): _____

People who may be able to help me:

Name: _____   Name: _____

Name: _____   Name: _____

Target date for achieving this goal: _____

is a strength, not a weakness. Accept change and be prepared for it. If you alter or even eliminate a goal, you haven't failed; you've simply responded to altered circumstances or changes in your perception of what's important to you. You'll find it helpful if, every six months or so, you use Organizer Sheet 46, Regular Review of Goals, to review your progress and to evaluate whether each of your goals still has meaning and value for you.

Organizer Sheet 46

Regular Review of Goals

Use this Organizer (one for each personal goal) three to six months after you first set your goals.

Goal:

_____

_____

My progress toward achieving this goal has been:

☐ Excellent   ☐ Good   ☐ Okay   ☐ Not good

My feelings now about this goal are:

☐ I'm still motivated and want to achieve this goal.
☐ I'm beginning to have doubts about whether I still want to reach this goal.
☐ I think it's probably time to discard this goal and rethink what I want.

Team Goal-Setting Action Checklist

- ☐ Compile a list of the key areas where you want to make improvements.
- ☐ Call a team meeting, explain the key areas for improvement, and ask the team to prioritize the list in order of urgency and importance.
- ☐ Along with the team, select two or three key areas to work with. Invite the team to consider all the possibilities for improvement.
- ☐ For each key area, define a SWEET objective—one that's sensible, written, easy to understand, easy to measure, and task-related. Aim for objectives that stretch and challenge your people but that are also realistic and attainable.
- ☐ Identify the individual tasks that need to be accomplished to achieve each objective.
- ☐ Delegate responsibility for each task, and, with the team, decide on the deadlines for each task and the target date for achieving each objective.
- ☐ When the team achieves the goal, celebrate success.

Personal Goal-Setting Action Checklist

- ☐ Examine all the areas of your life and decide where you want to make changes and improvements.
- ☐ For each area of your life, choose a goal that is both challenging and achievable, and make sure that it is SWEET. Remember, your personal goals represent your wishes, hopes, and dreams for a better future, so don't limit yourself.
- ☐ Run a risk analysis for any significant, life-changing goals you've chosen. Assess whether the rewards you will achieve will be worth the sacrifices you may have to make.
- ☐ Choose two or three goals to start with. Pick goals that are important, especially rewarding, or likely to be particularly pleasurable to work toward and achieve.
- ☐ For each of your chosen goals, identify the individual steps you'll have to work through to get where you want to be.
- ☐ Celebrate each success with a personal reward, something for yourself that you really enjoy.
- ☐ Review your goals regularly and be prepared to discard any that no longer serve your purposes or suit your needs.

Influencing

You use your influence whenever you try to persuade others to see your point of view, convince them that your idea will work, or explain to them how your proposition will be of benefit to them.

Influencing isn't about manipulation or the misuse of power. When you establish and maintain good working relationships so that other people will be receptive to your ideas and willing to consider your suggestions, you are using influencing skills. When you present your concepts logically and persuasively (and truthfully) so that people can understand and appreciate the value of your proposals, you are also using influencing skills.

How you go about influencing people requires an influencing strategy.

Creating an Influencing Strategy

Key question: What do I want?

The first step to creating an influencing strategy is to clarify your key objective—and to make clear, in your own mind, exactly what it is you want to achieve. (See Goal Setting.)

Key question: Who will be affected, and in what way, if I get what I want?

The second step is to actually plan your campaign. At this key planning stage, it is vital to carefully consider how your proposals will affect everyone involved. Who will benefit from your plan? Conversely, who might worry that your proposals are not in their best interests?

Think about the likely levels of opposition and support you can expect for your plan. Will anyone be totally opposed to your ideas? What objections are most likely to be raised? How will you deal with objections? What kind of evidence can you present to show that the benefits of your proposal are real? Who can you count on for total support?

Before you begin to run with the campaign, target those people who are likely to need extra attention and persuasion. Identify the personal benefits they'll enjoy if your plan takes off. Delineate any advantages for their department, function, or team. If you can answer the question "What's in it for me?" you can show people how your ideas will provide them with a positive outcome. Use Organizer Sheet 47, Support Versus Opposition, to list the people you need to influence and to identify the level of support or opposition you can expect from each person.

Effective communication is a key influencing skill and an important aspect of your strategy. The third step of the process is to communicate your ideas effectively. The best approach depends on your objective and the people involved. You may need to create opportunities for one-on-one informal meetings, or you may choose to set up a series of team meetings or formal presentations. The situation may call for you to produce written reports or use some combination of all of these approaches. Use Organizer Sheet 48, Communication Strategy for Influencing, to help you to decide how to communicate with each person on your influencing list.

Hearing, Understanding, Agreeing, and Taking Action

No matter what outcome you are working toward, you need the people on the receiving end of your influencing message to hear, understand, agree, and finally take the action you want them to take.

Hearing the message.

Although people may take the time to listen to you, they may not hear what you're saying. This happens when people:

Support Versus Opposition

Use this Organizer when you have identified the people you need to influence.

People I Want to Influence	Level of Opposition or Support Each Person Is Likely to Offer to My Ideas

Name: _____   ☐ High level of opposition

Telephone: _____   ☐ Some opposition

Fax: _____   ☐ Some support

E-mail: _____   ☐ High level of support

Name: _____   ☐ High level of opposition

Telephone: _____   ☐ Some opposition

Fax: _____   ☐ Some support

E-mail: _____   ☐ High level of support

Name: _____   ☐ High level of opposition

Telephone: _____   ☐ Some opposition

Fax: _____   ☐ Some support

E-mail: _____   ☐ High level of support

Communication Strategy for Influencing

Use this Organizer (one for each person you want to influence) before you start your influencing campaign.

Name of person I want to influence: _____

Communication strategy to use:

☐ One-on-one meeting   ☐ Group meeting

☐ Formal presentation   ☐ Informal get-together

☐ Telephone call   ☐ Letter or memo

☐ E-mail

- Have agendas that are very different from yours
- Believe your proposals are not in their best interests
- Don't recognize the importance of your strategy
- Are not convinced that you've considered all the implications

People can also make assumptions, based on past experience, that prevent them from being open to what you have to say (e.g., "I've heard it all before. I didn't like it then, so why should I like it now?"). Organizer Sheet 49, Benefits Versus Objections, will help you clarify the benefits people are likely to enjoy as a result of agreeing to your proposal and identify the objections these same people could raise.

To ensure that colleagues, customers, and bosses hear and understand your message, try these techniques:

1. Always make sure that you pitch your proposal at the right level: Make it technical for the techies, detailed for the data collectors, and general for the generalists.
2. Actively listen to what people have to say and ask open-

Benefits Versus Objections

Use this Organizer before you start your influencing campaign.

Person I want to influence: _____

The objections this person may raise to my plan:

1. _____

2. _____

3. _____

4. _____

The benefits this person will enjoy if my plan goes ahead:

_____

_____

_____

_____

_____

_____

_____

_____

_____

_____

_____

ended questions (e.g., How? Why? What? When? Where?) to discover their real concerns.

3. Answer questions thoroughly, and don't try to skip over the bad news in the hope that people won't notice.

4. Spell out your message's benefits, and use open and friendly body language (e.g., maintain eye contact, keep arms in a relaxed position) to communicate, nonverbally, your good intentions.

Each of these approaches will demonstrate, through words and actions, that you want to achieve a win-win outcome.

Getting to agreement.

The aim of any influencing strategy is, of course, to get people to agree with your point of view. You may face objections to your ideas because people feel threatened, are frightened of making a mistake, or believe you are overselling the proposition (e.g., "She's trying too hard. . . . He's getting desperate. . . . What's the downside?"). Of course, it could also be that they don't really understand the proposition (e.g., "I think I know where he's coming from . . . but I could be wrong. I'll say no; that's the safe route").

Taking action.

You can overcome objections by selling the benefits. Spell out, clearly and honestly, how someone is going to personally benefit from your plan. Provide reassurances and real-life examples of how your plan worked with other people, in other organizations.

Be careful not to oversell the proposition. No matter how enthusiastic you are, look objectively at the situation from the other person's point of view. If you go overboard with your idea, people are bound to think there's a catch.

Make sure your ideas are presented clearly and logically. (See Communication.) Invite questions and answer them patiently and thoroughly. Satisfy the other person's need to know, even if it takes more time than you would like. Use Organizer Sheet 50, Handling Objections, to work out the best way to respond to objections from other people.

Organizer Sheet 50

Handling Objections

Use this Organizer before you start your influencing campaign.

Objections likely to be raised by: _____ (see Organizer 49)

1. _____

To handle this objection, offer:
☐ Evidence of success elsewhere
☐ Reassurance
☐ More information
☐ Something else (explain): _____

_____

2. _____

To handle this objection, offer:
☐ Evidence of success elsewhere
☐ Reassurance
☐ More information
☐ Something else (explain): _____

_____

3. _____

To handle this objection, offer:
☐ Evidence of success elsewhere
☐ Reassurance
☐ More information
☐ Something else (explain): _____

_____

Finally, make sure that you keep track of your progress so that at regular points throughout your influencing campaign, you know who is "with you" and who's not. Organizer Sheet 51, Influencing Schedule, will help you keep a record of influencing meetings and conversations and the outcomes of each one.

Influencing Action Checklist

- ☐ Decide exactly what you want to achieve with your influencing strategy.
- ☐ Talk to the people who can make it happen.
- ☐ Present your proposals logically so that people can understand what you hope to achieve. Spell out the benefits and deal with the objections.
- ☐ Listen carefully to people's concerns.
- ☐ Offer solutions, not problems to be solved.
- ☐ Demonstrate, by what you say and what you do, that you are actively looking for a win-win outcome.
- ☐ Be patient.

Influencing Schedule

Use this Organizer (one for each person you need to influence) when you first begin your influencing campaign.

I plan to start my influencing campaign on: _____

I plan to have completed my influencing campaign and achieved my objective by: _____

Name: _____

Date of first contact: _____

Outcome of first contact:

_____

_____

Do I need to approach this person again:

☐ No   ☐ Yes   Date of next meeting: _____

The Internet

By now you're probably aware that just about everyone you know, at home and at work, is linked up, online, and busily surfing the Net. These days your organization, your boss, your colleagues, your clients, and your kids all expect you to access the Internet. In fact, customers notice whether or not your business stationery carries an e-mail address and the URL for your organization's Web site.

Although you might want to run, there's nowhere to hide. To make the most of this amazing technology, you have to be able to understand the jargon, get online, and finally, know how to use the Internet for whatever purpose suits you and your business best.

How Did It All Start?

In the 1960s, the U.S. military linked a number of computers, all of which were based in different locations. This network was designed to create a secure system of moving information around, just in case there was a national emergency and it wasn't feasible to use regular communication links. Thus, the Internet was born.

Academics, busily researching everything from nuclear fusion to the Ebola virus, quickly realized that they could rapidly exchange data if they, too, were linked by a network of computers. Instead of using regular mail, they could use the Internet to send electronic information from one computer to another, swiftly and cheaply.

In the 1980s, businesses began to realize that the Internet held the key to major global marketing and communication opportunities. Now, in the 1990s, key player corporations like Microsoft Corp., Sony, Ford Motor Co., Universal Pictures, Levi Strauss, The Body Shop, Virgin Records, FedEx, and many hundreds of thousands more use the Internet to make information about their products and services freely available, worldwide.

Every day millions of Internet subscribers around the world spend hours of their time at their computers looking for, finding, and reading or downloading this information. This pastime is known as "surfing the Net."

Understanding the Jargon

The Internet, the Information Superhighway, the World Wide Web, the Web, and the Net are all essentially interchangeable terms. All these phrases are used to describe a network of computers, based in countries around the world, owned and managed by different people, businesses, and organizations but connected together by information technology.

Anyone can join the network provided they have the right kind of hardware (a computer, a modem, and a telephone line), the right kind of software (communication software and a "browser"), and a subscription to a service provider (an organization that allows you to use its gateway onto the system).

Why Would Anyone Want to Surf the Net?

College students can use the Internet to find out just about anything from the Black Death that swept through Europe in the fourteenth century to the latest update from NASA. Investors can find the current price of stocks and shares. Patients can find out about the side effects of drugs prescribed by a physician earlier in the day. Travelers can find out which hotels have vacancies and which airlines have available seats—and they can even make their bookings via computer. Shoppers can use their computers to order everything from groceries to automobiles, without having to leave their homes. Realtors advertise properties for sale; banks advertise their banking facilities and services; recruitment agencies advertise job openings. These are just a few examples of the types of information available on the Internet.

Using the Internet for Real-Time Communication

It's possible, using electronic mail (e-mail), to send written information of all kinds from one computer to another. A mother in Portugal can send a "How are you, son?" message to her offspring in Japan. A finance director in Idaho can inquire, "Where are the up-to-date figures?" to her counterpart in London. A writer in Bombay can send a chapter of a book to his publisher in New York. A wife away on business in Toronto can send an "I won't be home tonight, honey" to her husband in Boston.

E-mail is fast, inexpensive, and perfect for communication between different time zones. Someone in London can e-mail someone in Florida without worrying about time differences. As soon as the person in Florida switches on his computer and checks for any new e-mails, the message appears on-screen. No more stressful or alarming 3 A.M. telephone calls!

Gateways to the Internet: ISPs

For your computer to be able to access and communicate with other computers on the Internet, you must subscribe to an Internet Service Provider (ISP). CompuServe and America Online (AOL) are two organizations that, for a monthly subscription fee, provide you with the necessary gateway onto the Internet. For your monthly fee, you get a communications software program that lets you onto the Internet, and an e-mail address so that anyone with access to the Internet can send information to your computer, and you can send information to theirs.

Both CompuServe and AOL offer subscribers access to special interest groups. These are places on the Net where like-minded people—teachers, cat lovers, parents, physicians, designers, writers, and every other kind of special interest group—can post messages for one another, make friends, and generally create online "communities" where they can share experiences, information, ideas, and opportunities. CompuServe and AOL also provide a

Organizer Sheet 52

Which Kind of Internet Service?

Use this Organizer (one for each Internet Service Provider) before you make your final choice.

Name of Internet Service Provider: _____

Address: _____

_____

Telephone: _____

Monthly subscription: $_____

Number of online hours included in this price: _____

Cost of additional online hours: _____

Additional information: _____

_____

limited amount of free access time, usually between twelve and twenty hours a month, depending on the monthly fee you choose to pay. Other ISPs offer unlimited free (or nearly free) access, but their service doesn't include special interest groups. Before you sign up with an ISP, use Organizer Sheet 52, Which Kind of Internet Service?, to identify the type of Internet service that is likely to suit you best.

Finding What You Want on the World Wide Web

Millions of people have e-mail addresses to which you can send information, just as you would send a letter through the postal system. E-mail addresses vary according to the type of Internet Service Provider you choose. A CompuServe address might be 2865145.22@compuserve.com; an AOL address might be jlowe@aol.com. If you compose a letter on your computer screen and, using the special software, send it to another e-mail address, your service provider routes the mail from your computer to the addressee's computer.

There are millions and millions of pages of information on the Internet. Each page has a specific address called a *uniform resource locator* (usually referred to as a URL). URLs always start with **http:// www,** followed by the specific address. For example, if you wanted to look at the information that Microsoft publishes about itself and its products, you would use the address **http//:www.microsoft.com.** If you wanted the latest headline news on-screen, you could go to **http://www.cnn.com.** For sports information, you can go to **http:// www.espnet.sportzone.com.** The URL that will take you to the CIA's Web site is **http://www.ODCI.gov.** And if you want to go to find out more about *The X Files*, you can visit **http:/www./ rutgers.edu/x-files.html** (among dozens of other sites for fans of this program).

If you want information about *anything* and you don't have the URL, you can ask one of several free online search facilities to find Web sites that match your search requirements. A few of the more popular search facilities (called *search engines*) can be located at the following URLs:

> http://www.**altavista.digital.com** (takes you to the Alta Vista search engine)
>
> http://www.**cyber411.com** (takes you to the Cyber 411 search engine)
>
> http://www.**dejanews.com** (takes you to the DejaNews search engine)
>
> http://www.**infoseek.com** (takes you to the Infoseek search engine)

To find out what you need to know about anything from atmospherics to zucchini, you need to type in (in the appropriate place on-screen) one or two key words and let the search engine do the rest. The results of a search can produce up to 1,500 different URLs where you can access information about your chosen topic. You can use Organizer Sheet 53, Useful URLs, to keep a record of the URL addresses of Web sites you like or visit repeatedly.

If you want to publish information about yourself or your organization on the Web, then your Internet Service Provider will

Useful URLs

Use this Organizer once you have access to the Internet.

Name of Organization or Person	URL
	http://www.
	http://www.
	http://www.
	http://www.
	http://www.
	http://www.
	http://www.
	http://www.
	http://www.
	http://www.
	http://www.
	http://www.
	http://www.
	http://www.
	http://www.

give you space for your data (i.e., text and pictures) and a URL so that people can find your Web pages.

If you have the time, computer skills, energy, and inclination, you can use a special software program such as Microsoft Front-Page or Adobe PageMill to create colorful and visually exciting pages of text and pictures for publication on the Web. Alternatively, you can hire one of the many professional design companies that specialize in creating web sites.

Getting Online

Key question: What do I need to spend money on?

To start you will need, at minimum:

1. A computer, a modem, and a telephone line.
2. A subscription to an Internet Service Provider. Two of the most popular services are CompuServe (5000 Arlington Centre Blvd., Columbus, OH 43220, telephone: 1-800-848-8990) and America Online (8619 Westwood Center Drive, Vienna, VA 22182, telephone: 1-703-448-8700).
3. Communication software and a browser (provided by your Internet Service Provider).
4. Some free time so you can sit down at your computer and begin to explore the varied, interesting, and exciting world of the Internet.

Internet Action Checklist

☐ Get the right kind of computer. Recommended is a Pentium PC with a minimum of 16 megabytes of memory (RAM) and a hard disk of 1 gigabyte, so you can store the necessary software.

☐ Select a modem with the fastest available speed because it is the modem that enables you to transfer information onto your computer screen from the Internet. The faster your modem, the easier it will be to access information.

☐ Consider whether you need a dedicated telephone line for your PC and modem. With only one telephone line, customers and colleagues won't be able to get through to your telephone number when you are online using the Internet. (See Teleworking.)

☐ Choose an Internet Service Provider that offers the deal that suits you and your organization best.

☐ Have your stationery printed with your e-mail address and the address of your Web site.

☐ Get whatever training you need to learn how to use the software and understand what you're doing.

☐ If you don't have much time, hire a professional to design and maintain your Web site and to take care of all the details.

Interviewing

Hiring and firing interviews need, for different reasons, a cautious and very focused approach. If you hire the wrong person, day after day you'll have to live with a constant reminder of your poor judgment and flawed decision-making skills. If you fire someone in the wrong way, without doing everything by the book, you may end up costing your organization a considerable amount of money.

Whether you are hiring or firing, take your time and evaluate all the facts. If you are having difficulty reaching a decision, gather more information, ask for a second opinion, and only act when you are absolutely sure that you are doing the right thing.

Hiring Interviews

Preparing a Job Description

Key question: What, precisely, is the job I want to fill?

When you are looking to hire someone, either for a completely new job or as a replacement for someone who is leaving, the first thing you need to do is to create a job description. This document spells out, simply and clearly, the main activities involved in the job as well as the specific responsibilities, lines of authority, working hours, job location, travel requirements, and any other important factors that someone doing the job needs to be aware of. Use Organizer Sheet 54, Job Description, to prepare a job description that covers all these key areas. Figure 1 presents a sample job description for a personal assistant.

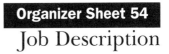

Organizer Sheet 54

Job Description

Use this Organizer before you start recruiting.

Job title: _____

The main activities someone doing this job will perform are:

1. _____

2. _____

3. _____

Specific responsibilities:

Main activity 1. _____

_____

_____

Main activity 2. _____

_____

_____

Main activity 3. _____

_____

_____

Lines of authority:

The person doing this job will be responsible *to* this person/these
people: _____

The person doing this job will be responsible *for* this person/these
people: _____

Hours: _____
Location: _____
Travel: _____
Other: _____

Figure 1. Job Description for a Personal Assistant

Main Activities:
1. Correspondence and documentation
2. Travel
3. Meetings
4. Scheduling appointments
5. Clients
6. Secretaries

Specific Responsibilities:
1. Correspondence and documentation
   - Replying to correspondence
   - Preparing transparencies and information sheets
2. Travel
   - Negotiating fares and costs
   - Making global travel bookings and hotel reservations
   - Preparing itineraries
3. Meetings
   - Evaluating and booking venues
   - Selecting and informing delegates
   - Booking speakers
   - Organizing delegate accommodations
4. Scheduling Appointments
   - Maintaining an office diary for the CEO
   - Maintaining a personal diary for the CEO
5. Clients
   - Organizing meeting with clients
   - Attending meetings with clients
   - Preparing documentation for client meetings
6. Secretaries
   - Supervising three junior secretaries
   - Monitoring work
   - Running appraisals
   - Preparing staff evaluation reports
   - Approving vacation schedules

Lines of authority:
1. Responsible only to the CEO
2. Responsible for three secretaries
3. Will be expected to work alone, unsupervised, for most of the time

Hours, Location, Travel:
1. Will be based in head office in Chicago
2. Will be expected to travel, when required, to meetings in Chicago and throughout the U.S.

Writing a job description will help you to clarify exactly what is involved in the job and will also help you move to the next stage, preparing a person specification.

Preparing a Person Specification

Key question: What skills, qualifications, qualities, and experience will the successful candidate need to do the job?

Your person specification should describe, on paper, the qualifications, skills, and qualities you're looking for in the ideal candidate (see Figure 2). You can split these factors into those qualifications that the successful person *must have* and those that the successful person *should have.*

Use Organizer Sheet 55, Person Specification, to create your blueprint for your ideal person. This organizer sheet will help you to set down on paper the qualifications, skills, and experience a successful job candidate must have and those that he or she should have. Then create and place your advertisement. Finally, check through the applications and see which people come closest to matching your blueprint.

Screening the Applications

If you can find someone who meets all the must-have requirements, as well as all of the should-have qualifications, skills, and qualities, then you may have struck gold. All the better if you think the team will also be able to get along with the new person. On a more realistic note, probably the best you can hope for is someone who has most of the must-have requirements and some of the should-have requirements.

As job applications come in, divide them into three separate piles:

- Pile 1: People who have *most* of the musts and *some* of the shoulds. These are people who (on paper at least) most closely match your specification. You'll probably need to interview all of these applicants.

Figure 2. Person Specification

	"Must-Have" Qualifications, Skills, and Qualities	"Should-Have" Qualifications, Skills, and Qualities
Education and Training	▪ High School diploma ▪ College degree	▪ One to two years' business experience
Skills	▪ Good communication skills ▪ MS Word for Windows ▪ MS PowerPoint ▪ MS Excel ▪ MS Access	▪ Able to influence key players in external organizations ▪ Shorthand ▪ French ▪ Spanish ▪ Knowledge of the travel industry
Experience	▪ Experience of supervising staff	▪ Experience of operating at board level
Personal Qualities	▪ Energetic ▪ Diplomatic ▪ Flexible ▪ Able to keep a cool head in a super-charged environment	▪ Capable of responding quickly to changing circumstances
Additional Requirements	▪ Willing to travel ▪ Able to work flexible hours including evenings and week-ends	

- Pile 2: People who have *some* of the musts and *one or two* of the shoulds. If no one in pile 1 is suitable, then it is certainly worth talking to some of these people.
- Pile 3: People who don't seem to have *any* of the qualifications, skills, or qualities you're looking for. These applications go to the shredder.

Person Specification

Use this Organizer before you start recruiting.

	"Must-Have" Requirements	"Should-Have" Requirements
Education and training		
Skills		
Experience		
Personal qualities		
Additional requirements		

Setting Up the Appointments

Interviewing is tough work because you need to be totally focused throughout the meeting. If you are tired or bored or pushed for time, you can make a major error of judgment. Think about how many people you are prepared to see in a day and how much time you're prepared to give to each person. Careful scheduling will help you to stay in control of the process.

Staging the Interviews

Make sure that you choose a space that is quiet and absolutely free from interruptions. If you risk being disturbed while you're interviewing, you won't be able to give people your undivided attention. You'll also be sending a negative message about your attitude toward the process and the importance of the job.

Don't sit behind an expansive desk. Sit next to the candidate, on a similar chair that is set at a similar height. This isn't an exercise in intimidation. The interviewee already knows how important you are.

Asking the Right Questions

Because you've prepared a job description and a person specification, you'll know what's involved in the job and what kind of person you're looking for. The only way you are going to find out about someone is to ask the right kinds of questions and listen, very carefully, to the answers. (See Communication.) You need to satisfy yourself, at the interview, with regard to the answers to these questions:

- Can this person do the job?
- Will this person do the job?
- Will this person fit into the team?
- Will I get along with this person?
- If I delegated an important job to this person, would I trust him to do it right?

Start off with the usual questions (e.g., Tell me about yourself. What do you know about our company? What did you enjoy most in your last job?). While answering these general questions, the candidate will have a chance to calm down and settle in, and you'll have an opportunity to evaluate his appearance, body language, and general manner.

Once you have covered the basic details, your next step is to dig deeper and try to find out how this person is going to operate in the job on a day-to-day basis.

The best way to find out how people will respond to real-life situations is to describe realistic scenarios and ask them to explain what they would do in these circumstances. One example would be to ask, "Tell me, what would you do if a computer virus got into the system and we lost all our data?" The what-if scenarios need to relate to your organization, your department, or the specific skills and qualities you are hoping someone is going to bring to the job. How people respond will give you a fairly accurate idea of how they would actually behave if faced with a similar situation in real life.

Recording the Details

After you've interviewed each person, write down your reactions. Don't rely on your memory. If you are seeing more than three people, by the end of the day the applicants will blur into one, and you probably won't remember much of importance. At the end of each interview, complete Organizer Sheet 56, Hiring Interview Evaluation. It will help you to keep track of the people you see and your reactions to them.

Forming a Judgment

By now you've asked all the right questions, and your candidate has answered with the right blend of knowledge, understanding, humor, or whatever else you're looking for. The words are right, but what about everything else? Before you hire someone, you need to be satisfied that she can do the job (i.e., skills, experience, qualifications), will do the job (i.e., motivation, enthusiasm, inspiration, courage, perseverance), as well as get along with you and fit in with the team. If you've spent time and energy building an effective, tightly knit team, you need to know that a new person

Hiring Interview Evaluation

Use this Organizer (one for each applicant) immediately after the interview.

Name: _____   Date: _____

Responses to standard questions
- ☐ Terrific   ☐ Good
- ☐ Okay   ☐ Not good   ☐ Appeared nervous

Responses to what-if scenarios
- ☐ Terrific   ☐ Good
- ☐ Okay   ☐ Not good   ☐ Appeared nervous

Appearance
- ☐ Terrific   ☐ Good   ☐ Okay   ☐ Not good
- ☐ Will fit in with our culture   ☐ Doesn't fit in with our culture

Body language
- ☐ Relaxed   ☐ Confident
- ☐ Appropriate   ☐ Not appropriate

Sense of humor
- ☐ Terrific   ☐ Good   ☐ Okay   ☐ What sense of humor?

General manner
- ☐ Good (approachable, professional)   ☐ Not good
- ☐ This person will fit into the team. Why? _____

_____

- ☐ This person won't fit into the team. Why? _____

_____

I would delegate an important task to this person and feel confident that he or she would handle it responsibly.
- ☐ Yes. Why? _____
- ☐ No. Why? _____

will fit in, contribute to the team, and work with the rest of the gang. Even if someone matches your blueprint perfectly and says all the right things, if there is anything that causes you to suspect that the individual may generate more problems than solutions, *don't hire the person.*

If you are not absolutely sure but you have a sense or instinct that someone is a possibility, call that person back for a second or even a third interview. Ask a colleague to sit in with you and get feedback from an objective third party. Involve someone on the team. Do whatever it takes, but don't make a final decision until you have covered all the angles and are comfortable that you've made the right choice.

Finally, make absolutely sure that you double-check references. Even if the applicant is your partner's best friend, follow up and do the reference check, and don't leave anything to chance.

Firing Interviews

Telling people that you have to let them go is one of the least pleasant tasks that any manager has to face. Sometimes you'll have to do this because people have broken the rules of engagement, so you can console yourself with the notion that, really, it's their own fault. But sometimes, because of restructuring or delayering or in response to budgetary constraints, you have to let good, hardworking, and valuable people leave the organization.

When you have to fire someone, follow your organization's procedures, arrange for an objective observer to be in the room, keep a written record of everything that was said and agreed on, and keep calm.

Follow procedures.

Every organization has its own procedures and paperwork. Don't ever try to cut corners or save time. Stick to the rules and go by the book.

Call in an observer.

Ask someone who has absolutely no vested interest in the proceedings to be in the room. This could be a colleague from another department or even another location. It could be someone in the same managerial grade as you or someone who is on the same pay scale as the person who is leaving. Whoever it is and whatever the person does in the organization, she should act as a disinterested observer who, if called upon later on, can give an objective and truthful account of what happened, what was said, and what was agreed on in the room.

Write everything down.

Don't rely on your memory. Later on, if there are problems, your written record may make an enormous difference to the outcome of any legal proceedings. Make sure your notes are legible, accurate, and dated.

Keep calm.

It doesn't matter if you are incandescent with rage or shocked and sympathetic, your role is to get the business done as calmly and efficiently as possible. In many cases, people will respond emotionally to the news of a dismissal or layoff, so be prepared for anger, tears, or even hysteria

Take into account that, for many people, losing their job represents their worst nightmare. This particularly applies to people who have been with the same organization for a number of years, unskilled workers who think they don't have the qualifications to appeal to another employer, or people who have reached a point in their lives where they consider themselves too old to find another job. Do your very best to stay calm, pleasant, nonjudgmental, and as neutral as possible. Before the firing interview takes place, complete Organizer Sheet 57, Firing Interview Record. It will help you prepare in advance so that, during the interview, you can keep track of all the key points you need to cover and deal with.

Firing Interview Record

Use this Organizer before the firing interview.

Name: _____

Date: _____

Reason(s) for dismissal: _____

Supporting evidence: _____

_____

Dates when the problems occurred: _____

Witnesses: _____

Dates of previous warnings: _____

Leaving date: _____

Severance pay: _____

Vacation pay: _____

Other payments: _____

Other topics I need to mention: _____

_____

Hiring Interviews Action Checklist

☐ Prepare a job description.

☐ Prepare a person description that lists the qualifications, skills, qualities, and experience the successful applicants must have, as well as those that they should have.

☐ Sort the applications into three piles:
  1. The people who match your specification well
  2. The people who match some parts of your specification
  3. The people who don't match at all

☐ Interview the people in pile 1. Put the people in pile 2 on hold for the time being. Put the applications in pile 3 into the trash can.

☐ Set up interviews in a comfortable environment where you won't be disturbed.

☐ Ask a range of probing what-if questions to determine how the applicant would respond to tricky situations.

☐ Listen carefully, watch the interviewee's body language, and pay attention to your intuition. Remember, once you hire someone, you're stuck with him.

Firing Interviews Action Checklist

☐ Follow your organization's procedures in every respect.

☐ If you have to provide hard evidence of someone's wrongdoing, then make sure that you gather, sift, and evaluate everything so that the reasons for the dismissal can be supported by hard facts.

☐ Don't run dismissal interviews on your own. Call in a disinterested observer and, if possible, someone to take notes.

☐ Even if you have to do it yourself, write everything down. You need an accurate, written record of what was said and agreed on. Date the notes and, if possible, get the dismissed member of staff to sign them, as an acknowledgment that the notes represent a true record of what took place during the dismissal interview.

☐ No matter what is said to you or how you personally feel about the situation, you have a responsibility to your organization to remain calm and nonjudgmental. Whatever you say or do at the firing interview should be suitable for presentation in court.

☐ After the interview, keep your own counsel and say as little as possible to other staff members.

☐ No matter who is going or why, hold on to the fact that it is not your fault.

Marketing

Ultimately, the purposes of marketing are to gain and keep a competitive edge, stay in business, expand the business, and maximize productivity and growth. To achieve these key objectives, you must understand what your existing and potential customers really want to buy (and make sure you are able to supply it), be clear about the image you want your product or service to project, be clear about your marketing goals, be confident that you have the right marketing mix, and use the right marketing strategies to achieve the results you want.

Managing Marketing

Step 1: Understanding Your Customers and Potential Customers

Key question: Who are our customers and what do they want?

Generally, people buy what they want to buy, rather than what they need to buy. (See Selling.) For example, people generally *need* a soap powder they can use in a washing machine to get clothes clean. Most people *want* to buy a soap powder that gives "the fresh, clean smell of clothes air-dried on a summer's day."

This is where market research is vital to ensure that your product or service matches customer wants, hopes, dreams, and expectations. Market research involves finding out from customers and potential customers what they think about your product or service. Specialist companies run mail and face-to-face surveys to get the answers to such questions as "How does our product compare to brand XYZ?" "If we made a pocket-size version, would you buy it?" and so on. The results of the market research lead organizations to develop newer, faster, brighter, fresher, more competitive products. If customers want palm-size personal computers, let's make them! If customers want modems with faster speeds for downloading from the Internet, we'll do it! If customers want ninety-eight percent fat-free chocolate cake, we'll find a recipe that works!

The bottom line is that even if you have a superb product, at the right price, if no one *wants it,* then you've got a flop on your hands.

Step 2: Creating a Suitable Image

Key question: How do we want our customers to perceive us?

Clever marketing allows an organization of any size to choose how it wants its customers to perceive the company and the products or services it offers. Clever marketing tailors every single aspect of the organization so that it matches the chosen image.

For example, picture a new, small consulting company that specializes in head-hunting senior management personnel for large organizations. There are two consultants and one receptionist working out of a small office. The consultants want to market the consultancy as a large and thriving organization. Their market research has shown that customers don't want to do business with small consultancies; customers want to hire high-energy, high-cost businesses. So, this small consultancy uses information technology to replace staff. All incoming calls are routed direct to voice mail with an option for the caller to speak to a personal assistant (in reality the receptionist); both consultants have constant access to e-mail and the Internet via their laptop computers. Clients are kept away from the office, and business meetings are arranged at upmarket venues. The consultants dress impeccably and drive top-of-the-line, state-of-the-art vehicles. All the items that leave the office—letters, business cards, brochures, information packets—are specifically designed to reinforce the image of a professional, competent, and expensive company. Potential customers buy in to the image and, within a very short space of time, because of the way in which they have marketed the business, the consultants can afford to expand, hire additional staff, and move to upgraded offices.

Knowing what kind of image you want your company to project to the outside world is key to your marketing success. Once you know how you want to be perceived, then you can match everything you do and say to that image, and thereby influence the way in which your existing and potential customers view the business. Use Organizer Sheet 58, Marketing Your Image, to assess the key aspects of your organization's image and to think about ways in which you could improve.

Step 3: Clarifying Your Marketing Goals

Key question: What do we want to achieve?

Once your market research has identified what people think about your product, how they think it compares to rival brands or services, and what kind of changes they like would to see in the product or service, your next step is to clarify what you hope to achieve. Do you want to appeal to a different segment of the market? For example, your service is purchased mainly by young, low-income families, but your market research shows that there are many older, high-income families who might also buy. Do you want to appeal to these specific people, or do you want to increase sales by two, five, or ten percent across the board? Or, do you want to start exporting to Asia or Europe?

You can only measure your progress against clearly defined goals. If you want to increase sales, then your goal might be "to increase sales by ten percent within a six-month period." If you want to increase profitability, then your goal might be "to increase profitability by ten percent by the end of the financial year." Organizer Sheet 59, Your Marketing Goals, will help you to identify the marketing goals you hope to achieve over the next twelve months and the next two years.

Step 4: Getting the Right Marketing Mix

Key questions: Have we got the right product, selling at the right price, being promoted in the right way, in the right places? If not, are we willing to change?

Marketing Your Image

Use this Organizer before you start making changes to your company's image.

Communication

The way we communicate with our customers and suppliers
- [ ] We project a positive and professional image.
- [ ] We project a mediocre image.
- [ ] We could do better.

The way we communicate internally
- [ ] We project an efficient and professional image.
- [ ] There are problems sometimes, and this filters through to customers and suppliers.
- [ ] We could do better.

The way customers and suppliers are able to communicate with us
- [ ] We make it easy for them.
- [ ] It's not always easy, but we do okay.
- [ ] We could do better.

Presentation

The way we present our products and services
- [ ] We project a positive and professional image.
- [ ] We project a mediocre image.
- [ ] We could do better.

The way our people present themselves
- [ ] Everyone projects an efficient and professional image.
- [ ] Some people have problems with our image.
- [ ] We could do better.

The image our building, stationery, vehicles, and equipment projects
- [ ] Every aspect of our business looks the way it should.
- [ ] Some aspects may need to be improved and upgraded.

☐ We need to make major improvements because we're projecting the wrong image.

Efficiency and Timeliness
☐ Our customers and suppliers are dealt with courteously and efficiently, and we always meet our deadlines.
☐ We know where we need to make improvements, and we're working on it.
☐ We need to make major improvements because we're projecting the wrong image.
☐ We project a mediocre image.
☐ We could do better.

The marketing mix is used to reinforce an organization's chosen image and to sell the product or service. The marketing mix—often referred to as the 4 Ps—is a combination of four key factors: the product, the price, the promotion, and the place or point of sale.

For example, take a company that wants to be perceived as the market leader in soft drinks. The product is a carbonated fruit juice, and the company's goal is "to stack 'em high, sell 'em fast, and outstrip the competition." In this case, the marketing mix might be:

- *Product.* High-volume production using standard ingredients.
- *Price.* Cheap, or certainly the same as (or slightly less than) similar rival brands.
- *Promotion.* Bright and brash TV advertising; snazzy plastic bottles. Main message: "It's cheap, it's refreshing, and it tastes good."
- *Place.* Supermarkets, gas stations, and similar retail outlets.

On the other hand, the marketing mix for an herbal health drink, where the company's goal is to produce a high-quality product for a discerning market, might be:

- *Product.* High-volume production using specialized and imported ingredients.

Your Marketing Goals

Use this Organizer before you make final decisions about your marketing strategy.

Goals we plan to achieve over the next twelve months	Goals we plan to achieve over the next two years
☐ Continue to sell our existing products and services to the kinds of customers we sell to now	☐ Continue to sell our existing products and services to the kinds of customers we sell to now
☐ Sell our existing products and services to different kinds of customers	☐ Sell our existing products and services to different kinds of customers
☐ Develop new products and services and sell them to the kinds of customers we sell to now	☐ Develop new products and services and sell them to the kinds of customers we sell to now
☐ Develop new products and services and sell them to new kinds of customers	☐ Develop new products and services and sell them to new kinds of customers
☐ Increase our market share in this country If so, by how much? _____	☐ Increase our market share in this country If so, by how much? _____
☐ Expand our operations and market our goods and services abroad If so, where? _____ By what date: _____	☐ Expand our operations and market our goods and services abroad If so, where? _____ By what date: _____

- *Price*. Expensive. Certainly the same price as (or slightly more than) the main competition.
- *Promotion*. Subtle TV advertising; expensive and carefully designed packaging. Main message: "It's expensive. It is revitalizing and rejuvenating. It can make a difference in your life. And it tastes wonderful."
- *Place*. Holistic health food stores, health clubs, and upmarket vegetarian food outlets.

Identify and use your unique selling point, often known as the USP. This is the key factor that makes your product or service different from similar products or services offered by your competitors. For example, is your product:

- More compact?
- Faster?
- Fresher?
- Softer?
- Suitable for use both inside and outside?

Whatever your USP is, it should be that certain something that will appeal to potential customers and persuade them to buy from you, rather than from your competitors.

Importance of the product life cycle.

Apart from making sure that your marketing mix is appropriate, you also need to understand where your product or service is in relation to the product life cycle. The product life cycle consists of five stages: introduction to the world, growth, boom, decline, and, finally, death.

When a new product or service is first introduced and marketed, it's at stage one of the product life cycle. This is a risky time because considerable sums of money will have been spent on research and development, production, packaging, marketing, advertising, and in-house staff development and training. At this stage, no one can say for sure whether the product will survive or fade away if it fails to catch the consumer's interest or attention.

A product or service is at stage two—growth—when it catches the public imagination and begins to sell.

169

Stage three—boom—occurs when the product or service is hot news. It's the flavor-of-the-month and everyone wants to buy. At this point, demand may exceed supply.

Stage four—decline—takes hold when the product or service is starting to look tired. New, fresher, more exciting alternatives are available. Customers increasingly want products that are bigger, better, faster, neater, or smarter.

Stage five—death—is when no one wants the product or service anymore. It is obsolete or no longer fashionable, or it has been outstripped by its competitors.

Regular Coca-Cola and PepsiCola, for example, have both survived the product life cycle. From time to time, the packaging changes and the advertising looks different, but the products remain more or less the same as they have always been, and customer demand remains high. On the other hand, two prime examples of products that have fallen victim to stage five, death, in the product life cycle are vinyl records and Teenage Mutant Ninja Turtle games, toys, and associated goods.

By monitoring where your product or service is in relation to the product life cycle, you can plan ahead and prepare for change by developing new products and services to replace those that are in decline or dead. Organizer Sheet 60, The Product Life Cycle, will help you to identify where you are in relation to the product life cycle. Also, use Organizer Sheet 61, Marketing Mix, to analyze how you want your product or service to be perceived, and to assess whether you need to make any changes to the mix of product, price, promotion, and place or point of sale.

Step 5: Using the Right Marketing Strategies

Key question: How do we get them to buy?

As consumers become more sophisticated, they become bored by conventional marketing strategies—money-off coupons, free lottery tickets, scratch cards, holiday prize drawings, BUY TWO AND GET ONE FREE OFFERS, FIFTY PERCENT MORE IN THE PACK, FIFTY PERCENT OFF THE PRICE, and on and on and on.

The Product Life Cycle

Use this Organizer (one for each product or service) every six months.

Product or Service:

_____

_____

Where this product or service is in the product life cycle:

- ☐ Introduction
- ☐ Growth
- ☐ Boom
- ☐ Decline
- ☐ Death

☐ We have a product or service in development that will replace this existing one.

☐ We have a product or service ready to launch that will replace this existing one.

☐ We need to decide what we develop next.

The right marketing strategy for your product or service depends, to a large extent, on the marketing mix of product, price, promotion, and place. For example, if you are selling frozen dinners, you could probably afford to run BUY TWO AND GET ONE FREE; but if you are selling sports cars, this strategy probably wouldn't be an option for you.

The strategies you use to tempt customers to buy from you, rather than from the competition, will make the difference between success and failure. Organizer Sheet 62, Marketing Strate-

(text continues on page 174)

Organizer Sheet 61

Marketing Mix

Use this Organizer (for each product or service) every twelve months.

Product or Service:

_____

_____

We want this product or service to be perceived as:

_____

_____

Current marketing mix (product/price/promotion/place):

☐ We've got the marketing mix exactly right.
☐ We need to make some changes to the product.
☐ We need to make some changes to the price.
☐ We need to make some changes to the promotion.
☐ We need to make some changes to the place of sale.

Suggestions:

The product: _____

_____

The price: _____

_____

The promotion: _____

_____

The place: _____

_____

Marketing Strategies

Use this Organizer before you make any changes to your marketing mix.

Product or Service:

_____

Marketing strategy worth considering to help us achieve our marketing goals:

- ☐ Increase the price.
- ☐ Reduce the price.
- ☐ Change the packaging.
- ☐ Change the distribution.
- ☐ Change the advertising.
- ☐ Increase the advertising.
- ☐ Change the advertising. How? _____

_____

_____

_____

- ☐ Change the product or service. How? _____

_____

_____

_____

- ☐ Withdraw this product or service.

- ☐ Do something else. What? _____

_____

_____

_____

gies, will help you identify marketing strategies that are appropriate to the marketing goals you outlined in Organizer Sheet 59.

Marketing Action Checklist

- ☐ Look at every aspect of your business—from the way your receptionist answers the phone, to the color and quality of your packaging, to the kind of coffee you offer to your clients. What do these things say about your organization?
- ☐ Think about the kinds of customers you want to attract. Is your organization, product, or service likely to appeal to this segment of the market? If not, what changes do you need to make?
- ☐ Marketing is, to some extent, about selling hopes, wishes, and dreams. Think about the hopes, wishes, and dreams of your customers. What do they hope to fulfill when they deal with your organization, buy your product, or use your service?
- ☐ Consider your unique selling point. Your USP is that extra special something that makes your chocolate shake, or automobile tire, or bookstore, or art gallery, or design and print service different from what's offered by your competitors.
- ☐ Plan your budget carefully and spend according to where you are in the product life cycle. If you are at the beginning, then marketing should take a high priority. If you are coming toward the end of the cycle, seriously think about new research and development.
- ☐ Watch how your competitors market products and services that are similar to yours.
- ☐ Recognize that marketing is a highly specialized activity. If you can, use expert guidance to steer you through the statistics and the strategies, but rely on your own instincts to tell you when a strategy is right for you and your company and when it's not.

Meeting Planning

For whatever reason you need to plan a meeting—whether your business wants to market or publicize a new product, promote new research findings, reward your salespeople, or prepare the staff for major in-house changes—the keys to success are organization, organization, organization. You must prepare your plan, work your plan, and stick to your plan—but always have a backup plan ready, just in case you need it.

To prepare your plan, you need to ask some important questions. Why are we having a meeting? What's the budget? Who should be there? Who's going to speak? Where will we hold the meeting? When should it be? Who's going to be in charge of planning? And who's going to be on the planning team? The answers to these questions will help you to create a workable strategy for overcoming most of the usual problems associated with planning a major event for a large number of people.

Meeting Planning Strategy

Stage 1: Preliminary Decisions

Why are we having a meeting?

Key question: What do we hope to achieve?

First of all, you need to clarify the purpose of the occasion. To some extent, the purpose dictates the amount of money you are going to spend and the profile of the event. Distill the purpose of the meeting into a simple, written goal. For example:

- *To introduce new and existing customers to our latest product*
- *To increase sales of our latest product*
- *To reward, encourage, and motivate our salespeople*
- *To tell our employees about the forthcoming changes to company structure and the way we'll be paying and promoting people in the future*

What's the budget?

Key question: How much can we spend?

This is a key item of information. You may decide that the best way to achieve your objective is to fly everyone to a wonderful hotel for five days of sun, sand, surf, and sensational food. But you can only do that if you have the budget to spend. Before you make any further decisions, find out what your budget allocation for meetings is, and, if necessary, argue for an increase. Don't try to operate on a shoestring budget. Always try to secure additional funding, if only for emergencies that might crop up.

Who should be there?

Key question: Whom do we invite?

If it's an occasion for marketing or publicizing your organization, you need to think about which existing and which new customers should be invited. You'll probably be limited to a specific number of meeting delegates, so establish criteria for your guest list. For example, you may wish to include customers who have been with your company for over a year, or customers who spend more than $100,000 a year, or customers who haven't bought from you for at least a year. You must also make a decision about whether you plan to invite official delegates only or their partners as well.

Who's going to speak?

Will you be looking for outside specialists to make some of the presentations, or will you be relying on people from within your organization? How many people will you invite to present, and what amount of time will you allocate to each one?

Once you've decided on the people you are going to invite to speak at the meeting, you also need to decide on the topic for each presentation and the running order for the speakers. In addition to your preferred speakers, make a list of reserve speakers, just in case the main players are unable to attend. Use Organizer Sheet 63, Meeting Presenters, to create your list of main and backup speakers.

Where will we hold the meeting?

Look for venues that offer:

- Easy access for people who have to travel some distance
- Parking
- Suitable meeting rooms
- Suitable (and sufficient) accommodations for your delegates if they are staying overnight
- Good food
- In-house business facilities (e.g., access to fax, e-mail)
- Pool and other in-house leisure facilities

Before you make a decision about which venue to choose, use Organizer Sheet 64, Venue Plan, to draw up a list of your own criteria (e.g., close to our head office, daily rate of less than $100). Once you are clear about what you want, you can start narrowing down a list of suitable venues. Go through the brochures and information packets, and select the venue that most closely matches your specification.

When should it be?

You may need to speak with other people in your organization (e.g., sales, marketing, or administration) before you decide the

177

Meeting Presenters

Use this Organizer before the meeting.

Main Presenters

Name _____

Topic: _____

Length of talk: _____

Telephone: _____

Fax: _____

E-mail: _____

Address: _____

Name _____

Topic: _____

Length of talk: _____

Telephone: _____

Fax: _____

E-mail: _____

Address: _____

Backup Presenter

Name _____

Topic: _____

Length of talk: _____

Telephone: _____

Fax: _____

E-mail: _____

Address: _____

Venue Plan

Use this Organizer before you choose your meeting venue.

Location
Close to:
- ☐ Airport
- ☐ Beach
- ☐ City
- ☐ Our head office
- ☐ Other:

_____

Room rate
- ☐ Less than $70 per day
- ☐ $70 to $100 per day
- ☐ $101 to $150 per day
- ☐ Other:

_____
_____

Conference Room
Seating for (circle one):
25   50   75   100
Other: _____

- ☐ Natural daylight
- ☐ Audiovisual requirements
  (if needed, describe here):

_____
_____
_____
_____

Guest Rooms
- ☐ Standard and executive rooms
- ☐ Standard rooms only
- ☐ Executive rooms only
- ☐ Other type of room:

_____
_____
_____

Parking
- ☐ Less than 25
- ☐ 26 to 50
- ☐ 51 to 75
- ☐ 76 to 100
- ☐ More than 100
- ☐ Other requirements: _____

_____

Menu Options
- ☐ Vegetarian
- ☐ Kosher
- ☐ Low salt
- ☐ Gluten free
- ☐ Other food requirements:

_____
_____

Recreational Facilities
- ☐ Pool
- ☐ Gym
- ☐ Golf
- ☐ Tennis courts
- ☐ Other:

_____
_____
_____

most appropriate time to hold the meeting. Should the meeting be scheduled for midweek? Friday and Saturday? A long weekend? Make sure you select a date and time when you believe your most important delegates and your key speakers will be able to attend.

Who's going to be in charge of planning?

Key question: Who's going to lead the project?

You can lead the planning team yourself or delegate this responsibility. (See Delegating.) You'll need someone with experience in handling large to medium-size projects and with a good eye for detail.

Who's going to be on the planning team?

As well as the project leader, you are going to need secretarial and administrative support. Anyone with previous meeting planning experience should be assigned to the team. You want people who are flexible, can handle unexpected situations calmly, and can achieve miracles in under twenty-four hours. Use Organizer Sheet 65, Your Meeting Planning Team, to help you to decide who to assign to the planning team.

Stage 2: Final Arrangements

Once you have made some preliminary decisions about who, what, where, and when, someone needs to get down to the real business of finalizing the arrangements.

Book the meeting venue.

Key question: What kind of venue do we need and can we afford?

Don't rely on PR or marketing brochures. If it's an important meeting, the venue is key to the success of the event. Check it out yourself or delegate the task to someone you trust. Make sure that the venue is pleasant and of a suitably high quality overall.

Organizer Sheet 65

Your Meeting Planning Team

Use this Organizer (one for each person on the team) before you start to organize the meeting.

Name: _____

The skills and expertise this person will bring to the team: _____

_____

I want this person to be responsible for:

☐ Creating a delegate database
☐ Designing delegate information packets
☐ Mailing information packets and invitations
☐ Organizing conference room and equipment
☐ Organizing the welcome desk
☐ Creating a database of suitable venues
☐ Serving as the liaison with the venue
☐ Organizing rooms and meals
☐ Coordinating presenters
☐ Managing the budget

Check out the rooms, meals, and service (remember, the staff at the venue can make or break your event). Scrutinize the meeting room itself. You'll need adequate light, good air-conditioning/heating, comfortable seating, a good public address system, and efficient, up-to-date audiovisual equipment. Remember, if you are expecting people to spend a day or more listening to presentations, they'll appreciate and require a light, airy, and comfortable environment.

Invite the delegates.

Key question: Which key players need to attend?

Make sure that you give people plenty of advance notice. Send out a delegate information packet with full details of the meeting—where it is to be held and when. Include a map so people can find the venue easily. If, for instance, you are having a formal black-tie dinner as part of the event, make sure that the delegates are told.

As soon as you receive confirmation back from the delegates, you can inform the venue of the number of rooms and meals you require.

Book the speakers and arrange the schedule.

Key question: Who has something to say and can say it in a way that's both interesting and informative?

Arrange with every speaker the length of their presentation, and discuss the topic you want them to present. You might want to ask every presenter to provide an advance draft of their presentation. Not only will the draft give you an idea of the speaker's approach to the topic, but it offers you the opportunity to make some creative suggestions and arrange the order of speakers.

Work out your schedule and allocate time slots to each of the presenters. Bear in mind that no matter how hard you try, most people go over their allocated speaking time. Allow ten minutes leeway for each presenter. Aim for a good mix of presenters. For example, try to follow heavyweight material with something a littler lighter, for variety. Your goal is to keep the delegates interested and informed. Don't forget to schedule meal and comfort breaks, plus any social events you plan to run. And don't forget to book your reserve speakers as well.

Organize a welcome desk at the venue.

Appoint two or three people to take care of delegates as they arrive, to provide information, and generally to offer a point of contact for your organization. The people on the desk should be confident and experienced team members, able to interface with your guests and with the venue staff if there are problems of any kind with rooms, food, or service. Remember, your delegates deserve the best.

Don't expect to relax until everyone has gone home.

If you are project managing the meeting, then you'll need to be on your toes the whole time the delegates are at the venue. Anything can (and often does) go wrong. People won't like their rooms; the venue hasn't prepared enough meals for those with special diets; the air-conditioning breaks down; salmonella breaks out; arguments and disagreements can begin to spark all over the place. Be prepared for any eventuality and accept that you won't be able to relax until the event is over and everyone, including you, has gone home.

Meeting Planning Action Checklist

- ☐ Find out what's in the budget and appoint your team.
- ☐ Prepare a draft delegate invitation list and a draft speaker invitation list.
- ☐ List the criteria you are looking for in a meeting venue. Compare your list with three or four possibilities. Pare the list down to one or two venues and check them out yourself.
- ☐ Settle on a time that is suitable for the key players, and make the final decision about the venue.
- ☐ Prepare and send out delegate information packets and book your speakers.
- ☐ Arrive at the venue early, set up the welcome desk, and check everything, down to the last detail.
- ☐ Expect the unexpected.

Meetings

Some managers constantly drift or dash, depending on their style, from one meeting to another. They have meetings about when to call a meeting; meetings about the strategy they'll use at the next meeting; meetings about how the last meeting went; and so on. Of course, some meetings are necessary, important, significant, and productive. Many are not. Take care that much of your precious time and energy aren't wasted at meetings that achieve very little.

Do We Really Need to Meet?

Key question: Can we share information and ideas some other way?

At the end of most meetings, someone usually says, "Okay, when shall we get together again?" and everyone pulls out a diary. Another meeting is agreed on, and everyone dutifully notes the time and date.

Instead, why not ask, "Do we really need to meet?" Quite often it is possible to update colleagues on progress, share information, or float a new idea using the telephone, fax, or e-mail. Don't fall into the trap of arranging a meeting just because that's how it has always been done. By arranging for the group to communicate in other ways, you can cut down on the number of meetings, which means that the meetings you do arrange assume more importance and are likely to be more productive and more worthwhile.

Once you have decided that a meeting is necessary, then it is important to plan ahead and create a positive strategy to make sure that the time and energy you invest in the meeting will move you closer to your goals. Your strategy depends on whether you are chairing and leading the meeting or whether you are attending the meeting as one of the people around the table.

Strategy for Chairing and Leading a Meeting

As chairperson, you can do a great deal to make sure that the meeting is successful and productive.

Before the Meeting

Key questions: Why? Who? Where? When?

- *Why is the meeting taking place?* Do you hope to reach a decision or some kind of agreement? Are you hoping to leave the meeting with a specific plan, strategy, or list of key actions? As an outcome of this meeting, what do you hope to achieve, gain, know, or do?
- *Who needs to attend the meeting?* Sometimes it is extremely difficult to get everyone together on a specific date. If there are problems with scheduling a meeting, target the key players and arrange the meeting to suit them. These are the people with the authority, specialized knowledge, or influence whom you need to be there. Less important players will have to either miss the meeting or rearrange their schedules so they can attend. Use Organizer Sheet 66, Why and Who?, to clarify why you need to have a meeting and who needs to be there.
- *Where will the meeting take place?* You'll need somewhere quiet where you can talk without interruptions. People function more efficiently and think more clearly when they are reasonably comfortable. So it is in your own interest to make sure that the heating, ventilation, lighting, seating, and refreshments are all sufficient and suitable. You'll need to think about how you can best delegate responsibility for making sure that the details are taken care of. (See Delegating.) You also need to choose who is going to take the minutes of the meeting. Ideally this person should be an

Organizer Sheet 66

Why and Who?
(Meeting Purpose and Attendees)

Use this Organizer before you arrange the meeting.

1. Why do we need to have a meeting? _____

   _____

2. Can we do this by telephone, fax, or e-mail? ☐ Yes ☐ No

   > If you answer yes to question 2, you don't need to complete the rest of this chart.

3. What do we want to achieve at this meeting?

   ☐ Create (explain): _____

   ☐ Approve (explain): _____

   ☐ Arrange (explain): _____

   ☐ Decide (explain): _____

   ☐ Something else (explain): _____

4. Who are the key players who must attend if the meeting is going to be successful?

Name: _____

What will this person contribute?
   ☐ Information   ☐ Authority   ☐ An opinion   ☐ Skills
   ☐ Resources   ☐ Something else (explain): _____

Name: _____

What will this person contribute?
   ☐ Information   ☐ Authority   ☐ An opinion   ☐ Skills
   ☐ Resources   ☐ Something else (explain): _____

observer, not someone who is attending the meeting as a participant, because you need someone who can focus completely on taking notes without having to worry about making a contribution to
the discussion.

■ *When should the meeting be held?* If you are chairing the meeting, then you'll probably have significant input regarding the
schedule. Set a start and a finish time. Schedule the meeting for a
time that is good for you. Don't be railroaded into a breakfast
meeting if that's not your best time of day. Think about whether
you really want to meet in the late afternoon at the end of a hectic
week. Try to organize your diary so that you have a little free time
before the meeting actually starts. That way you'll have an opportunity to gather your thoughts and arrive at the meeting cool, com-
posed, and on time. Organizer Sheet 67, Where and When?, is a
tool to help you arrange the details of where and when the meeting should be held, and to whom you are going to delegate responsibility.

Spread the word.

Send out an agenda so that everyone is clear about the purpose of the meeting, the start time, and where the meeting is going
to be held. In the agenda, provide a SWEET (i.e., sensible, written,
easy to understand, easy to measure, and task-related) objective
for each topic that is up for discussion. For example, if the topic is
marketing, the agenda may be "to consider and discuss the presentations made by external consultants and choose the campaign we
intend to use." This way people will come to the meeting knowing
what you expect from them.

If appraisal is a key topic for discussion, your SWEET objective may be "to set a date for introducing annual appraisals and
decide the method we are going to use to communicate this information to all staff." By including your objectives in the agenda,
everyone can clearly see the purpose of the meeting and what you
hope to achieve. At the end of the meeting, people can judge for
themselves whether or not the objectives have been achieved.

It is also a good idea to remind people, in the agenda, that
you want them to bring certain documents or files to the meeting.
The key point is that you should do everything possible to mini-

Where and When? (Meeting Place and Time)

Use this Organizer before you organize the meeting.

1. Where are you going to hold the meeting?

   Before you decide, think about:
   ☐ The number of people you are going to invite
   ☐ The distance some people may have to travel
   ☐ The expectations some people may have

2. When are you going to hold the meeting?

   ☐ Date: _____

   ☐ Start time: _____

   ☐ Finish time: _____

3. To whom are you going to delegate responsibility for making the arrangements?

   _____

4. When making the arrangements for the meeting, is there anything special this person needs to consider with regard to:
   ☐ Seating?   ☐ Lighting?   ☐ Ventilation?
   ☐ Refreshments?   ☐ Resources (e.g., telephones, flip charts, etc.)?

5. To whom are you going to delegate responsibility for:
   ☐ Taking the minutes?

   _____

   ☐ Producing the minutes?

   _____

   ☐ Distributing the minutes?

   _____

mize misunderstandings and prevent time wasting once the meeting gets under way. Use Organizer Sheet 68, What's on the Meeting Agenda?, to identify the topics you want to discuss at the meeting and to set a SWEET objective for every topic.

During the Meeting

If you are chairing the meeting, a key part of your role is to control the people and the process and to keep a careful eye on the clock.

Start on time.

Start promptly, explain why the meeting has been called, run through the agenda, and be clear about when you expect the meeting to finish. Let people know that you want a result by the end of the meeting; if you achieve a result before the anticipated finishing time, then at that point the meeting will be over, and everyone can leave.

Keep people focused.

Keep people on track. Much time can be wasted because people go off on a tangent and start to discuss matters that are often interesting but irrelevant. A big part of your role as chairperson and meeting leader is to ensure that people contribute information, opinions, ideas, and suggestions about the topics under discussion.

Involve everyone.

Ideally, everyone around the table has something to contribute—that's why they were invited—and it is your responsibility to make sure that everyone has a chance to air their views or ask questions. Don't allow the more senior or more outgoing people to take over. Don't allow the quiet types to retreat behind a wall of silence. Don't allow any attendees to distance themselves from the discussion or to say, "This is not my problem." If they are sitting at the table, the discussion does involve them, their opinion is important, and the outcome will, in one way or another, have an effect on them.

What's on the Meeting Agenda?

Use this Organizer when you are preparing a meeting agenda.

Example: S = sensible   W = written   E = easy to
understand   E = easy to measure   T = task-related
Topic: Budget management
SWEET objective: By the end of the meeting, we've decided who
is going to take control of the budget.

Topics for Discussion

1. _____

    SWEET objective: _____

2. _____

    SWEET objective: _____

3. _____

    SWEET objective: _____

4. _____

    SWEET objective: _____

5. _____

    SWEET objective: _____

6. _____

    SWEET objective: _____

Deal with the difficult people.

At meetings, people use a range of tactics to manipulate the proceedings. If you are chairing the meeting, it is your responsibility to notice and take care of difficult behavior. (See Delegating.) Some of the most popular manipulation tactics are:

- *Topic-jumping.* Someone aims to dissipate group energy and cause a loss of direction by continually jumping to other topics. Bring these people back into line by saying something like, "Tom, that is an important issue, but right now we're focusing on schedules. I want to deal with schedules before we move on."

- *Raising red herrings.* Someone raises a topic that is related but irrelevant to the topic under discussion and attempts to make it a key issue. Regain focus by saying something like, "Carrie, that's a side issue, and right now we're focusing on the main issue, which is whether or not we keep our current law firm or move to another one. Let's address that first and reach a decision."

- *Blocking.* Someone blocks an idea or a suggestion made by someone else on the basis that "It just won't work." To manage this situation, say something like, "Okay, I'd like to hear, specifically, why you think this won't work. Give me three good reasons."

- *Pulling rank.* Some people use their seniority, rather than logic or reason, to override someone else's ideas and opinions. Take a diplomatic approach by saying something like, "I appreciate your input, Suzanne, but I also think it's important that we look at this issue from every angle. I'd like to hear what Steve has to say—it could give us a fresh perspective."

- *Tuning out.* Someone avoids contributing or getting involved because "This really doesn't affect me." Draw these people into the discussion by saying something such as, "You're here because whatever we decide today will, ultimately, affect your department. You have a lot of experience in this area, and I'd like to hear what you think."

- *Getting mad.* Some people get angry or even lose (or pretend to lose) their temper in an attempt to intimidate quieter or less senior people. Take control by saying something like, "Hold it! We're here to discuss these issues calmly and professionally. Now, let's start again and focus on the key facts."

Summarize regularly.

Help everyone to keep track of what is going on by regularly summarizing what has been said or agreed on (e.g., "Okay, Dolores is going to talk to the European people about deadlines, and Tom is going to check out the exchange rates. What we need to do now is to look at how we're going to slant the proposal").

Encourage the team to reach a decision.

When you are leading the meeting, you are not there to make the decisions, but you are responsible for pushing the team toward some kind of agreement. You can do this by asking for further information or clarification, by building on other people's ideas, or by summarizing the arguments for and against. If you think it would be helpful, list the advantages and disadvantages of each possible decision on a large sheet of paper and pin it on the wall. Make it difficult for people to remain undecided. Try not to allow the meeting to end in disarray and indecision—you'll only have to call another meeting and go through the process all over again.

Of course sometimes, despite your best efforts, the team won't be able to reach a decision, and there needs to be another meeting. In this case, make it clear that you expect people to do some research or some clear thinking before the next meeting and that, next time around, everyone should expect to stay at the table until agreement is reached.

Close the meeting.

Briefly run through the decisions that have been reached, highlight the decisions that remain to be made, summarize the key actions for which people have agreed to accept responsibility, and clarify the next step. This could be another meeting, of course, but it doesn't have to be.

After the Meeting

Distribute the minutes.

As soon as possible after the meeting, have the minutes prepared and distributed to everyone who attended. This document should give truthful and accurate details of the date, time, and place of the meeting; who was there; the key points discussed; the agreements reached; the actions for which individuals accepted responsibility; and the arrangements for the next meeting (if there's to be one).

Strategy for Contributing to a Meeting

If you have been asked to attend a meeting, then it is to be hoped that you've been invited because you have a real contribution to make. If you honestly believe that your presence at the meeting is irrelevant, have a word with the person who will be chairing and leading the meeting, and explain your concerns. If there is a good reason for your attendance, it should be clarified. Otherwise, you'll be able to cancel.

Before the Meeting

Ideally, you'll receive the agenda in advance. Read it through and think about the purpose of the meeting and the contribution you'll be expected to make. Do you need to obtain any information? Talk to anyone? Read any documents?

Think about what you must do to make sure that you are well informed and prepared, and consider the position you're going to take at the meeting. Prepare your arguments carefully if you think that your view is likely to be in the minority. Who is likely to oppose you, and who is likely to support you? Whom do you need to influence before the meeting, and what will your strategy be? (See Influencing.)

Organizer Sheet 69, Meeting Agenda Strategies, if filled out before the meeting, will help you to identify the:

- Research you need to do or information you need to gather
- Position you intend to take when discussing each topic
- Objections other people may raise to your ideas, and the ways in which you can handle them

During the Meeting

Arrive on time.

Being punctual shows that you are both professional and eager to get down to business. It also means that if any pre-meeting deals are struck, you'll be aware of what's going on.

Contribute.

Listen carefully and don't make assumptions or jump to conclusions. If you don't understand something, ask for clarification. Don't allow other people to disguise their views or intentions behind a smokescreen of jargon or overly complex arguments.

Keep asking questions until you are satisfied that you have sufficient information to make an informed decision. Contribute your views and opinions. This may be the only opportunity you'll have to influence the process, so don't waste it.

Accept the decision.

It is possible that the agreements that are reached are not in line with your views and objectives. If you have presented your case clearly and persuasively and the majority decision goes against your wishes, then your options are limited. If this is a team meeting and the decision has been reached democratically, then you have a responsibility to the team to accept the agreement and do your best to make it work. If this isn't a team meeting, then calmly say why you are unable to go along with what has been

Meeting Agenda Strategies

Use this Organizer (one for each agenda topic) before you attend the meeting.

Agenda topic: _____

My Strategy

- ☐ What do I need to read? _____
  _____
  _____
  _____

- ☐ What do I need to find out? _____
  _____
  _____

- ☐ What documents or files do I need to take with me? _____
  _____
  _____

- ☐ What's my position on this agenda topic? What's an ideal outcome for me? _____
  _____
  _____

- ☐ What objections might other people raise? _____
  _____
  _____

- ☐ How will I deal with objections? _____
  _____
  _____

Post-Meeting Action Plan

Use this Organizer after the meeting.

Agenda topic: _____

_____

I've agreed to:

☐ Write

  What? _____

  To whom? _____

☐ Meet

  Whom? _____

  When? _____

☐ Read

  What? _____

☐ Find out

  What? _____

☐ Arrange

  What? _____

  When? _____

☐ Write

  What? _____

  To whom? _____

Deadline for completion: _____

agreed on. Remember that the key points of what you say will be noted in the minutes of the meeting.

After the Meeting

When the minutes are distributed, read them and make sure that any comments or opinions attributed to you are accurate. Check to make sure that your understanding of what you are supposed to do, or what you've agreed to do, matches the information documented in the minutes. If there are any discrepancies, contact the chair and discuss the issues you are unhappy about.

The minutes of the meeting are a formal record of what took place, and, six months down the line, they can come back to haunt you. If they are not accurate, say so as soon as possible after receiving and reviewing the minutes. After the meeting, use Organizer Sheet 70, Post-Meeting Action Plan, to keep track of the responsibilities you've assumed as a result of attending the meeting.

Action Checklist for Chairing a Meeting

- ☐ Carefully consider whether a meeting is really necessary. Can you achieve your objective by letter, telephone, or e-mail?
- ☐ Delegate responsibility for:
  1. Arranging a suitable venue and checking that the lighting, heating, ventilation, seating, and refreshments are all taken care of
  2. Taking, preparing, and distributing the minutes
- ☐ Prepare an agenda (and distribute it in advance) that gives information about the meeting's:
  1. Venue (i.e., where is the meeting being held?)
  2. Date, and start and finish times (i.e., when is the meeting taking place?)
  3. Attendees (i.e., who needs to be at the meeting?)
  4. Objectives (i.e., why is the meeting taking place?)
- ☐ Start on time and keep a careful eye on the clock. Don't allow irrelevancies to steal time so that the meeting ends without a decision.
- ☐ Give everyone an opportunity to contribute, keep people focused on the important issues, and summarize throughout the meeting.

☐ Stay objective. Your role is to focus and drive the meeting, not to force people to see things your way.

☐ Read the minutes before they are distributed, and make sure they are truthful and accurate.

Action Checklist for Contributing to a Meeting

☐ When the agenda is distributed, read it. If you suspect that you have been invited to make up the numbers or for some other un-productive reason, contact the chairperson and explain your concerns. If it isn't useful or necessary for you to be there, don't go.

☐ Prepare thoroughly—read documents, gather information, and talk to people. Clarify your position so that you have a clear idea of what you intend to say at the meeting.

☐ Think about whether you need to influence others to consider your point of view, and, if so, prepare an influencing strategy.

☐ Arrive on time.

☐ Work with, not against, the chairperson. Explain your position calmly and assertively. Ask questions and listen to the answers.

☐ Don't lose your temper, and don't try to railroad people into seeing things your way.

☐ Even if, in your opinion, someone is deliberately pushing or baiting you, stay cool.

☐ When the minutes are distributed after the meeting, read them through and query anything about which you are unsatisfied.

Mentoring Partnerships

Is there someone in your life who acts as a role model for you? Someone who gives you the benefit of his experience and knowledge, and who helps you to avoid the pitfalls and grasp the opportunities? If so, that person is your mentor.

Many organizations realize just about everyone can benefit from partnering with someone who has "been there, done that." These mentoring partnerships work well—provided, of course, the person with the wisdom and experience is prepared to work hand in hand with the protégé. And it is equally important that the protégé makes an effort to get along with the mentor. If both people in the partnership recognize that it's a mutually beneficial deal, then everyone—including the organization—wins.

It's not enough to passively hope that your people will find someone they can relate to. A partnership program has to be developed carefully so that the people involved—mentors and protégés—get the right kind of training and ongoing support.

If you are looking to set up partnerships within your organizations, you need to consider four key questions: Who will benefit from having a mentor? Which people will do a good job as a mentor? What kind of training do mentors need? How will you monitor the program to make sure that everything is working in the way it should?

Who Will Benefit From Having a Mentor?

Just about everyone can benefit from having a partner in the business who is a willing and enthusiastic mentor. Usually, the people who benefit the most are:

- Those who are facing the challenge of learning new skills and operating in new ways
- Those who have been promoted to more complex and demanding jobs
- Senior-level, fast-track people who are heading to the top of the corporate ladder
- Junior personnel who are just beginning to find their niche within the organization

Which People Will Do a Good Job as a Mentor?

Conscripting people into mentorship partnerships usually doesn't work too well. Generally the best mentors are people who want to share their time and their knowledge. Successful mentor partners do not regard the role as a time-consuming burden, but as an opportunity to make a meaningful contribution to the organization and to maximize their own professional development.

Mentors need a good understanding of the organization, its objectives, and its culture. They need effective communication skills, patience, and the ability to establish and maintain good working relationships. Good mentors are motivational and inspirational, and they serve as a role model for their protégés. They understand the importance of the mentoring partnership, take their responsibilities seriously, keep partnership confidences, maintain integrity, and act with the utmost professionalism at all times.

The very best mentors understand that they will personally benefit by achieving a higher profile within the organization that allows them access to a broader range of resources (often including access to more senior-level people in the business). They also realize that their self-confidence and job satisfaction will increase, and they'll be on the right track and in the right place for any career development opportunities that come along.

What Kind of Training Do Mentors Need?

Even the most enthusiastic people need some help with understanding the ground rules of this kind of partnership. Potential partners need to be told what's involved and what their roles and responsibilities are. They need to know what they have to do and how they should behave (e.g., the level of support and encouragement they should offer their protégés, and the skills and knowledge they're expected to provide). They also need to know how long the partnership is expected to last, what to do if problems occur, and how to network and find support among the other mentors in the business.

How Should We Monitor the Program?

Monitoring is important because the people involved in the partnerships shouldn't feel that mentoring is just another buzzword initiative that will, in time, fall by the wayside and be forgotten.

Include the mentoring partnership as a topic for discussion at appraisal time. Invite both mentors and their protégés to submit short feedback reports at regular intervals. This helps to keep everyone up to date and is a good way to detect if a partnership isn't working out. Recognize the partnerships as special relationships by celebrating successes, and make sure that both the mentor and the protégé get positive, appreciative feedback. By encouraging everyone in the business to get involved you'll cultivate team spirit and a real sense of people working together to achieve common goals.

Strategy for Developing a Mentoring Partnership Program

Step 1: Identify the people who are going to be the protégés.

> *Key question: Who will make the most of challenging development opportunities as well as ongoing advice, support, and encouragement?*

Choose your criteria for selecting protégés. Are you going to select new employees who've recently joined the company? Middle managers? Women or minorities? People who've been promoted to more demanding jobs with new responsibilities? Organizer Sheet 71, Your Target Mentoring Group, will help you to identify the types of people within your organization who will benefit the most from this kind of program.

Step 2: Identify the people who are going to be the mentors.

Key question: Who has the right mix of skills, personal qualities, and professional experience?

Advertise the program and ask for volunteers. Remember, conscripts won't work with this kind of program. Arrange a get-together with the volunteers and talk them through the program and their prospective roles. Openly discuss the downsides of mentoring. Mention the time and energy it takes. Talk about the level of commitment that's going to be expected. Anyone who isn't serious will drop out at this stage.

Of those people who are left, consider whether you need a formal selection process. Use Organizer Sheet 72, Mentor Skills, to identify the skills, qualities, and experience each potential mentor might bring to this role.

Step 3: Organize a training program.

Key question: How much time and money is the organization prepared to invest?

Work with your training department or an external consultant to come up with a two- or three-day training program to familiarize the mentors with the task that lies ahead. Training should take mentors through the purpose of the partnership and the goals they should be working toward; their role in the partnership and the skills they'll need to use; how to organize and keep to a consistent schedule of meetings; how to avoid pitfalls and deal with problems; and finally, how they, as mentors, can get advice, support, and encouragement for themselves, when needed. Use Organizer Sheet 73, Training Program Topics for Mentors, to list topics you want to see covered by the mentor training program.

Your Target Mentoring Group

Use this Organizer before the mentoring program starts.

☐ Senior managers
☐ Middle managers
☐ Junior managers
☐ Nonmanagerial staff

Criteria for inclusion in the mentor partnership program:

From which departments? _____

_____

_____

_____

_____

From which functions? _____

_____

_____

_____

From which specialties? _____

_____

_____

_____

Length of time with the organization? _____

Other criteria (explain): _____

_____

_____

Mentor Skills

Use this Organizer (one for each potential mentor) before the program starts.

Name: _____

Job title: _____

Skills, knowledge, and experience this person can bring to a partnership:

- ☐ Solid understanding of the culture of the business
- ☐ Specialist knowledge or expertise
- ☐ Good communication skills
- ☐ Patience
- ☐ Sense of humor
- ☐ Flexibility
- ☐ Creativity
- ☐ Integrity
- ☐ Ability to model the skills and attitudes we want our people to develop
- ☐ Ability to create and sustain a supportive relationship

Step 4: Decide the structure and frequency of partnership meetings.

Key question: What's the best format for the program?

Do you want to arrange a specific schedule (e.g., weekly or monthly) for meetings, or are you going to leave it to the partnerships to work out what's best for them? Are you going to organize regular partnership get-togethers where everyone involved in the program can meet, formally or informally, to share ideas and information?

Training Program Topics for Mentors

Use this Organizer before you run the training program for mentors.

- ☐ Our objectives (i.e., why we're running the partnership program and what we hope to achieve for both the protégés and mentors)
- ☐ The benefits of the partnership program for the organization, the protégés, and the mentors
- ☐ The kinds of people who will be the protégé half of the partnership
- ☐ What's involved in being a mentor (i.e., roles and responsibilities)
- ☐ The skills, qualities, and experience a mentor should bring to the partnership
- ☐ The behaviors and attitudes a mentor should model for the protégé
- ☐ The kinds of problems that could occur in the partnership, and how to deal with them
- ☐ What to do if a partnership breaks down
- ☐ How to schedule and organize partnership program meetings
- ☐ How long the partnership is likely to last
- ☐ How and where mentors can get advice, guidance, support, and encouragement
- ☐ How to provide feedback on the partnership
- ☐ How protégés will provide feedback on the partnership
- ☐ How the success of the program will be evaluated
- ☐ How to run the first partnership meeting
- ☐ How to celebrate partnership success
- ☐ Other topics:

1. _____

2. _____

3. _____

4. _____

Step 5: Fine-tune the program.

Key question: How do we handle potential conflicts and partnership problems?

You need to think about how you are going to partner each mentor with the right protégé, as well as how you're going to handle partnerships that, for one reason or another, don't work out. You also must establish a procedure whereby people can obtain honest feedback on what's happening and how useful the partnership is to both protégé and mentor. Finally, you must create a support system for the mentors so that, when they need guidance, answers, or just a sounding board, they know where to go.

Decisions regarding each one of these issues need to be made *before* the program starts. Organizer Sheet 74, Mentoring Partnership Program Schedule, will help you to prepare a realistic schedule and decide who should be responsible for different aspects of the program.

Mentoring Program Action Checklist

- ☐ Decide why a mentorship program would be beneficial for your organization, and clarify who would benefit most.
- ☐ Call for volunteers who are prepared to become mentors and who have the skills you need. Recognize that the people who want to get involved in the program are most likely to be the people who'll make the program work.
- ☐ Choose as mentors those people who will model the attitudes and behaviors that you want to permeate the organization, and train them thoroughly so they understand their role.
- ☐ Choose the protégés and introduce them to the program.
- ☐ Create partnerships between mentors and protégés, but recognize that sometimes, for a range of reasons, partnerships don't work and changes have to be made.
- ☐ Make sure that the mentors have the time to network with one another, and recognize that they need support and encouragement, too.
- ☐ Don't expect too much, too soon.

Mentoring Partnership Program Schedule

Use this Organizer before the mentoring program starts.

Person responsible for **selecting mentors:** _____

Start date: _____ Completion date: _____

Person responsible for **selecting protégés:** _____

Start date: _____ Completion date: _____

Person responsible for **preparing mentor training program:**

_____

Start date: _____ Completion date: _____

Person responsible for **delivering mentor training program:**

_____

Start date: _____ Completion date: _____

Person responsible for **preparing protégé orientation program:**

_____

Start date: _____ Completion date: _____

Person responsible for **delivering protégé training program:**

_____

Start date: _____ Completion date: _____

Person responsible for **gathering feedback from protégés:**

_____

Start date: _____ Completion date: _____

Person responsible for **gathering feedback from mentors:**

_____

Start date: _____ Completion date: _____

Person responsible for **evaluating feedback:** _____

Start date: _____ Completion date: _____

Person responsible for **providing guidance and support to mentors:** _____

Start date: _____ Completion date: _____

Person responsible for **handling conflicts in partnerships and solving partnership problems:** _____

Start date: _____ Completion date: _____

Negotiation

Expert negotiation is about getting the best deal you can while, at the same time, keeping the goodwill of the other side. We can all be tough negotiators. Although standing firm may often get you the deal you want at the present moment, a too-rigid approach may affect your negotiating position in the future and sour future deals.

The best, toughest, and most professional negotiators know that if they want to get the very best deal for themselves and their organization *and* keep the door open for the future, they have to stay SHARP throughout the negotiation process. Staying SHARP involves taking a position that is supercool, honest, assertive, realistic, and prepared.

The Supercool Negotiator

Supercool negotiators go into the negotiation with icy determination. They never allow the other side to see how much they need to leave the table with a specific outcome. Even if the outcome for the supercool negotiator is a matter of bankruptcy versus solvency, or even life versus death, the supercool negotiator shows no emotion and stays calm under fire.

Supercool negotiators take what the other side throws at them, and, unruffled, they continue to pursue their own line. Supercool negotiators don't get angry, irritable, impatient, sarcastic, or otherwise upset. And they don't let the other side see that they are surprised, pleased, enthusiastic, or triumphant. They know that if they keep control of their emotions, they stand a better chance of achieving an acceptable deal and of keeping the relationship on an even footing for the future.

The Honest Negotiator

Honest negotiators know the extent of their authority. They never make promises they can't keep. Their word is absolute, and they don't agree to anything unless they are prepared to follow through. Honest negotiators do not trade concessions or concede any aspect of the deal unless they know that, when they leave the table, they can and will deliver.

The Assertive Negotiator

Assertive negotiators say what they mean and mean what they say. They recognize the other side's rights (see Communication), and they don't waste time or energy playing passive games (e.g., pretending not to have sufficient authority or understanding; pretending to flatter or be impressed) or aggressive games (e.g., pretending to lose their temper; pretending there is a deadlock when there isn't; pretending to be insulted or otherwise upset).

Assertive negotiators recognize that the process of negotiation involves working toward an agreement that is favorable for them and reasonably acceptable to the other side. They know that if they negotiate a deal that leaves the other side experiencing the trauma of total defeat, then they are leaving the door open for revenge and retaliation in the future.

The Realistic Negotiator

Realistic negotiators know what is achievable and what's not. Although their first offer or demand may, from the other side's point of view, be total madness, realistic negotiators recognize the difference between a starting and a finishing position. They do their homework before the negotiation process starts so they know perfectly well what is and isn't realistic.

The Prepared Negotiator

Prepared negotiators know that preparation is the secret of success. They will spend eighty percent of their time preparing to negotiate and, perhaps, twenty percent of their time actually conducting business. Prepared negotiators know that facing an important or complex negotiation demands a high degree of detailed and thorough preparation. They will know everything there is to know about the other side; they'll be clear about how far they are willing to compromise; and they will understand, absolutely, where to draw the bottom line.

Creating a Negotiating Strategy

Prepare your negotiating strategy *before* the process begins. That way you can give your full attention to the actual negotiations when you sit down with the other side. You'll be able to think on your feet and respond appropriately, no matter how the other side behaves and regardless of what they ask for. This applies whether the negotiation is fairly straightforward and brief (e.g., negotiating a promotion or pay raise, a small discount from a supplier, or an extra line of credit) or sensitive, complex, and likely to extend over a period of time (e.g., negotiating a six-book, five-year deal with a publisher; negotiating budgets and architectural blueprints for a major building program; negotiating changes to established working practices with the unions).

Before the Negotiation Begins

Gather information about the other side.

Key question: What do they really want, and how badly do they want it?

Find out about the individuals and the organization you'll be negotiating with. Use Organizer Sheet 75, Negotiating Skills and Expertise, to build a profile of the other team so that you can match your team's skills and expertise to theirs.

Run a SWOT analysis. (See Goal Setting.) What are your opponents' strengths and weaknesses? What opportunities and what

Negotiating Skills and Expertise

Use this Organizer (one for each person on your team) before the negotiation starts.

My Team	Their Team
Name: _____	Name: _____
Job title: _____	Job title: _____
Experience: _____	Experience: _____
_____	_____
Specialist skills or knowledge:	Specialist skills or knowledge:
_____	_____
_____	_____
_____	_____

threats do they face? What's their financial position? Their reputation? What's important to them? How much do they need to achieve a good deal for themselves? When they sit down to negotiate with you, are they:

- In a strong position (i.e., on balance, do they have what you badly want?)
- In a weak position (i.e., on balance, do you have what they badly want?)
- Fairly evenly matched with you (i.e., do you both have something the other badly wants?)

Do as much research as possible beforehand so that when you start negotiating, you can compare what is being said with the facts. This will help you to identify where your opponents are exaggerating, where they are bluffing, and where they are telling the truth.

Clarify your own position.

Key questions: What's the extent of my authority? How far can I go? How flexible can I be?

Before you start to negotiate, you have to be clear in your own mind about:

1. The limits of your own authority. You have to know how far you can go and to what extent you are free to negotiate cuts, increases, add-ons, changes, and new approaches.
2. What the best possible outcome is for you.
3. Your absolute bottom line (probably the worst possible outcome for you, but a deal you could learn to live with if you have to).
4. The concessions you are willing to trade. These will probably be related to one or more of the following key variables: cost, price, time, quality, quantity, personnel (e.g., "I can go to a ten percent discount if my back's against the wall," or "I can do ten days' delivery, but I must have a twenty-five percent cash payment up-front").
5. The concessions you are not, under any circumstances, willing or able to trade.
6. Your opening offer (probably unrealistic, but something to put on the table to get the ball rolling).

Organizer Sheet 76, Perfect, Realistic, and Bottom Line, will help you to identify these positions so that, when you go into the negotiation, you are clear about how much flexibility you have. Organizer Sheet 77, Key Variables During Negotiation, will help you to identify the key variables on which you may be able to make concessions during negotiations, and the level and types of concessions you would willing to make. Both of these organizer sheets should be completed well before the negotiation process begins.

Brief the team.

Key question: Do we all understand exactly what we have to do?

Perfect, Realistic, and Bottom Line

Use this Organizer before you start the negotiation.

In this negotiation, the perfect deal for me would be: _____

_____

_____

In this negotiation, a realistic deal for me would be: _____

_____

_____

In this negotiation, the deal that represents my bottom line and on which I am not prepared to move would be: _____

_____

_____

Important, high-profile negotiations often involve a team of people—the lead negotiator, a financial advisor, a subject specialist (an engineer, designer, microbiologist, or whoever has the specialist skills and knowledge to say what is and what isn't possible within their specialty), and an attorney.

The team should meet as many times as necessary before negotiations begin so that they can get to know one another, reach agreement on the key aspects of the negotiation (e.g., bottom-line positions and concessions), prepare and rehearse their proposals, agree on their overall strategy (e.g., formal or informal, relaxed or tough, limited time or as long as it takes), and finally, determine how they will handle tricky situations.

Discuss a range of what-if scenarios (e.g., what if the other side threatens to . . .) and agree on a common approach. Use Organizer Sheet 78, Key Issues During Negotiations, to establish those issues that will seriously affect the way the team negotiates.

Make sure that one person on the team has responsibility for

Key Variables During Negotiations

Use this Organizer before the negotiation starts.

Cost/Price
- ☐ Cost/price is a key issue and could be a sticking point for me.
- ☐ I'll negotiate on cost/price, provided I can get everything else I want.
- ☐ I'm prepared to be flexible on cost/price.
- ☐ I'd be willing to reduce the cost/price by $_____ or _____%.
- ☐ If I'm pushed into a corner, I'll reduce the cost/price by $_____ or _____%, but this is my bottom line.

Time
- ☐ Time is a key issue and could be a sticking point for me.
- ☐ I'll negotiate on time, provided I can get everything else I want.
- ☐ I'm prepared to be flexible on time.
- ☐ I'd be willing to increase/reduce the amount of time by:
  - _____ hours
  - _____ days
  - _____ weeks
  - _____ months
- ☐ If I'm pushed into a corner, I'll increase/reduce the amount of time by:
  - _____ hours
  - _____ days
  - _____ weeks
  - _____ months

Quality
- ☐ Quality is a key issue and could be a sticking point for me.
- ☐ I'll negotiate on quality, provided I can get everything else I want.
- ☐ I'm prepared to be flexible on quality.
- ☐ I'd be willing to improve quality.   ☐ yes   ☐ no

☐ I'd be willing to accept reduced quality. ☐ yes ☐ no
☐ If I'm pushed into a corner, my position on quality is: _____

_____

_____

Personnel
☐ Personnel is a key issue and could be a sticking point for me.
☐ I'll negotiate on personnel, provided I can get everything else I want.
☐ I'm prepared to be flexible on personnel.
☐ If I'm pushed into a corner, I'll make the following changes to personnel, but this is my bottom line: _____

_____

_____

writing down points of agreement as and when they are reached. Organizer Sheet 79, Points of Agreement, is a useful tool to use.

The team is ready to negotiate as a team when everyone has all the relevant information and is clear about how the others on the team are going to behave. At this point everyone is working toward achieving the same outcome. There should be no disagreements (these should be ironed out before you sit down with the other side), and no one on the team should spring any surprises during the negotiation meeting. There's ample opportunity for discussion and disagreement before and after the meeting. Make sure you present a united front during the actual negotiations.

During the Negotiation Meetings

Listen carefully and watch body language.

You know what you want. Now you have to find out what the other side wants. Listen carefully and ask as many questions as you need. If you don't understand something, say so. It'll be too late, once the deal is struck. Don't be afraid to say when something isn't clear to you. Using complex language or confusing arguments may

Key Issues During Negotiations

Use this Organizer before you start to negotiate.

It seems as though I am in the **strongest** negotiating position because I have what they want: ☐ Yes   ☐ No

It seems as though I am in the **weakest** negotiating position because they have what I want: ☐ Yes   ☐ No

It seems as though there is an **even balance**—we both want something the other is able to offer: Yes   ☐ No

Achieving a deal that is favorable for **me** is:

☐ Vital for me.
☐ Reasonably important for me.

☐ Important for me.
☐ I can afford to be flexible.

If I don't achieve a favorable deal, the consequences for me will be that: _____

_____

Achieving a deal that is favorable for **them** is:

☐ Vital for them.
☐ Reasonably important for them.

☐ Important for them.
☐ They can afford to be flexible.

If they don't achieve a favorable deal, the consequences for them will be that: _____

_____

I expect the key areas of disagreement or difficulty to be:

1. _____ I can handle this by: _____
2. _____ I can handle this by: _____
3. _____ I can handle this by: _____

I will be satisfied if: _____

I will call for an adjournment if they: _____

Points of Agreement

Use this Organizer during the negotiation process.

Key Negotiating Points

1. _____

_____

☐ Agreed   Date: _____

2. _____

_____

☐ Agreed   Date: _____

3. _____

_____

☐ Agreed   Date: _____

4. _____

_____

☐ Agreed   Date: _____

be part of your opponents' strategy, and they may be relying on your reluctance to admit you don't understand. Don't fall for it!

Pay attention as well to nonverbal communication. Does the body language match what is being said? Observe if the other side is saying the right things but using defensive or aggressive body language, or is saying the wrong things but using open and friendly gestures. Body language will give you a clue as to what the message really is.

Build agreement.

Negotiation is a process of give-and-take on both sides. Build on the areas where you can reach agreement. Be prepared to trade concessions, but be careful and don't go overboard. Say, slowly, "Well, I guess we might be able to . . ." when the other side offers to trade a concession, even if it is exactly what you want. Save the jumping up and down for later!

Move slowly from your opening offer to your ideal outcome. Recognize that, to close the deal, you may have to settle for your bottom-line position—the outcome you can learn to live with, if you really have to.

Summarize regularly.

At regular intervals, summarize what has been agreed on so far and where sticking points still exist (e.g., "So it looks like we're happy with the production schedule and the staff training program, but we still need to reach agreement on cost"). That way everyone has the same understanding at the same time. Also, be sure to summarize the agreement, point by point, at the end of the meeting to ensure there will be no disputes or disagreements later on.

Watch out for tactics and tricks.

Be especially aware of the following tactics and tricks, and know how to handle them:

- *The Bulldozer Tactic*. This involves taking the initiative in a big way, right at the start of the negotiating, then making assumptions and pushing hard (e.g., "I think we all know why we're here, so let's get on with it and get it over with"). Don't be intimidated and don't be bulldozed. Clarify your concerns, point by point, calmly ignoring any show of irritation or impatience from the other side.

- *The Let's Be Friends Tactic.* This involves assuming a level of intimacy and friendship that does not, in reality, exist (e.g., "We know each other well enough to be able to iron out any difficulties"). Don't lose sight of the fact that you are there to negotiate the best possible deal for yourself and your organization. Hold on to your ideal outcome for as long as you can, and don't be tempted to give away concessions just because the atmosphere of conviviality and goodwill is overwhelming.

- *The We Can Make Things Really Tough for You Tactic.* This involves making threats, either overtly or covertly. The implication is that if you don't go along with the other side, you will find yourself in a very difficult position, one way or another. Stay supercool and don't react. If you've done your pre-negotiation preparation, you'll have considered all the possible outcomes and will have reached your own conclusions. Don't be frightened into submission.

- *The Let's Not Worry About That Right Now Tactic.* This involves dismissing or glossing over your concerns (e.g., "That's not a major issue so let's not worry about that right now"). The issue may, in fact, be very important, and that could be precisely why this tactic is being used. Don't be lulled into a false sense of security just because it seems as if you are more or less getting everything you want. Stay SHARP.

After the Negotiation

Put your understanding of the agreement in writing and send the other side a copy. Make sure they check and agree on every point.

Keep your promises. Do everything humanly possible to make sure that you and your organization live up to the agreement you have so carefully and professionally negotiated.

Negotiation Action Checklist

- [ ] Pick your team carefully so that you can match the skills and expertise of the negotiators from the other side.
- [ ] Brief your team thoroughly, and make sure that everyone understands the team's objectives and the team's approach.
- [ ] Clarify what you want, what you will and will not accept, and the concessions you are prepared to make.
- [ ] Go into the negotiation with a positive attitude. Work on the basis that it is always possible to reach a mutually acceptable solution.
- [ ] Regardless of what happens, make sure you are SHARP:
  Supercool
  Honest
  Assertive
  Realistic
  Prepared
- [ ] Be on your guard for tactics and tricks.
- [ ] Verify and agree on every point, and put everything in writing.

Presentations

All managers must face the fact that, at some time in their career, they'll have to make an important presentation. They realize, with the onset of a slight nervous tic and a very distressing migraine, that, finally, the moment of truth is here and there's no escape.

No matter what you think of the prospect of delivering information in a fairly formal way to a group of people (possibly important decision makers), there are strategies you can use to make the process less painful for yourself and more interesting for your audience.

Preplanning

Before you get down to the serious business of actually preparing your presentation, you need to first choose the appropriate strategy, then find out how much your audience already knows about your topic, and finally decide on the key elements of your message.

Preplanning Stage 1: Choose Your Presentation Strategy

Depending on what you hope to achieve, you can choose to prepare either an informative presentation or a persuasive presentation. The differences between these styles of presentations are as follows:

- *Informative presentations.* These presentations focus on delivering factual information (e.g., "This is how the new system works," "This is the procedure we're going to use from now on," "This is the plan for upgrading the network"). Choose this strategy if you are simply passing on data and information that people need to know.

- *Persuasive presentations.* Choose the persuasive strategy when you are selling an idea, a service, or a product, or when you want to motivate people or persuade them to adopt your point of view or do things your way.

Preplanning Stage 2: Analyze Your Audience

Find out who your audience will be and how much they already know about the topic you intend to discuss. This information will help you to pitch your presentation at the right level. If your target audience knows nothing at all about your presentation topic, then you'll need to guide them through the basic information to help them make sense of your ideas or your proposals. If you launch straight into your material without giving them some background, they'll be lost and your presentation will fail because the audience won't understand and will quickly lose interest.

If your audience is already up to speed, then you should skip the basics and move swiftly into the new information or proposals you are there to present. Covering old ground or presenting basic details to people who don't need them will not be helpful because your audience will tune you out. Use Organizer Sheet 80, Presentation Preplanning, to determine which presentation strategy to use and to analyze the audience you'll be presenting to.

Preplanning Stage 3: Decide on the Key Elements of Your Message

If your goal is to present information so that people get it the first time or quickly learn to do what you want them to do, then you must decide on the key points to include in your presentation.

Think about what you want your audience to remember and take away with them. At the end of the presentation, what key facts must these people remember? What specific systems or procedures do I want the people to use? You'll find it helpful if you keep these questions in mind when you are deciding on the key elements to include in the presentation.

Presentation Preplanning

Use this Organizer before the presentation.

◼ **My Presentation Strategy**
The main purpose of my presentation is to:
- ☐ Provide an update of information
- ☐ Provide new information

If you have checked either of the boxes, you should use the news format.

The main purpose of my presentation is to:
- ☐ Persuade the audience to see my point of view
- ☐ Persuade the audience to agree to do something (e.g., buy something, give their approval, or accept change)

If you have checked either of the boxes, you should use the persuasive solution format.

◼ **My Audience**
- ☐ My audience knows absolutely nothing about the topic. Everything will be new to them.

If you've checked this box, you should give a thorough (but not overly lengthy) description of the background and history.

- ☐ My audience knows something about the topic, but they'll need some history and background.

If you've checked this box, you should give a brief introduction, outlining the key points and dates.

- ☐ My audience knows nearly as much as I do about this topic. They don't need any background information.

If you've checked this box, just introduce the topic, bring your audience up to speed with any new information, and then make the presentation.

The Four Key Stages of Preparing Your Presentation

Once your preplanning is complete, you are ready to move on to the four key stages of:

1. Preparing your message
2. Preparing your visual aids
3. Preparing yourself
4. Preparing the venue

Preparing Your Message

Key question: Am I presenting information or asking for a decision?

Informing your audience.

If you are presenting information, without any need to persuade or sell, you can make it easy for people to understand your message by using a news format. This approach is used by anchor people on news programs all over the world to present complex and detailed information in a straightforward, easy-to-understand format. You give your audience a brief personal introduction, then you give them the headlines, then the news; then you give them a summary of the news. The news format works as follows:

- *A brief personal introduction.* Always begin with a brief introduction. Say who you are, where you're from, and how long you intend to speak. For example, "Hello, I'm Maria Cortez. I'm the marketing director, and I'm planning on taking the next twenty minutes to speak to you about the way we're going to launch Lemon Sauce Cookies."

This brief introduction sets the scene for your audience and puts your presentation into context. They now know who you are, why you're addressing them, and, perhaps most important of all, how long they are expected to give you their attention. It's also wise, in the introduction, to say how you intend to handle questions. You may be happy to field questions as they occur during the presentation (although this may interrupt your flow and throw you off balance), or you may prefer to say something like, "I'm sure that there are going to be questions, and I'll be happy to deal with those at the end of the presentation."

- *The headlines.* To help people to key in to the information you are going to present, give them the headlines. Headlines usually include a little background information. For example, "As you know, back in 1995 we started to look at ways in which we could provide training and support for all our people. We started by introducing a coaching scheme, and last year we began the process of creating an individual learning program for each employee. Today I want to tell you about our new flexible learning courses, how these will operate, and the procedure for joining the program."

For an audience that knows very little about your topic, you'll need to give enough background information so that people can put the new information into context, with some logical sequence and order. Don't go into masses of detail that will only be of interest to the specialists in the room. Ask yourself the key question: "If I knew nothing about this topic, what facts would I need to know to help me understand the issues here?" For a well-informed audience, your background information can be kept to a minimum.

- *The news.* This is your main message, so you should present the key points of information in small chunks and in a logical sequence. Bear in mind the key word KISS (keep it simple and straightforward).

- *The summary.* At the end of the presentation, you should encapsulate the most important key points you've covered in the news. These are the facts that you particularly want your audience to remember. For example, "Okay, to summarize where we are and where we're going—the product launch is on August 21 and we are on target to meet that date. We are having our first focus group on September 10, and for that date I need you to prepare an updated sales forecast based on sales for the period August 21 to September 7."

226

Use Organizer Sheet 81, Planning the Content for Factual News-Style Presentations; this organizer sheet is designed to take you through the process of planning all four stages of a factual, informative presentation.

Persuading your audience.

When you are asking people to give you something (e.g., more time or more money, or approval or agreement), you need to present your information using the persuasive solution strategy. Using this approach, you divide your presentation into four segments, as follows:

1. *Scene setting*. Briefly introduce yourself, then set the scene for your audience. Give the background to the situation, presenting the level of detail that best suits the audience's needs, as this gives everyone a common starting point. For example, "As you know, over the past five years, our business has increased by over thirty-five percent. This is great news but, over the past six months, we've found ourselves in a position where we've had to refuse new clients so that we can give our full attention to our existing clients." Scene setting shows that you've done your research—especially important when you are pitching to a potential client.

2. *Specific situation*. Describe the current situation and mention the specific problems, issues, or challenges that must be addressed. For example, "Since January we have lost something approaching $250,000 potential revenue. That is our number one problem. Problem number two is that Linda is leaving us in November, which means that we will have four key accounts without a key account executive to take care of them."

3. *Suggestions*. In this segment of the presentation, describe all the available options and alternatives, and explain the advantages and disadvantages of each one, making sure that your own preferred option is included among the possibilities. For example, "There are four ways we can go. First, we can do nothing. When Linda leaves, we don't replace her, which means that we are going to save her salary but probably lose her key accounts. Option number two is . . ."

Planning the Content for Factual News-Style Presentations

Use this Organizer before the presentation.

1. Personal Introduction

My personal introduction (key facts about me): _____

_____

The reason(s) I'm making the presentation: _____

_____

The way I'm going to handle questions:

☐ As they occur during the presentation
☐ At the end of the presentation

The length of time I plan to speak in this segment: _____ minutes

2. The Headlines

The main theme or topic of the presentation: _____

_____

The background information: _____

_____

The history: _____

_____

The key areas I'll be covering:

_____

_____

_____

3. The News

Key point: _____

Key point: _____

Key point: _____

Key point: _____

The length of time I plan to speak in this segment: _____ minutes

4. The Summary

My brief summary of the key points: _____

_____

_____

_____

_____

The action I want people to take: _____

_____

_____

_____

The deadline for this action: _____

Any other important information: _____

_____

_____

_____

_____

The length of time I plan to speak in this segment: _____ minutes

By dealing with the positive and negative aspects of all the possibilities, you put the spotlight on what you want to do and also preempt those people in the audience who want to offer their preferred option as the best course of action. If you mention all options, and feature their disadvantages, they won't be able to say at the end of the presentation, "But what about . . . ?"

4. *Solution.* Finally, say which course of action you believe to be the right solution and sell the benefits. For example, "Okay, this is how I believe we can solve the problem. I suggest that we do this because . . ." Present your solution with confidence and enthusiasm, and make it easy for your audience to approve your plan. Also, make sure that you tell people what you want them to do (e.g., "I need you to give me your verbal approval today, and your written approval by Monday").

Ending your presentation.

Finally, check to make sure you've dealt with all the questions and thank people for their time and attention. Use Organizer Sheet 82, Planning the Content for Persuasive Solution Presentations, to plan and prepare a persuasive presentation. Organizer Sheet 83, Handling Questions, will allow you to plan, in advance, the best possible answers you could give to the most likely questions you could be asked during either a factual or a persuasive presentation.

Preparing Your Visual Aids

Key question: How can I make the visuals highly interesting and relevant so that people can see what I mean?

Use pictures to help your audience understand your presentation. Charts, maps, graphs, diagrams, and photographs can all help to illustrate your key points and allow people to better see what you mean. Computer software programs such as Microsoft PowerPoint or Lotus Freelance Graphics can help you create stunning visuals. You can easily and quickly print them straight onto transparencies using a laser printer.

You can also use flip charts (pads of A1-size paper) that fit

Planning the Content for Persuasive Solution Presentations

Use this Organizer before the presentation.

1. Personal Introduction

My personal introduction (key facts about me): _____

_____

The reason(s) I'm making the presentation: _____

_____

The way I'm going to handle questions:
- ☐ As they occur during the presentation
- ☐ At the end of the presentation

The length of time I plan to speak in this segment: _____ minutes

2. Scene Setting

The main theme or topic of the presentation: _____

_____

_____

The background information: _____

_____

_____

The history: _____

_____

The key areas I'll be covering: _____

_____

_____

The length of time I plan to speak in this segment: _____ minutes

3. Specific Situation

These are the key facts that best describe the specific situation:

_____

_____

_____

_____

The length of time I plan to speak in this segment: _____ minutes

4. Suggestions (including the advantages and disadvantages of each plan)

Plan 1: _____

_____

_____

Plan 2: _____

_____

_____

Plan 3: _____

_____

_____

Plan 4: _____

_____

_____

My preferred plan is number _____

The length of time I plan to speak in this segment: _____ minutes

5. Solution

The reasons the audience should go for my preferred plan: _____

_____

_____

_____

_____

The specific action I want people to take: _____

_____

_____

The deadline for taking this action: _____

Any other important information: _____

_____

_____

The length of time I plan to speak in this segment: _____ minutes

Handling Questions

Use this Organizer before the presentation.

Likely Question: _____

_____

_____

Suitable Answer: _____

_____

_____

Likely Question: _____

_____

_____

Suitable Answer: _____

_____

_____

Likely Question: _____

_____

_____

Suitable Answer: _____

_____

_____

neatly onto a flip-chart easel to present interesting lists and diagrams. Flip charts can be prepared in advance. A good trick is to draw, in pencil, your diagram or map and then, during your talk, work over the pencil lines with thick colored pens. Your audience won't see your preparatory drawing, and they'll be impressed with your ability to produce a well-thought-out visual on the spot. Flip charts are also good for noting down questions and suggestions from the audience as the presentation proceeds.

If you hand out information sheets, make sure you do so at the end of the presentation, after you've finished speaking. Otherwise your audience will be tempted to read the notes and tune you out while you're speaking.

Make sure that your visuals are clear and easy to read. Good colors to use are blue, black, and dark red because they can be seen from the back of the room. Avoid paler colors such as yellow, orange, and pink for text because they are much more difficult to see.

Don't overload your visuals with too much detail. Avoid lines and lines of text, or rows and rows of numbers. Keep your visual presentation clean and sharp (less is more). Organizer Sheet 84, Visual Aids for Factual News-Style Presentations, will help you to plan the kinds of visuals aids you are going to use at each stage of the presentation; Organizer Sheet 85, Visual Aids for Persuasive Solution Presentations, can be used to plan visual aids for those presentations.

Preparing Yourself

Key question: How do I make sure that I'm prepared?

You are the key element in the equation that will make the difference between a mediocre presentation and a terrific one.

Rehearsing the material.

Before making your presentation, the best gift you can give yourself is the gift of time to prepare and rehearse. There is no substitute for actually going through the presentation and speaking the words out loud. Try to practice in front of someone you

Organizer Sheet 84

Visual Aids for Factual News-Style Presentations

Use this Organizer before the presentation.

The Headlines

Key point: _____ transparency/slide/flip chart/information sheet (*circle one*)
Person responsible for finding or preparing this information:

_____

Key point: _____ transparency/slide/flip chart/information sheet (*circle one*)
Person responsible for finding or preparing this information:

_____

Key point: _____ transparency/slide/flip chart/information sheet (*circle one*)
Person responsible for finding or preparing this information:

_____

Key point: _____ transparency/slide/flip chart/information sheet (*circle one*)
Person responsible for finding or preparing this information:

_____

The News

Key point: _____ transparency/slide/flip chart/information sheet (*circle one*)
Person responsible for finding or preparing this information:

_____

Key point: _____ transparency/slide/flip chart/information sheet (*circle one*)
Person responsible for finding or preparing this information:

_____

Key point: _____ transparency/slide/flip chart/information sheet (*circle one*)
Person responsible for finding or preparing this information:

_____

Key point: _____ transparency/slide/flip chart/information sheet (*circle one*)
Person responsible for finding or preparing this information:

The Summary

Key point: _____ transparency/slide/flip chart/information sheet (*circle one*)
Person responsible for finding or preparing this information:

Key point: _____ transparency/slide/flip chart/information sheet (*circle one*)
Person responsible for finding or preparing this information:

Key point: _____ transparency/slide/flip chart/information sheet (*circle one*)
Person responsible for finding or preparing this information:

Key point: _____ transparency/slide/flip chart/information sheet (*circle one*)
Person responsible for finding or preparing this information:

Key point: _____ transparency/slide/flip chart/information sheet (*circle one*)
Person responsible for finding or preparing this information:

Visual Aids for Persuasive
Solution Presentations

Use this Organizer before the presentation.

Scene Setting

Key point: _____ transparency/slide/flip chart/information sheet
(*circle one*)
Person responsible for finding or preparing this information:

_____

Key point: _____ transparency/slide/flip chart/information sheet
(*circle one*)
Person responsible for finding or preparing this information:

_____

Key point: _____ transparency/slide/flip chart/information sheet
(*circle one*)
Person responsible for finding or preparing this information:

_____

Key point: _____ transparency/slide/flip chart/information sheet
(*circle one*)
Person responsible for finding or preparing this information:

_____

Specific Situation

Key point: _____ transparency/slide/flip chart/information sheet
(*circle one*)
Person responsible for finding or preparing this information:

_____

Key point: _____ transparency/slide/flip chart/information sheet
(*circle one*)
Person responsible for finding or preparing this information:

_____

Key point: _____ transparency/slide/flip chart/information sheet
(*circle one*)
Person responsible for finding or preparing this information:

_____

Key point: _____ transparency/slide/flip chart/information sheet (*circle one*)
Person responsible for finding or preparing this information:

_____

Suggestions
Plan number: _____ transparency/slide/flip chart/information sheet (*circle one*)
Person responsible for finding or preparing this information:

_____

Plan number: _____ transparency/slide/flip chart/information sheet (*circle one*)
Person responsible for finding or preparing this information:

_____

Plan number: _____ transparency/slide/flip chart/information sheet (*circle one*)
Person responsible for finding or preparing this information:

_____

Plan number: _____ transparency/slide/flip chart/information sheet (*circle one*)
Person responsible for finding or preparing this information:

_____

Solution
Key point: _____ transparency/slide/flip chart/information sheet (*circle one*)
Person responsible for finding or preparing this information:

_____

Key point: _____ transparency/slide/flip chart/information sheet (*circle one*)
Person responsible for finding or preparing this information:

_____

Key point: _____ transparency/slide/flip chart/information sheet (*circle one*)
Person responsible for finding or preparing this information:

_____

Key point: _____ transparency/slide/flip chart/information sheet (*circle one*)
Person responsible for finding or preparing this information:

_____

trust and feel safe with. Ask for feedback on your performance and, if there are any criticisms, don't get upset. Instead, work on what needs to be changed so that, when it's showtime, you can give a good performance and sound and look confident.

Checking your voice and your body language.

Speak clearly and loud enough to be heard, but without shouting. Don't rush through the words to get it over with, but do keep a smart pace so that people don't get bored. Stand tall, don't slouch or fidget, and look out toward the audience, not down at the transparencies or the floor. Figure out, before the presentation, what you are going to do with your hands. Practice in front of a mirror to see whether you look or feel more comfortable holding something (maybe a clipboard or laser wand), putting your hands behind your back, or putting them in your pockets. There are no hard-and-fast rules. Do whatever feels right for you.

Presenting the right image.

What you wear for the presentation will depend on your organization, whether you're making a formal or an informal presentation, and, of course, your own personal style. Whatever you choose, do not choose anything that is too tight, too short, too loud, or even too new. You won't be able to remember the words, manage the visuals, smile, maintain eye contact, speak clearly, stand confidently, and answer questions thoroughly if your new shoes are taking your mind off the main event.

Stay within the time slot you've been allocated. If you've agreed to present for an hour, then stick to that. This is especially important if there are other people lined up to present after you. If you go over the time limit, the next person will start late and possibly finish late, and this can have a domino effect on the whole day's program.

Preparing cue cards.

Do not, under any circumstances, read from a script. This looks unprofessional, and it's mind-numbing for your audience. If you need backup, prepare cue cards by writing key words or phrases onto small record cards. Number each card and staple or clip them together. That way, if you drop the pack, it's not a problem.

Anticipating questions.

Anticipate the most likely questions and frame your answers in advance. Of course you won't know exactly what people are going to ask, but if you know your subject, you'll have a fair idea of the kinds of questions that are most likely to come up. If at all possible, run through the presentation in front of a small, invited audience—your partner or a couple of close friends. Ask your audience to note down, during the presentation, the questions that occur to them as you speak. At the end of your trial run, invite questions, see what comes up, and run through your prepared answers. You may find, after this session, that you need to rethink some of your responses. It's better to make the changes now rather than discover, on presentation day, that your answers sound dismissive or ill-considered.

On the day you are to give your presentation, if you don't know the answer to a question, say so and confirm that you will get back to the questioner with the information, by a specific deadline. Make a note of what you've agreed to do, and make sure you do it.

Preparing the Venue

Key question: What do I need to check when I get there?

Get to the venue with time to spare and check the room to see if you have everything you need. Try out any equipment you'll be using to make sure that everything works in the way you want it to. Put a transparency onto the projector and check it out from the back of the room; it should be in focus and easy to read.

Lay out your transparencies and your information sheets, and set up your flip charts, if you're using them. Make sure you have pens and markers, a glass of water, and some tissues. Use Orga-

Key Information for Presentations

Use this Organizer before the presentation.

Date of presentation: _____

Start time: _____   Finish time: _____

Venue address: _____

_____

_____

Venue telephone: _____   Venue fax: _____

Venue e-mail: _____

Venue contact name: _____

Number of people expected to attend the presentation: _____

Names and job titles of the key players/key decision makers:

1. Name: _____   Job title: _____

2. Name: _____   Job title: _____

3. Name: _____   Job title: _____

4. Name: _____   Job title: _____

5. Name: _____   Job title: _____

Written information I must take with me: _____

_____

Equipment or samples I must take with me: _____

_____

Additional important information: _____

_____

nizer Sheet 86, Key Information for Presentations, to record the details of the venue and to help you remember some key facts about the time, the place, and the people who'll be there.

When you are happy that the room is well organized and properly equipped, you can take a deep breath and start to focus your mind on what you have to say and how you're going to say it.

Presentation Action Checklist

- ☐ Choose your presentation strategy:
    1. The news format if you are going to present information
    2. The persuasive solution format if you are going to persuade, sell, influence, and convince
- ☐ Analyze your audience. You want to make sure that what you have to say makes sense for the uninitiated and isn't patronizing for the people who know almost as much as you do. Ask these questions:
    1. How much does the audience already know about the topic?
    2. How much background and history do I need to include in the presentation?
- ☐ Prepare the content. Begin with your personal introduction, then move into:
    1. Informative news presentation: Give the headlines, the news, and a summary.
    2. Persuasive solution presentation: Focus on scene setting, the specific situation, suggestions, and a solution.
- ☐ Make sure your visual aids are clean and sharp and that you've followed the rule "less is more."
- ☐ Rehearse everything in advance—from how you are going to answer questions through to what you're going to wear.
- ☐ Go to bed early the night before the presentation. You need to be bright-eyed and bushy tailed!
- ☐ Get to the venue ahead of time and check everything—from whether the projector works to whether people at the back of the room will be able to read your visuals.

Project Planning

Projects come in a variety of shapes and sizes, wrapped in all kinds of criteria and constraints. There are large and important projects that, if delivered on time, will enhance your reputation and your career. And there are small and tricky projects that offer little satisfaction or reward but, if delivered to a high standard, just may lead to more challenging and interesting deals in the future.

No matter how prestigious or mundane, all projects should be brought in on time, within budget, and with the highest possible quality. Fortunately, you can achieve these goals of time, cost, and quality by using the same set of skills, regardless of the size or importance level of the project. Whether you are launching a new product on a global basis, creating a prototype nuclear warhead, or simply reorganizing your team's work space, the planning and management principles are the same.

For each new project, you need to follow a strategy that will take you from planning through to a successful conclusion.

Creating a Project Strategy

For any project, there are four key steps: defining the project, planning the project, running and monitoring the project, and completing and reviewing the project. By adhering to this strategy you'll progress from the initial (and often hysterical) reaction of "How am I supposed to do this?" to self-confident completion of the project ("Okay, that's done; what's next?").

Step 1: Defining the Project

Key question: What am I supposed to achieve?

First, you need to define what you want to achieve and by when. You can best do this by creating one or more SWEET project goals. These goals are statements that are sensible, written, easy to understand, easy to measure, and task-related (e.g., develop our own version of the MMX chip by January 2001; lay off one-third of the labor force by the end of the year; develop, write, and produce a new staff orientation program by December 2002).

Once your project goals are clarified on paper, then you know exactly what you need to achieve and by when. Defining your project will also help you to gather a suitable team of people with the right mix of skills, knowledge, and experience you need. As time passes and the project progresses, you can measure and compare what is happening with what is supposed to be happening and judge your progress.

Step 2: Planning the Project

Key question: How much time and money do I have?

The first stage of the planning process is to prioritize the three important factors at work in any project: time, cost, and quality. For example, time may be of the essence or, perhaps, quality is of paramount importance. In either situation, you could be given an almost unlimited budget and the freedom to spend whatever you like, as long as you bring the project in on time or to the highest possible quality standards. Alternatively, if your budget is strictly limited, then every decision you make will be driven by cost. You may have to sacrifice quality or speed to ensure that you keep the costs down. The way in which you prioritize time, cost, and quality has a direct bearing on the way you plan and manage the work.

Your next step is to clarify the resources you're going to need. To some extent, your needs depend on how you've prioritized time, cost, and quality. You may have to say, "Money's tight, so we'll make do with one specialist," or you may be able to say, "Money's not an issue, so we'll have the team of five specialists we really need."

The resources you need may be people, time, work space, information, contacts, equipment, or materials. Sometimes you may

245

be given a project to manage, but someone else is making the decision about what resources are adequate for you to accomplish the project's goal. If there is a mismatch between what has been made available to you and what you believe you need to complete the project to your standards, then you must say, loud and clear, where the shortfall lies. Although you may not always get what you want, it is important that you ask, right at the start, for the additional resources you need. Explain why you need these additional resources and how inadequate resources could affect the success of the project. That way everyone is aware of the issues and the potential problems that may occur.

Once you know what it is you have to do, and you are clear about the resources you need to do it, the next step is planning each stage of the project against the calendar. Start off by putting some key dates down on paper. For example, the project start date is May 7; the presentation to the faculty board is May 12; we'll have completed application for external funding by June 5. These are your major milestones.

If you achieve what you have set out to achieve by each milestone, then the project is on target. If you haven't completed the work by a specific milestone, then you'll need to take remedial action, fast.

When you are satisfied that you have listed all key dates for each stage of the project, the next step is to turn your list into a visual schedule. This way everyone on the team can see, at a glance, what needs to be done and by when. Figure 3 is an example of how a list of key tasks can be turned into a bar chart. There are a number of software programs available that you can use for creating project schedules.

Before the project gets off the ground, use Organizer Sheet 87, Key Project Milestone Dates, to clarify the key dates that will serve as milestones for the completion of each stage of your project. Then you also need to delegate responsibility for tasks and their milestone delivery dates to individual members of the team, making sure that you allocate the right tasks to the right people.

Finally, don't expect everything to go according to your original plan. Build in flexibility by preparing a list of possible problems and suitable solutions. Include all the major problems you are most likely to encounter on the project, so you can anticipate them

Figure 3. Turning a List of Key Actions and Milestone Dates Into a Bar Chart

List of key actions:
1. Start project on July 2 (first team meeting)
2. Complete initial tests by August 28
3. Evaluate preliminary findings and discuss by September 21
4. Write up preliminary findings by October 19
5. Present preliminary findings to the board on November 24
6. Wind up project on December 3

Task	July	August	September	October	November	December
Start project	■ 2					
Complete initial tests	■■■	■■■ 28				
Evaluate preliminary findings		■■	■■ 21			
Write up preliminary findings			■■■	■■ 19		
Present to the board				■■	■■■ 24	
Wind up project					■■■	■ 3

and be ready to respond. For example, "What if our supplier cannot meet our demand for the five million cross-thread fasteners we need? Who can identify an alternative source of supply?" or "What if Juan can't handle the statistics on his own? Who can I call on to help him out?"

Generally, most project problems stem from:

- A lack of resources
- The wrong people being assigned to the team

Key Project Milestone Dates

Use this Organizer before you prepare a visual chart of key dates and milestones.

Project title: _____

Project goal(s): _____

Start date: _____

Milestone 1: By _____ we need to achieve: _____

Milestone 2: By _____ we need to achieve: _____

Milestone 3: By _____ we need to achieve: _____

Milestone 4: By _____ we need to achieve: _____

Milestone 5: By _____ we need to achieve: _____

Milestone 6: By _____ we need to achieve: _____

Milestone 7: By _____ we need to achieve: _____

Milestone 8: By _____ we need to achieve: _____

Milestone 9: By _____ we need to achieve: _____

Milestone 10: By _____ we need to achieve: _____

Milestone 11: By _____ we need to achieve: _____

Milestone 12: By _____ we need to achieve: _____

Project completion date: _____

- The right people doing the job wrong
- Unrealistic expectations and poorly planned milestones
- Unexpected situations

Even before the project actually gets under way, think about all the things that could go wrong and be prepared. Use Organizer Sheet 88, Project Problems and Solutions, to identify potential problems and generate some practical solutions.

Although it is only a paper exercise, let your imagination run wild. Write down the major disasters that might befall you and your team. These problems may be internal and, for example, connected to the budget, to workload, or to staffing. Or the problems may be related to external conditions such as suppliers, changes to the law or the political situation, or a downturn in the economy. When your list is complete, call a team planning meeting, present the list, and ask your people to brainstorm solutions. As the team generates ideas, write down the best solutions and keep the chart in a safe place, just in case it's needed later.

Step 3: Running and Monitoring the Project

Key question: How do I keep the project on track?

Stay calm.

The first few days of any project are normally tense, as people settle into their roles, get comfortable with one another and the expectations they have to meet, and generally get their bearings. At this stage, as a manager, you need to remain levelheaded and allow the highs and lows, dramas and disappointments, to simply wash over you. The members of the team will take their lead from you. If you remain calm and optimistic, so will they. If you overreact to problems (and problems are bound to crop up, even at the earliest stages of a project), then the team is likely to overreact too. At this stage, you don't need to hear people complain, "Nothing's going right; this project is doomed to failure." Never mind what you think when you close your office door. In front of the team, you need to smile and appear to take everything in your stride. Of

Project Problems and Solutions

Use this Organizer (as many as you need) before the project starts.

Potential Problem

What if: _____

_____

_____

Possible Solution

If this happens, we could: _____

_____

_____

_____

If that solution doesn't work, we could always, as a last resort:

_____

_____

Potential Problem

What if: _____

_____

_____

Possible Solution

If this happens, we could: _____

_____

_____

If that solution doesn't work, we could always, as a last resort:

_____

_____

course, this is a worst-case scenario, and the project may progress very smoothly—but then again, it may not.

Encourage communication.

Many projects hit hard times because people on the team don't share information about what's happening within their segment of the project. Consequently, because other people on the team don't know what's happening, mistakes, confusion, and bad decisions flow through the project. Every minor slipup contributes to the whole, until finally, despair and desperation set in. Team members darkly mutter, "Well, I didn't know," and "No one told me." But, of course, by then it's too late.

Schedule regular team briefings and team meetings. Team briefings can comfortably be held every day, need take no more than ten or fifteen minutes, and can be used to disseminate key information to the team. Such briefings are also useful for highlighting any potential problems or specific areas of concern.

Team meetings need to be held at least once a week. The purpose of the meetings is to provide a focal point for the project. Team meetings should be used to discuss key issues, share ideas, brainstorm solutions, and also provide positive feedback and encouragement to everyone involved in the project. Short, informative, enjoyable team meetings can be productive, inspirational, and motivational, and they build team spirit. Long, drawn-out team meetings that are unfocused serve no useful purpose. At the start of the project use Organizer Sheet 89, Project Communication, to devise a practical communication strategy for your team.

Monitor everything.

The only way to keep on top of a project is to monitor everything. Monitor time and compare progress against milestone dates. Monitor spending and compare it against the budget. (See Budgets.) Monitor people (both inside and outside the organization) and make sure that everyone is doing what they are supposed to be doing.

As soon as anything appears to be going off course, take remedial action. Look at your problems and solutions list (Organizer

Project Communication

Use this Organizer before the project starts.

When I need to give the team data and hard facts, I'll:

- ☐ Call a special team meeting.
- ☐ Deliver the information at the daily team briefing.
- ☐ Deliver the information at the weekly team meeting.
- ☐ Send an e-mail.
- ☐ Send a memo.

When I need to alert the team to potential problems or changes to procedures, I'll:

- ☐ Call a special team meeting.
- ☐ Deliver the information at the daily team briefing.
- ☐ Arrange an informal get-together.
- ☐ Do something else (explain): _____

When I need to generate new ideas and solutions within the team, I'll:

- ☐ Call a special team meeting.
- ☐ Arrange an informal team get-together.
- ☐ Take the team to a hotel for two to three days.
- ☐ Do something else (explain): _____

Sheet 88). If the solution isn't there, call a team meeting and brainstorm ideas. Involve your people; let them take ownership of the work together and create a solution that they can buy into. This is likely to be much more effective than simply choosing a solution on your own and then imposing it on the team. The key point to remember is, if things start to go wrong, don't expect the problems to sort themselves out. Look at the problem, discuss the alternatives, and prepare to take action.

Use Organizer Sheet 90, Project Monitoring Systems, to

Project Monitoring Systems

Use this Organizer before the project starts.

To monitor TIME, I'll use:

☐ Bar chart showing milestone dates

☐ Large chart showing days left to complete project

☐ Computer program to generate achievements against milestones

☐ Weekly presentations by team members describing their progress

☐ Written reports provided by team members describing their progress

☐ Another system (explain): _____

_____

To monitor COST, I'll use:

☐ An allocation/expenditure sheet similar to Organizer Sheet 9 (Monthly Expenditure Versus Budget)

☐ An allocation/expenditure sheet I've devised myself

☐ A computer program designed to monitor expenditure

☐ Weekly presentations by team members describing and explaining their expenditure against their budget allocations

☐ Written reports provided by team members describing and explaining their expenditure against their budget allocations

☐ Another system (explain): _____

_____

To monitor QUALITY, I'll use:

☐ Weekly presentations by team members describing and explaining how they are making sure they achieve the required quality standards

- ☐ Written reports provided by team members describing and explaining how they are making sure they achieve the required quality standards
- ☐ Written status reports provided by suppliers
- ☐ Verbal status reports provided by suppliers
- ☐ Another system (explain): _____

_____

choose, right at the start of the project, the best strategies for keeping on top of how the project is progressing.

Step 4: Completing and Reviewing the Project

Key question: If I have to do this all over again in the future, what should I do differently?

Regardless of what happens during the life of the project always make sure that, on completion, you carry out a detailed project review with your team. This review will provide many valuable lessons for everyone. Avoid blame and criticism. Stick with the facts and objectively consider:

- What went well and should be repeated in the future on another project
- What didn't go well and should be avoided in the future

If you have the courage and are prepared to listen, ask the team for feedback on your performance. Accept the praise gracefully, but listen carefully to any criticisms. There may be actions that you, as a manager and project leader, need to avoid next time around.

Organizer Sheet 91, Project Review, will help you to review the project and rate how well you managed time, cost, and quality issues. Use this information to identify changes and improvements for the next project you are involved with.

Project Review

Use this Organizer when the project is completed to rate your and your team's performance.

Managing Time
☐ Excellent: We met all our time targets and milestones on time.
☐ Good: We met most of our time targets and milestones on time.
☐ Not good: We missed a number of time targets and milestones.
☐ Dismal: We were way behind on everything.
For the next project, we can improve the way we manage time by:

_____

_____

Managing Cost
☐ Excellent: We stayed within our budget allocations.
☐ Good: We overspent a little, but this was due to changing circumstances, beyond our control.
☐ Not good: We overspent in quite a big way.
☐ Dismal: The budget went out the window, and spending went out of control.
For the next project, we can improve the way we manage cost by:

_____

_____

Managing Quality
☐ Excellent: We delivered everything to the required standard.
☐ Good: We delivered most of the project to the required standard, but due to changing circumstances beyond our control, some of the deliverables could have been better.
☐ Not good: We had to sacrifice quality to finish on time.
☐ Not so good: We had to sacrifice quality to stay within the budget.
☐ Dismal: Quality was so poor that we stopped talking about it after a while.
For the next project, we can improve the way we manage quality by: _____

_____

Project Planning Action Checklist

- ☐ Define the project and set your goals.
- ☐ Prioritize, in order of importance, the three key areas of time, cost, and quality, and identify the resources you are going to need (e.g., time, people, money, space, information, contacts, equipment, and materials).
- ☐ Establish the key dates that will be the major milestones in your project, and produce a visual schedule for the team so that everyone can see what needs to be done and by when.
- ☐ With the team, generate a list of potential problems and possible solutions.
- ☐ Communicate constantly; hold daily team briefings and weekly team meetings, and encourage people to share information and ideas.
- ☐ Monitor relentlessly. If things look like they may be going off course, get ready to take action.
- ☐ Stay calm because, if the people on your team see that you are falling apart, they'll quickly follow suit.

Public Relations

Public relations is about projecting and communicating the right message to the right people at the right time. When you and your organization are facing a crisis situation (see Troubleshooting and Crisis Management), the way in which the company handles public relations will make the vital difference between success and failure. Conversely, when things are going well, the only way people may find out about your success is if you tell them. Like everything else in business, good public relations doesn't just happen, it has to be managed.

Your organization has numerous stakeholders—people who, one way or another, have a vested interest in how the business is doing and the kind of reputation the business is acquiring. These people are existing customers who buy your product or service, potential customers, suppliers, competitors, banks and financial houses, shareholders, and, of course, your staff. These people need to know that what you are selling is legal, ethical, reliable, and effective, and that the corporation itself can pay its debts and keep operations running smoothly, even when the going gets tough.

The basic role of any public relations campaign—whether it's driven internally by your company or externally by a specialist PR agency—is to present, to the outside world, the good news about what's happening. Even in times of crisis and drama, good PR takes the view that every cloud has a silver lining.

Public opinion is a powerful force. If your stakeholders start to buy in to the idea that your organization appears unhealthy, you may find yourself on a slippery downhill slope leading nowhere fast. Even if you employ a high-profile consultancy to manage your external image, you still need to know how to make the news in the right way, manage the media when things go wrong, and consistently spread the right kind of message about the business.

Strategy for Managing Public Relations

The Press Office

Key question: Are we managing our public relations, or is it just happening?

Even if you employ an outside consultancy to manage most of your organization's PR, it is sensible to delegate some responsibility internally. Some element of PR can usually be included in the job description for someone working in the marketing group. (See Marketing and Interviewing.) The key point to remember is that you need someone inside the business who can deal with the media when necessary, in good times and bad.

If you don't have an outside PR agency, then ideally hire an experienced press officer who will be responsible for building a network of positive contacts and dealing with the media; checking the media for interviews, reports, and articles that relate to the company; preparing "good news" press releases; arranging press meetings; preparing campaigns to offset the effects of bad news; and coaching senior managers before they give interviews to anyone outside the organization.

Who's Interested?

Who is especially interested in finding out about your organization? Who will be most influenced by what's happening in your organization? Who can influence what happens to your organization? What kind of papers, magazines, and trade journals do these people read? Which TV programs do they watch?

These people are your target audience, and when you have good news about the business—whether about an upturn in profits, expansion, awards, a breakthrough in research, or an exciting new product—these are the people to whom your message should be targeted.

What's the Key Message?

Before undertaking any kind of contact with the media, it is vital to clarify your key messages. Decide what information you are prepared to disclose and what's strictly off limits, and make sure that everyone in the organization understands the difference.

Follow the Rules of Engagement

Your PR campaign can be proactive or defensive. In a proactive campaign, you take the initiative to tell people about what's happening. In a defensive campaign, your goal is to prevent people from finding out too much. Either way, there are certain rules of engagement you need to follow when dealing with the media.

Issuing press releases.

Key question: What are the messages we want to send out to the world?

Press releases need to be short, snappy, and to the point. They should catch the imagination and offer exciting news or a fresh angle; otherwise they won't make publication. Organizer Sheet 92, Press Releases, will help you clarify the key messages you need to include in a press release. Always make sure your press releases are sent to the right people and in time to meet publication deadlines. If you've had trouble getting your press releases into print, think about hiring a professional copywriter to do the work for you.

Speaking to journalists and TV news reporters.

Key question: Which topics do I need to avoid?

Journalists have a good eye and a good ear for what makes news. They're not interested in facilitating your PR campaign; they're interested in getting a good story that will appeal to their viewers and readers.

When dealing with journalists, keep your wits about you.

Press Releases

What event is the press release focusing on? _____

_____

_____

_____

Why is this event important and interesting? _____

_____

_____

_____

Who's involved in this event, and what's important and interesting about them? _____

_____

_____

When did this event occur? _____

Where did this event occur? _____

What key message is this event sending about your organization, your people, your product, or your service? _____

_____

_____

_____

_____

Don't say anything that you not are prepared to see splashed over the front page. Don't be drawn into making unguarded comments, and, in public, watch your body language. You may be holding your head because a migraine is coming on, but never lose sight of the fact that this could be the photograph of you that hits the front page. Avoid saying "No comment" in response to questions because many people in the media interpret this answer as, "Yes, you're right, but I'm not prepared to discuss the matter."

Appearing on TV.

Key question: Who is the best person to project the right image?

Whether you are on the news or a talk show, everything you say and do will, in one way or another, have an impact on your organization.

Dress carefully. Your appearance sends a major signal about you and your business. Avoid anything that is flashy, keep jewelry to a minimum, and wear smart but not-too-tight clothing. You can expect to get hot under the lights in a TV studio, so take that into consideration when choosing what you'll wear.

Prepare your key messages and rehearse them. Although the option may not be open to you, ask to submit a list of the questions you are prepared to answer and a list of topics that are off limits.

Take your time answering questions, and don't be pushed or bluffed into saying something that you'll regret. Interviewers are paid to get reactions, and they're highly skilled interrogators. Pause before answering and think about what you are going to say; don't be drawn into reacting emotionally. Keep cool and stick to your key message. Use Organizer Sheet 93, Media Interviews, to clarify the topics you are and are not prepared to deal with, the questions you will and won't answer, and the answers you are prepared to give.

Organizing a press meeting.

Key question: Whom do we want to invite, and whom do we have to invite?

Media Interviews

Use this Organizer before the media interview.

Topics I'm prepared to discuss:

_____

_____

_____

_____

_____

Topics that are strictly off limits:

_____

_____

_____

_____

_____

Questions I'm prepared to deal with:

1. _____

   My response: _____

   _____

   _____

2. _____

   My response: _____

   _____

   _____

If you are organizing a press meeting—either to advertise good news or to put a courageous face on when responding to bad news—think carefully about where the event is to be held, who will be invited, and who will be on hand to represent your organization:

- *The venue.* Is your message serious or upbeat? Are you projecting success and stability, or innovation and excitement? Do you want to speak to the press inside or outside (e.g., the Oval Office or the Rose Garden)?
- *The guests.* Your PR consultancy or in-house press officer should have a complete and up-to-date list of the journalists who need to be invited. Any news hounds worth their salt will tag along, anyway.
- *The organization's representative.* If extremely bad news will be covered, then the most senior people in the organization must be there. Use Organizer Sheet 94, Organizing a Media Conference, to make the appropriate arrangements before you hold a conference with the media.

PR Action Checklist

- ☐ Make someone in the business responsible for handling public relations and disseminating information both externally and internally.
- ☐ Hire a PR consultancy or, at the very least, a professional copywriter to prepare press releases.
- ☐ Target your PR messages so that they reach the right people (e.g., shareholders, customers, suppliers, banks, and one of the most important audiences—your staff).
- ☐ Before you meet with the media, prepare and rehearse your key messages.
- ☐ Clarify the topics you are prepared to discuss and the questions you are prepared to answer—as well as those that are off limits.
- ☐ Don't say or do anything that could be open to misinterpretation. Avoid responding with ''No comment,'' since some people will take this to mean ''Yes.''
- ☐ Always remember to engage your brain before you open your mouth!

Organizing a Media Conference

Use this Organizer before the press meeting.

When will the meeting be held?

Date: _____

Start time: _____

Expected finish time: _____

Where will the meeting be held?

Venue: _____

_____

_____

Who should be invited?

_____   _____

_____   _____

_____   _____

_____   _____

What do I need to organize?

☐ Drinks   ☐ Fax   ☐ Food   ☐ E-mail
☐ Parking   ☐ Phones
☐ Other:

_____

_____

_____

Who should be there to represent my organization?

_____

_____

_____

What approach is the conference going to take?

☐ We're advertising the good news.
☐ We're presenting the facts—it's damage control.

What are the key messages? _____

_____

_____

Quality

All kinds of organizations, in just about every country in the world, are coming to realize that if they want to stay in business, prosper, and thrive, then they have to put quality at the top of their agenda. In the most successful organizations, quality filters down through the business and affects every aspect of what the company does, what the company makes or sells, and how the company treats its customers.

Customers doing business with a quality-oriented organization are confident that they are purchasing and using a product or service that does what it is supposed to do, first time and every time. An organization that is serious about quality takes the time and trouble, and spends the money, to ensure that its customers believe the business is interested in establishing and building a working relationship with them. Customers who do business with quality-oriented organizations are consistently made to feel that they are highly valued and very important.

Companies committed to quality start off by analyzing every aspect of their business to make sure that customers' needs are met, on time, in the right way, every time. Such organizations look at everything—the way that people in the business answer the telephone, the wording of standard letters sent out to customers, the attitude and appearance of the security staff, the length of time it takes to deliver an estimate or quotation, the professionalism and product knowledge of the salespeople, the way queries and complaints are handled, even the flowers in the reception area. They identify where and how improvements can be made, and they make them. But they don't stop there. They commit to continuous improvement so that everything they do, inside and outside the business, and everything they provide, for both internal and external customers, is continually examined, developed, improved, and upgraded.

Quality doesn't happen overnight, and it certainly isn't, initially at least, the cheapest way to run a business. But it is only through dedication to quality that an organization can hope for stability and growth in the future. Ultimately, taking this approach will ensure that customers remain loyal and that employees gain confidence, self-esteem, and motivation, so they work harder and more effectively, and the company maintains its profitability and competitive edge. As a manager, it is important that you understand how to establish and maintain not only an awareness of quality, but also a total dedication to the concept throughout the business.

Strategy for Establishing Dedication to Quality

Step 1: Start at the Top

Key question: Is everyone at the top totally committed to quality?

Like most major initiatives in business, a push for quality must be initiated from the top down, by the most senior people in the organization. If you don't have the wholehearted commitment of the people at the top, then forget it, because it won't work.

Step 2: Sell the Concept of Quality to Your Staff

Key question: How can we make quality real for our people?

The only way to achieve quality in an organization is through the people who work there. Everyone in the business needs to understand what quality means and why it's important.

A key concept that everyone in the organization must understand is that every employee has both external customers and internal customers. People understand, absolutely, that their external customers are the people who buy and use the company's products or services. But they also need to realize that their internal customers are their colleagues and coworkers within the business to whom they supply a product or a service.

For a receptionist in a beauty parlor, for example, the external customers are the people who have appointments for treatments. The receptionist's internal customers are the hairdressers, manicurists, masseurs, and holistic therapists who supply services to the external customers. If the receptionist confuses the appointment times, books customers for the wrong service, or arranges for customers to see the wrong therapist, then the whole concept of quality goes out the window. The external customers will almost certainly get upset and take their business elsewhere.

For someone working on a production line making strawberry desserts, clearly the external customers are the people who will eventually buy the dessert product in a store. But the internal customers are the people further up and down the production line. For example, the people further up the line, who send the pastry shells along for filling, need to know that there will be a clear run through for them and that the shells will be filled and then forwarded down the line. The person filling the pastry shells has to do it fast and do it right—otherwise the people further down the line (more internal customers) who are inspecting and packing the product will, in turn, have their own problems as a result of delays or shoddy work.

People need to see that quality is the responsibility of every single person in the business, and that includes them. Use Organizer Sheet 95, Building Quality In, to formalize thinking about how you can build quality into the most important areas of the business, including contracts, documentation, specifications, payments, and procedures for handling problems and complaints.

Step 3: Examine All Your Processes

Key question: What are we doing, and how well are we doing it?

In quality terms, a process is a task where you put thought, energy, labor, and materials in, so that you get something out. Dictating a letter is a process. Creating a work schedule, designing a new label, dealing with a customer complaint, answering the telephone, fill-

Organizer Sheet 95

Building Quality In

Use this Organizer before you start your drive toward quality.

Contracts
Is there a procedure for checking contracts before they are accepted?
- ☐ Yes.
- ☐ No.
- ☐ We don't need a procedure.
- ☐ We need to organize a procedure.

Specifications
Is there a system for confirming customer specifications and requirements before work starts?
- ☐ Yes.
- ☐ No.
- ☐ We don't need a procedure.
- ☐ We need to organize a procedure.

Changes
Is there a process for reviewing and confirming required customer changes before the changes are actually made?
- ☐ Yes.
- ☐ No.
- ☐ We don't need a procedure.
- ☐ We need to organize a procedure.

Legal Requirements
Is there a process for making sure that all systems and procedures conform with current legal requirements?
- ☐ Yes.
- ☐ No.
- ☐ We don't need a procedure.
- ☐ We need to organize a procedure.

Payments
Is there a procedure to make sure that payments are made correctly, and on time?
- ☐ Yes.
- ☐ No.
- ☐ We don't need a procedure.
- ☐ We need to organize a procedure.

Products and Services
Are there procedures to check that the products and services are delivered according to the quality standards promised to customers?
- ☐ Yes.
- ☐ No.
- ☐ We don't need a procedure.
- ☐ We need to organize a procedure.

Documentation
Are there systems to check that all the documentation used within the organization is simple, straightforward, clear, and easy to understand?
- ☐ Yes.
- ☐ No.
- ☐ We don't need a procedure.
- ☐ We need to organize a procedure.

Suppliers
Are there procedures for checking that suppliers are keeping their promises?
- ☐ Yes.
- ☐ No.
- ☐ We don't need a procedure.
- ☐ We need to organize a procedure.

Statistics
Are there systems for recording statistics on sales, outputs, productivity, and targets?
- ☐ Yes.
- ☐ No.

☐ We don't need a procedure.
☐ We need to organize a procedure.

Training
Are there systems for recording the training undertaken by each member of the staff?
☐ Yes.
☐ No.
☐ We don't need a procedure.
☐ We need to organize a procedure.

Problems and Complaints
Is there a procedure for recording customer problems and complaints?
☐ Yes.
☐ No.
☐ We don't need a procedure.
☐ We need to organize a procedure.

ing a box, delivering a parcel, holding a team meeting to make a decision—all these activities are processes.

Some processes add value, while other processes simply cost money. For example, the processes involved in combining raw ingredients into tasty and attractive strawberry desserts, and then packing them into an appealing gift box, all add value. This is because the organization can sell the ingredients as a whole product and make a profit.

But the process of examining the desserts for defects doesn't add value; it simply costs money. There are the labor costs for the people who are paid to examine the product, plus the materials costs for the ingredients in any defective product that is discarded because it's not good enough to be sold.

You must examine all your processes and decide which add value and which cost money. Then you need to delegate responsibility for each process so that someone in the business is accountable for making that process the best it can be. Finally, you need to look at each process and ask, "How can we make this process more efficient? How can we add more value? How can we make this process cost less?" To answer these questions, you have to set quality standards.

Stage 4: Set Your Quality Standards

Key question: How can we do things better?

Ideally, there should be zero defects in your goods or services. This means that if you are designing and manufacturing software programs, every single program that leaves your factory will work first time, every time, and be free of bugs, viruses, and any other blips, problems, or defects. If your company repairs dishwashers, then every technician will identify and fix the fault first time, every time, and the appliance will not suffer from the same problem again in the future. If your company delivers management training, then every participant will confirm at the end of the course that the training has met their expectations; has achieved its stated goals; was interesting, helpful, and informative; and couldn't in any way be improved.

In the long term, it is more economical to build quality into what you do (and get it right the first time) rather than inspect for defects and fix them before they get to the customer. Achieving zero defects is absolutely possible, but it certainly doesn't happen overnight.

To begin working toward zero defects, you must set quality standards for each of your processes. A quality standard is a statement that describes to what standard a process should be carried out. Some examples of quality standards are:

- Answer the telephone within three rings.
- Send brochures and information packs to customers within eight hours of receiving a request.
- Fill each pastry shell using four ounces of strawberry puree and two ounces of fresh cream.
- Repair electrical faults within twenty minutes.
- Produce word-processed reports that are free from spelling and typing errors.

- In the event of a fire, clear the building within three minutes.

To create meaningful quality standards, you need to know what is happening right now, what your customers expect and want, what you can do so you can meet your customers' expectations, and how you can monitor the situation to determine whether the quality standards are being met. For example, take just one aspect of the work that goes on in a major financial institution—the processing of existing customer applications for an increased credit limit. You may come up with a matrix of information such as shown in Table 1.

Once your people know to what standard they should be doing something, they can start to think about the improvements they need to make to processes so that they can actually achieve those standards. Use Organizer Sheet 96, Setting Quality Standards, to examine your existing quality standards, set the improved standards you'd like to introduce, and work out details of the monitoring processes you can use to check that what should be happening is happening.

Stage 5: Focus on Quality

Key question: How do we involve everyone in the business in the pursuit of quality?

Having identified the processes and the people who are responsible for each process, and having set the quality standards, the next step is to get your people together to focus on how, working together, they can make improvements.

In essence, you give the people who are actually doing the job the opportunity to get involved, take responsibility, and become interested in how they can do things better. This is moving away from the concept of "I'm the boss and I want you to do it this way because that's what will get the best results" to "You're the expert because you're actually doing it; so tell me, how can we make improvements?"

Table 1. Establishing Quality Standards

Current Quality Standard	New Quality Standard	Method of Monitoring
1. Applications are looked at within forty-eight hours of receiving them.	1. Applications will be looked at within twenty-four hours of receiving them.	1. Managers will examine a cross-section of customer applications every day.
2. Customers are informed of their increased credit limit by standard letter within five days of a decision being reached.	2. Customers will be informed of their increased credit limit by a personal phone call within twelve hours of a decision being reached. The phone call will be followed up with an individual letter.	2. Staff will complete telephone call sheets that will be looked at by managers every day. Random samples of individual letters will be examined each day.
3. Customers are informed that their request has been refused by standard letter within seven days of a decision being reached.	3. Customers will be informed that their request has been refused within twenty-four hours of a decision being reached.	3. Random samples of customers will be telephoned and taken through a customer satisfaction questionnaire.
4. Most customers wait nine to fourteen days to hear whether or not their application has been successful.	4. No customer will have to wait more than three days to hear whether or not their application has been successful.	4. Random samples of customers will be contacted by mail and asked to complete a customer satisfaction questionnaire.

Setting Quality Standards

Use this Organizer every six months to help you review your quality standards.

Existing Quality Standards (What's currently happening)	Improved Quality Standards (What you'd like to see happening in six months)
_____	_____
_____	_____
_____	_____
_____	_____
_____	_____
_____	_____
_____	_____
_____	_____
_____	_____
_____	_____
_____	_____
_____	_____
_____	_____
_____	_____
_____	_____
_____	_____
_____	_____
_____	_____

Training for Quality

Moving an established labor force from a position where they do the job in the way they are told to a position where they devise new and better ways of doing the job takes time and training. Asking people to think about their jobs, to evaluate what they are doing, to solve problems and make decisions, and to create new and better working methods often means that the employing organization has to provide training in a number of skills such as communication, problem solving, decision making, and teamwork. Everyone should participate in the training, including the people packing boxes and joining wires and lifting heavy loads and counting packages.

Your people will respond because, suddenly, they'll be able to see the purpose and importance of their jobs. They'll recognize that their input is valuable, recognized, and appreciated. They will be involved in what they're doing, and they'll get personal satisfaction out of doing a job well and contributing ways in which they can do it better.

Put the spotlight on quality by creating small teams, each one led either by the person who is responsible for the process or by a manager, supervisor, or departmental team leader. These teams, which can be called quality circles or focus groups or process teams, should meet each day, either in the morning before work starts or in the evening as work finishes. The purpose of the meetings should be to discuss problems that occurred during that day, agree on possible solutions, share new ideas and suggestions for improvement, and learn from each person's experience, triumphs, and failures.

At quality meetings, people continuously look for ways in which processes can be improved, defects can be eradicated, problems can be solved, and quality standards can be raised. Generally, everything can get better, day by day, on an ongoing basis. This meeting of minds is what lies at the heart of continuous improvement, and it makes the difference between retaining your competitive edge and losing business to your rivals.

Quality Action Checklist

☐ Sell quality to your employees, and make sure that everyone in the business knows what it is and why it is important.

☐ Examine all your processes to see exactly what is happening.

☐ Think about what your customers expect and want. If you're not sure, ask them.

☐ Set meaningful and achievable quality standards and communicate them to all your employees.

☐ Organize meaningful training so that everyone in the business has the knowledge and skills they need to communicate, solve problems, make decisions, and work as part of a dynamic and focused team.

☐ Organize quality circles, focus groups, or process teams to be responsible for examining the processes daily and looking for ways to do things even better.

☐ Encourage everyone to be creative problem solvers and solution finders.

☐ Monitor progress so that you can see what is being achieved and what is not.

Selling

If you are a professional involved in medicine, engineering, software development, academic research, or a thousand and one other specialties, you may be tempted to believe that selling is not part of your job. The truth of the matter is, if you are a manager, you need to be able to sell. You have to sell your ideas and your vision to your boss, the CEO, the board, the shareholders, your team, your colleagues and coworkers, and all the other people with whom you come in contact on a regular basis. It isn't enough to believe that your idea is best or that what you want to do will benefit the organization. You have to be able to sell the benefits.

Creating a Strategy for Selling Your Ideas

Let's say, for example, that you want an increase in your budget. Or you may need an additional person on your team. Perhaps you want to invest in some new technology, or you want to persuade the marketing department to change the way it's positioning a product. Whenever you want something that someone else can supply—whether it's time or money or approval or even a change of heart—you must be able to present your request in such a way that the other party will see the benefits of giving you what you are asking for. That's what selling is all about.

Step 1: Explain the Benefits

Key question: How can I explain and show other people that this deal will be good for them?

When you choose to buy a particular car from a particular salesperson, you are probably basing your decision on the benefits you were told you'll enjoy once you've made your purchase. The salesperson wants your money and, in return, is offering benefits.

The best salespeople know that most people buy with their emotions, rather than with logic. If we bought with logic, we'd choose the most sensible, safest, and economical car on the market. But we don't. We long for the sleekest, fastest, sexiest car in the showroom—the one that most definitely isn't the cheapest. And we base this choice on the benefits of owning such a car—the prestige, the comfort, and the wonderful in-car toys. Forget logic; we want pleasure!

Whenever you have to sell other people on an idea, you need to explain the benefits they'll enjoy if they go along with you. If you ask someone to do something for you and you can show them that they will get something out of it—they'll save time, work, money, or hassle—then those are the benefits.

Every time you want someone to buy from you, clearly explain the real benefits that they'll enjoy as a result of saying yes to you. Here are some examples:

1. Instead of saying, "I need an extra five percent on the budget," explain the situation in a more compelling way. For example, "What I really need is for you to approve a five percent increase to the budget. If you can go along with that, then I can call in some part-time workers and I can absolutely guarantee that we'll finish the project on schedule. My take on that is that Karen's going to be impressed with the way you've handled the deal."

2. Instead of saying, "I need another PC," you could say, "If you can let me have another PC, then I'll be able to get the figures through to you at least forty-eight hours before they're needed at the head office. That way, you'll have much more time than you have now to make sure that everything is accurate."

3. Instead of saying, "I need more time," you could say, "If you could hold back for two more days, then I can send the data to Iowa for checking. Then, when you present to the board, you're going to know that everything has been

verified twice. You'll be able to deal with whatever they try to throw at you."

Use Organizer Sheet 97, Selling the Benefits, to clarify the benefits of any proposal for which you want to obtain agreement from someone else.

Step 2: Anticipate Objections

Key question: Why might someone say no?

When you are trying to sell something to people, you can expect them to raise objections. These may sound like reasons why they don't want to buy in to your idea, but often they're not reasons but a smoke screen raised in self-defense. You ask your boss to allow you to hire an additional member of staff. Your boss immediately swings into panic mode and thinks, "If I approve this request, then Joe and Chris and Karen are all going to want extra people too. I'd better say there's no money left in the budget."

Make it easy for people to say yes to you. Plan ahead and anticipate the objections they are likely to raise. And offer solutions. People raise objections for many different reasons. They are worried they may not be doing the right thing. They're not sure it is in their best interests. They wonder if they could get a better result if they do nothing or something else entirely. They haven't really understood what you want, why you want it, and why it will be good for them.

It is important to understand that when someone raises an objection, he's not saying, "No, I don't want to do this now or ever." What he is saying, most of the time, is, "I'm not sure. Convince me. Persuade me. Reassure me that I'm doing the right thing."

To overcome objections, you need to make sure that people understand your proposition and how they will benefit. Explain as many times as you need to until you are sure they understand. Provide reassurances. "Perhaps you're worried about. . . . I've thought that through, and it seems to me that. . . ." Calm their fears and show them how this deal will be good for them. Orga-

Selling the Benefits

Use this Organizer before you start selling.

The benefits my prospective buyer will enjoy if he/she says "Yes" are:

_____

_____

_____

_____

_____

_____

_____

nizer Sheet 98, Getting Past Objections, will help you to anticipate objections someone may come up with when you are selling your idea. Take the opportunity to determine, in advance, how you can respond.

Step 3: Close the Deal

Key question: How can I make it easy for this person to say yes?

Always ask for a yes. Don't assume that because you've explained the benefits and you've handled the objections, people are going to actually volunteer their approval. Nine times out of ten, they won't. They'll wait for you to close the deal.

All you need do is say something like, "Okay, shall I go ahead on that basis?" (a statement that requires a simple yes response), or "Shall I order the PC or will you?" (a statement that gives someone the opportunity to choose—either me or you, Monday or Wednesday, morning or afternoon). Remember, too, that sometimes selling the benefits and handling the objections will be part of a wider influencing campaign that takes place over a period of time. (See Influencing.)

Getting Past Objections

Use this Organizer before you start selling.

The objections my prospective buyer might raise:

Objection: _____

_____

_____

How I'll respond: _____

_____

_____

Objection: _____

_____

_____

How I'll respond: _____

_____

_____

Objection: _____

_____

_____

How I'll respond: _____

_____

_____

Selling Action Checklist

- ☐ Anticipate all of the likely objections and, in advance, prepare your responses.
- ☐ Speak to the right person—that's the person who has the authority to buy or say yes to your proposition.
- ☐ Spell out how people will benefit if they buy in to your proposition. If you cannot think of benefits, change the deal so that benefits exist for the buyer.
- ☐ Handle objections by providing reassurance. People need to know that they're doing the right thing if they say yes. Don't back off when an objection is raised. It just means they need more information.
- ☐ Close the deal by actually asking for agreement.
- ☐ Make it easy for people to say yes.
- ☐ Recognize that, sometimes, you'll have to adopt a long-term influencing strategy to persuade someone to see your point of view and buy the deal you're selling.

Strategic Planning

Some businesses make it from year to year, surviving but never really hitting the big time. These organizations are satisfied if they can keep their labor force without the need for downsizing, stay in credit at the bank, and maybe, just maybe, increase their profitability by one or two percent. Sadly, when change occurs, as change must, these businesses are ill-equipped to cope. Some manage to keep their heads above water, and some sink. It's a depressing scenario, but very real for many organizations throughout the world.

On the other hand, some businesses go from strength to strength until, ultimately, they touch just about everyone's lives in one way or another. Microsoft and Sony are just two examples of companies that have never been content to rest on their laurels and watch the world go by. Instead, they have consistently expanded their vision and anticipated new products and markets. And much of their success has largely been due to the amount of care and attention that has been lavished on their strategic planning program.

Any organization that is involved in a strategic planning program must ask three critical questions: Where are we now? How did we get here? Where do we want to be?

Where Are We Now?

Key question: How are we doing?

Before you can start to think about where you want to be two, five, or ten years down the road, you have to be clear about precisely where it is you are now. Clarifying your current position means you have to address some tough questions, such as:

- What do our customers think of us?
- What do our competitors think of us?
- What's our market share?
- What's our profitability?
- How do our market share and profitability compare to our competitors' market shares and profitability?
- What's our mission—what are we here to do? Are we doing it? Is everyone in the business aware of our mission?

Ask your customers.

Key question: Why do our customers continue to do business with us?

Find out from your customers—through face-to-face contact, on the telephone, or by a postal questionnaire—what they think about the business. Does the business meet their needs now? Do they think it will meet their needs in the future? What are those needs likely to be? How do your customers perceive your business as compared to your competitors'? What do they like best and what do they like least? Send out copies of Organizer Sheet 99, Customer Questionnaire, to find out what your customers think about the business.

Ask your staff.

Key question: Is everyone in the business trying to achieve the same things?

Find out from your employees what they think of the business and where they would position the organization in relation to its competitors. Also, ask your people to define the company's mission statement. This is crucial because if they don't know precisely what the business is trying to achieve, they won't be able to achieve it. Use Organizer Sheet 100, Staff Questionnaire, as the basis for a

Organizer Sheet 99

Customer Questionnaire

Use this Organizer before you finalize your strategic plan.

1. What delights you about our service or product? ⎯⎯⎯⎯⎯⎯

⎯⎯⎯⎯⎯⎯⎯⎯⎯⎯⎯⎯⎯⎯⎯⎯⎯⎯⎯⎯⎯⎯⎯⎯⎯⎯

2. What disappoints you about our service or product? ⎯⎯⎯⎯

⎯⎯⎯⎯⎯⎯⎯⎯⎯⎯⎯⎯⎯⎯⎯⎯⎯⎯⎯⎯⎯⎯⎯⎯⎯⎯

3. Are we easy to buy from?
☐ No ☐ Sometimes ☐ Usually ☐ Always

4. Do we make buying a pleasurable experience for you?
☐ No ☐ Sometimes ☐ Usually ☐ Always

5. Why do you choose to buy from us? ⎯⎯⎯⎯⎯⎯⎯⎯⎯⎯

⎯⎯⎯⎯⎯⎯⎯⎯⎯⎯⎯⎯⎯⎯⎯⎯⎯⎯⎯⎯⎯⎯⎯⎯⎯⎯

6. Are we responsive to your needs?
☐ No ☐ Sometimes ☐ Usually ☐ Always

7. What do you think we do best? ⎯⎯⎯⎯⎯⎯⎯⎯⎯⎯⎯

⎯⎯⎯⎯⎯⎯⎯⎯⎯⎯⎯⎯⎯⎯⎯⎯⎯⎯⎯⎯⎯⎯⎯⎯⎯⎯

8. What do you think we do least well? ⎯⎯⎯⎯⎯⎯⎯⎯

⎯⎯⎯⎯⎯⎯⎯⎯⎯⎯⎯⎯⎯⎯⎯⎯⎯⎯⎯⎯⎯⎯⎯⎯⎯⎯

9. If you could make three changes to the way we do business with you, what would they be? ⎯⎯⎯⎯⎯⎯⎯⎯⎯⎯⎯⎯⎯

⎯⎯⎯⎯⎯⎯⎯⎯⎯⎯⎯⎯⎯⎯⎯⎯⎯⎯⎯⎯⎯⎯⎯⎯⎯⎯

10. How are we at solving your problems?
☐ Not good ☐ Okay ☐ Good ☐ Terrific

11. How do you feel about our timeliness?
☐ Not good ☐ Okay ☐ Good ☐ Terrific

12. Do you feel we give value for your money?
☐ No ☐ Sometimes ☐ Usually ☐ Always

13. Do you buy similar products or services from anyone else? If so, how do we compare?
☐ Yes, I do. ☐ No, I don't. ☐ There's not much difference.
You're better than your competitor because: ⎯⎯⎯⎯⎯⎯
You're not as good as your competitor because: ⎯⎯⎯⎯⎯⎯

14. How do you rate our staff?
☐ Not good ☐ Okay ☐ Good ☐ Terrific
15. How can we improve? _____

16. What would you like to be able to buy from us in the future? _

17. What would you like us to do differently in the future? _____

staff survey. Compile a questionnaire, using all or just some of the questions provided on this organizer sheet, and send it to everyone who works in your company. This should give you a good idea of how your people feel about the organization.

Ask your team.

Key question: What kind of future do we want?

Pull the team together and find out what every individual on it feels about the business. Do they all share the same vision? Do they all agree on where the business is now and where it's heading? What, if anything, would they choose to change?

You may find some of the answers unpalatable, and you may disagree with some of the perceptions. For example, customer surveys may show that your customers believe there is room for improvement in the area of quality, service, or timeliness. Or, if no one in the business is clear about what the business is really about and trying to achieve, then you will have to raise awareness of your mission statement throughout the business. Everyone in the organization should know exactly what the business is about—whether it is providing top-quality cars at rock-bottom prices, or offering the best available medical care, regardless of cost, to all patients, or creating innovative advertising campaigns that sell products.

You may begin to wish you had never started the process of asking for feedback from customers and employees in the first place. But, regardless of how you feel about the responses, if you

Staff Questionnaire

Use this Organizer before you finalize your strategic plan.

1. What is this organization's mission statement? _____

_____

What does this statement mean to you? _____

_____

Do you feel that your manager and others on the management team stick to the spirit of our mission statement?
☐ No   ☐ Sometimes   ☐ Always   ☐ Not too sure

2. If you were a customer, what impression would you get of the business? _____

_____

_____

3. What do you think we do really well? _____

_____

_____

4. What do you think we don't do so well? _____

_____

_____

5. How do you think we compare to our competitors in terms of price?
☐ We're better.   ☐ We're about equal.   ☐ We're not as good.

6. How do you think we compare to our competitors so far as quality is concerned?
☐ We're better.   ☐ We're about equal.   ☐ We're not as good.

7. How do you think we compare to our competitors with regard to value for money?
☐ We're better.   ☐ We're about equal.   ☐ We're not as good.

8. If you could change or improve three things in the business, what would they be? _____

_____

_____

9. How could we make it easier for our customers to enjoy buying from us? _____

_____
_____
_____

10. How could we make it more enjoyable for you to work here?

_____
_____

are serious about planning for the future, the feedback you get has to be addressed.

How Did We Get Here?

Key question: So far, what has propelled us forward or held us back?

The next step is to focus on the factors that have driven the business over recent years. What challenges has the business had to face in the past, and how has it coped with those challenges? What, if any, opportunities has the business grasped and made the most of? What does the business do best and what does it do least well? Where are the strengths and where are the weaknesses?

Organizer Sheet 101, Historical SWOT Analysis, will help you to clarify the strengths the business has developed, the weaknesses the business has displayed, the opportunities the business has seized, and the threats the business has faced over the past three to five years.

Where Do We Want to Be?

Key question: How can we turn our dreams into reality?

The final step is to clarify your vision for the business. Where do you want to be this time next year? In two years' time? In five years? What kind of reputation do you want to have? What levels

Historical SWOT Analysis

Use this Organizer before you finalize your strategic plan.

Over the past three to five years, these are the strengths the business has developed:	Over the past three to five years, these are the weaknesses the business has displayed:
_____	_____
_____	_____
_____	_____
_____	_____
_____	_____
_____	_____
_____	_____
Over the past three to five years, these are the opportunities the business has seized:	Over the past three to five years, these are the threats the business has faced:
_____	_____
_____	_____
_____	_____
_____	_____
_____	_____
_____	_____
_____	_____
_____	_____

of market share and profitability do you hope to achieve? What kind of global presence do you envision? How do you want to compare with your competitors? Organizer Sheet 102, Where Are We Going?, will help you to define, on paper, your vision for the future.

When your vision for the future is clarified, you must start thinking about how you are going to make the journey from where you are to where you want to be. Some of the key issues you'll need to look at are:

- *The values in the business.* What do you, as an organization, believe in?
- *The skill sets in the business.* What skills and qualities do your people have in abundance, and what skills and qualities are missing? What levels of leadership and teamwork already exist in the business, and what leadership and teamwork efforts are you going to need to develop to achieve the future you want?

Use Organizer Sheet 103, The Way Forward, to generate new ideas that you can use to move the business forward.

Some businesses back off from serious strategic planning because they know that, once they start, every aspect of the organization will have to stand in the spotlight and be examined and evaluated. Some companies don't want to change; some think they don't need to change; and some companies know that, to make a new future for themselves, they must change.

Change may have to occur from the top down, bottom up, and right across the board, at every level of the business. And it may mean investing time and money in people, technology, training, marketing, and just about any other function you can think of. Those businesses that appreciate the need for change, and have the courage to envision a new and better future, will be those that survive into the new millennium and beyond.

Where Are We Going?

Use this Organizer before you finalize your strategic plan.

My vision for the business two years from now:	My vision for the business five years from now:
Market share increased by _____%	Market share increased by _____%
Profitability increased by _____%	Profitability increased by _____%
Global penetration increased by _____%	Global penetration increased by _____%
Will be operating in the following new areas:	Will be operating in the following new areas:

_____ _____

_____ _____

_____ _____

_____ _____

_____ _____

_____ _____

Will be delighting our customers by:	Will be delighting our customers by:

_____ _____

_____ _____

_____ _____

_____ _____

_____ _____

_____ _____

The Way Forward

Use this Organizer before you finalize your strategic plan.

Goals
What are our current goals for this financial year? _____

_____

What long-term goals do we want to achieve two years from now?

_____

Resources Needed to Help Us Reach Long-Term Goals
What kind of new technology? _____

_____

What kind of new machinery or equipment? _____

_____

What kind of space? _____

_____

What kind of additional staff? _____

_____

What kinds of training programs? _____

_____

What kinds of additional finance? _____

_____

Our People (What They Must Do to Help Us Reach Our Long-Term Goals)
Do we need to raise awareness of quality standards?
☐ Yes ☐ No
Do we need to raise awareness of customer service?
☐ Yes ☐ No
Do we need to raise awareness of timeliness? ☐ Yes ☐ No
Do we need to raise awareness of teamwork? ☐ Yes ☐ No

Do we need to improve our product or service? If so, how?

_____

_____

Do we need to diversify? If so, in what way?

_____

_____

Do we need to expand? If so, to what extent?

_____

_____

Do we need to appeal to a different customer base? If so, which one?

_____

_____

Do we need to change our corporate image? If so, how?

_____

_____

Do we need to change our operating style? If so, to what?

_____

_____

Do we need to change our position on the environment? If so, in what way?

_____

_____

Do we need to change our attitudes? If so, which ones?

_____

_____

Do we need to change our approach to anything? If so, what?

_____

_____

Strategic Planning Action Checklist

- ☐ Shine a spotlight on every area of your business to get a clear picture of where you are now.
- ☐ Ask your customers if the business meets their needs now, and if they think the business can meet their needs in the future.
- ☐ Ask your staff how they feel the business rates in comparison to your competitors.
- ☐ Ask the members of your team where they think the business is heading and what, if anything, they would choose to change.
- ☐ Clarify what the business is about and create a clear and dynamic mission statement.
- ☐ Distribute the mission statement throughout the company so that everyone knows what the business is aiming to achieve.
- ☐ Create a vision that encapsulates the very best of what the business does, and live the vision every day until it becomes a reality.
- ☐ Be prepared to change as the business changes.

Stress Management

Stress and stress-related illnesses, both physical and emotional, kill people, damage relationships, and cost companies billions of dollars each year. In the high-octane atmosphere of the 1980s, it was fashionable to be totally available, faxable, mobile phonable, living on the edge, and stressed out. As the millennium approaches, attitudes are changing. These days managers are expected to manage their stress, along with everything else.

We live in stressful times. We are surrounded by technology that appears to be infinitely more intelligent than we are. The competitive marketplace is more cutthroat than ever before. Companies are leaner and meaner. Employees are constantly aware of the possibility that, at any moment, they could be downsized, delayered, synergized, or rationalized. Men at work live in fear of being accused of sexual harassment. We worry constantly about whether our management style fits the new corporate profile. Women exhaust themselves trying to be faster, sharper, and brighter than their male counterparts in the workplace while running a home and raising a family. All managers wear themselves out trying to keep abreast of the jargon, the most recent initiative, and the latest flavor-of-the-month.

On top of all this, managers have to build, support, and lead the team; give constructive feedback; disseminate communications in all directions; meet the targets; stay within the budget; reduce downtime; increase productivity; love and delight customers; and innovate, innovate, innovate! Is it any wonder there's a lot of stress in today's workplace?

Understanding Stress

Long, long ago, everyone survived by hunting and gathering food. Over the course of time, we evolved a physiological system for survival. Nowadays you feel the symptoms of stress because your body responds automatically to external events that you perceive as threatening. This is the fight or flight syndrome, and it simply means that your body is preparing itself to either stand and fight or take flight and run away from a threatening situation. In the good old hunter-gatherer days, the threatening situation may have been a dinosaur. These days it is much more likely to be an invitation from the IRS, a helpful suggestion from your partner, a snarl-up of traffic on the freeway, a looming deadline, or an irate client.

Whatever you perceive as a threatening situation will cause certain physiological changes in your body. Your heart will beat faster to ensure an abundant blood supply; in response your blood pressure rises and blood-clotting agents are released into the bloodstream to deal with anticipated wounds. Your breathing rate increases to allow an additional supply of oxygen, and your liver swings into action by providing extra cholesterol for energy. Blood flows to the brain to help with the thinking process but drains away from the surface of the skin to minimize bleeding from wounds. Your perspiration rate increases—a mechanism designed to cool you down while you're fighting or running. Your bladder and bowels get ready to empty because a lighter body moves more quickly, and adrenaline, noradrenaline, cortisol, and adrenocorticotropic hormones (among others) flood your system.

This automatic response is extremely useful if you are, in fact, facing a genuinely dangerous situation and you need to stand and fight or run away. But if you are simply having a disagreement with someone at the next desk, or becoming irritated with the driver in the car in front of you, your body is on red alert and there isn't any way to switch off the fight or flight response. When this happens, hour by hour, day by day, and week by week, you're moving down the road to a heart attack. Use Organizer Sheet 104, Your Stress Levels, to identify the physical and emotional stress levels you are currently experiencing.

Your Stress Levels

Use this Organizer to check your stress levels.

Stress Symptom	How Often I Experience This Stress	My Level of Concern About This Stressful Situation
Sleep I need to sleep much more than I used to:	☐ Never ☐ Occasionally ☐ Sometimes ☐ Frequently ☐ Almost all the time	☐ I know the cause of the problem, and it's just temporary. ☐ I'm a little anxious. ☐ I'm worried. ☐ I know I should do something about this situation.
Sleep I'm unable to get to sleep; I wake in the middle of the night or wake very, very early:	☐ Never ☐ Occasionally ☐ Sometimes ☐ Frequently ☐ Almost all the time	☐ I know the cause of the problem, and it's just temporary. ☐ I'm a little anxious. ☐ I'm worried. ☐ I know I should do something about this situation.
Food I'm eating much less than usual and losing weight:	☐ Never ☐ Occasionally ☐ Sometimes ☐ Frequently ☐ Almost all the time	☐ I know the cause of the problem, and it's just temporary. ☐ I'm a little anxious. ☐ I'm worried. ☐ I know I should do something about this situation.

Food I'm eating much more than usual and putting on weight:	☐ Never ☐ Occasionally ☐ Sometimes ☐ Frequently ☐ Almost all the time	☐ I know the cause of the problem, and it's just temporary. ☐ I'm a little anxious. ☐ I'm worried. ☐ I know I should do something about this situation.
Digestion I experience nausea, vomiting, or other digestive problems:	☐ Never ☐ Occasionally ☐ Sometimes ☐ Frequently ☐ Almost all the time	☐ I know the cause of the problem, and it's just temporary. ☐ I'm a little anxious. ☐ I'm worried. ☐ I know I should do something about this situation.
Muscular I have back, shoulder, or neck pain for which there is no identifiable cause:	☐ Never ☐ Occasionally ☐ Sometimes ☐ Frequently ☐ Almost all the time	☐ I know the cause of the problem, and it's just temporary. ☐ I'm a little anxious. ☐ I'm worried. ☐ I know I should do something about this situation.
Emotional I have feelings of anxiety, uncertainty, exhaustion, and/or depression:	☐ Never ☐ Occasionally ☐ Sometimes ☐ Frequently ☐ Almost all the time	☐ I know the cause of the problem, and it's just temporary. ☐ I'm a little anxious. ☐ I'm worried. ☐ I know I should do something about this situation.

Emotional I have feelings of powerlessness, inadequacy, and failure:	☐ Never ☐ Occasionally ☐ Sometimes ☐ Frequently ☐ Almost all the time	☐ I know the cause of the problem, and it's just temporary. ☐ I'm a little anxious. ☐ I'm worried. ☐ I know I should do something about this situation.
Emotional I have feelings of being stuck or trapped in a hope-less situation from which there is absolutely no way out:	☐ Never ☐ Occasionally ☐ Sometimes ☐ Frequently ☐ Almost all the time	☐ I know the cause of the problem, and it's just temporary. ☐ I'm a little anxious. ☐ I'm worried. ☐ I know I should do something about this situation.

Once you've identified your stress symptoms, you need to find a technique to bring your body out of fight or flight mode and back into a normal, nonalert mode. Use Organizer Sheet 105, Your Key Stress Factors, to identify those people and situations that you find most threatening and that tend to prompt a fight or flight reaction.

Strategies for Returning Your Body to Normal Mode

Whatever techniques you use, your goal should be to return your heartbeat, respiration, blood pressure and flow, breathing, blad-der, bowels, and perspiration rate back to normal and release the powerful cocktail of hormones from your system.

Because everyone is different, different strokes work for dif-ferent folks. So choose the techniques that appeal to you most.

Find the Joy

Do those things that give you most pleasure, and don't feel guilty. If you want to sit and watch the sunset with your mind in

Your Key Stress Factors

Use this Organizer before your stress level gets out of control.

Key Factor	How I Feel About This Factor	The Level of Stress This Key Factor Causes Me
My relationship with my partner:	☐ Terrific. ☐ Good. ☐ Okay. ☐ Not good. ☐ Don't even ask. ☐ I don't have a partner.	☐ No stress at all ☐ Hardly any ☐ Some ☐ A fair amount ☐ A lot of stress ☐ Almost unbearable stress
The kind of job I do:	☐ Terrific. ☐ Good. ☐ Okay. ☐ Not good. ☐ Don't even ask.	☐ No stress at all ☐ Hardly any ☐ Some ☐ A fair amount ☐ A lot of stress ☐ Almost unbearable stress
The kind of organization I work for:	☐ Terrific. ☐ Good. ☐ Okay. ☐ Not good. ☐ Don't even ask.	☐ No stress at all ☐ Hardly any ☐ Some ☐ A fair amount ☐ A lot of stress ☐ Almost unbearable stress
The kind of people I work with:	☐ Terrific. ☐ Good. ☐ Okay. ☐ Not good. ☐ Don't even ask.	☐ No stress at all ☐ Hardly any ☐ Some ☐ A fair amount ☐ A lot of stress ☐ Almost unbearable stress

Key Factor	How I Feel About This Factor	The Level of Stress This Key Factor Causes Me
The kind of place I work in (my working environment):	☐ Terrific. ☐ Good. ☐ Okay. ☐ Not good. ☐ Don't even ask.	☐ No stress at all ☐ Hardly any ☐ Some ☐ A fair amount ☐ A lot of stress ☐ Almost unbear- able stress
The kind of technology I have to cope with:	☐ Terrific. ☐ Good. ☐ Okay. ☐ Not good. ☐ Don't even ask.	☐ No stress at all ☐ Hardly any ☐ Some ☐ A fair amount ☐ A lot of stress ☐ Almost unbear- able stress
The kinds of changes I have to get used to:	☐ Terrific. ☐ Good. ☐ Okay. ☐ Not good. ☐ Don't even ask.	☐ No stress at all ☐ Hardly any ☐ Some ☐ A fair amount ☐ A lot of stress ☐ Almost unbear- able stress
The kinds of customers and clients I have to deal with:	☐ Terrific. ☐ Good. ☐ Okay. ☐ Not good. ☐ Don't even ask. ☐ I don't have too many customers.	☐ No stress at all ☐ Hardly any ☐ Some ☐ A fair amount ☐ A lot of stress ☐ Almost unbear- able stress
My boss:	☐ Terrific. ☐ Good. ☐ Okay. ☐ Not good. ☐ Don't even ask.	☐ No stress at all ☐ Hardly any ☐ Some ☐ A fair amount ☐ A lot of stress ☐ Almost unbear- able stress

Key Factor	How I Feel About This Factor	The Level of Stress This Key Factor Causes Me
The way my career is progressing:	☐ Terrific. ☐ Good. ☐ Okay. ☐ Not good. ☐ Don't even ask.	☐ No stress at all ☐ Hardly any ☐ Some ☐ A fair amount ☐ A lot of stress ☐ Almost unbear- able stress
The place where I live:	☐ Terrific. ☐ Good. ☐ Okay. ☐ Not good. ☐ Don't even ask.	☐ No stress at all ☐ Hardly any ☐ Some ☐ A fair amount ☐ A lot of stress ☐ Almost unbear- able stress
My life outside work:	☐ Terrific. ☐ Good. ☐ Okay. ☐ Not good. ☐ Don't even ask.	☐ No stress at all ☐ Hardly any ☐ Some ☐ A fair amount ☐ A lot of stress ☐ Almost unbear- able stress
My relationship with my children:	☐ Terrific. ☐ Good. ☐ Okay. ☐ Not good. ☐ Don't even ask. ☐ I don't have chil- dren.	☐ No stress at all ☐ Hardly any ☐ Some ☐ A fair amount ☐ A lot of stress ☐ Almost unbear- able stress
The kind of friends I have:	☐ Terrific. ☐ Good. ☐ Okay. ☐ Not good. ☐ Don't even ask. ☐ I don't have too many friends.	☐ No stress at all ☐ Hardly any ☐ Some ☐ A fair amount ☐ A lot of stress ☐ Almost unbear- able stress

neutral, do it. Turning off work is not a time waster. It could, in fact, save your life.

Find an interest that is not, in any way, related to the dollar-earning work you do. This could be anything from fishing to growing orchids; from watercolor painting to canoeing; from yoga to playing chess. It doesn't matter what it is as long as it is an activity that you enjoy and that gives you an opportunity to focus your mind on something other than the work you do or the problems you're experiencing in your life. Schedule this activity into your daily or weekly calendar.

Body Play

Provided you don't approach your exercise program as yet another competition where you need to succeed, physical exercise can help you to flush the adrenaline out of your system. Exercise also releases endorphins into the body. These are your system's natural painkillers and mood enhancers. If you have any kind of medical condition, check with your physician first and, if you're out of practice, start an exercise routine slowly and build up gradually. Walking, dancing, jogging, working out at the gym, swimming—all are proven stress busters. Many alternative therapies are also wonderful for helping to release stress. For example:

- Aromatherapy massage uses the healing qualities of the essential oils taken from fruits, flowers, and plants.
- Reflexology massage focuses on clearing the energy centers in the feet, each of which is connected to a part of the physical body (e.g., lungs, kidneys, and lymphatic system). Reflexology can soothe the emotions, calm the mind, and help the body to rebalance and repair itself.
- Health kinesiology uses muscle testing to detect, from your own body's responses, what you need to heal physically, mentally, and emotionally and to disperse accumulated stress-related toxins.

Mind Play

Use meditation and mind games to quiet your thought processes. Studies at the best and most important hospitals and universities in the world have convinced physicians and psychiatrists to accept that there is a strong link between the mind and the body. If you calm and settle your mind, you'll calm and settle your body.

Each of the following techniques can be practiced once or twice daily, for between ten minutes and an hour. Use Organizer Sheet 106, Stress Management Action Plan, to identify which of these stress management tools will be most helpful to you in your life:

- *Focused breathing*. Sit quietly and focus all of your attention on your breathing. Slowly and gently inhale and exhale, and as you breathe in and out, notice how your breathing sounds and feels. Don't try to change or improve anything you are doing; just be aware of each breath as you breathe in and out.

- *Power sounds*. Sit in a quiet, private space; breathe in; and as you breath out, say the word *om*. Extend the sound so that it becomes "*Ooooommmm*," and with each intake of breath and each exhale, you'll find yourself becoming calmer and more centered.

- *Mindful walking*. The best way to practice this technique is beside the sea or in the country, although that may not be an option for many people. If you are walking in the city, sunrise is the best time because there is less traffic and fewer people around. Walk slowly and in silence. Be mindful and aware of everything, paying attention to your inner world (i.e., the sound of your breathing and the way your body moves and feels as you walk) and the outer world (i.e., the colors, smells, and sounds of the world about you). At this moment in time, walking is your purpose and the most important thing you can do.

Don't think about getting from one place to another; just focus on the process of moving your body through time and space. As you walk in this way, your heart rate will slow, your breathing will relax, and you will feel focused and centered.

- *Visualization*. Daydreaming and imagining your desired positive future can help you to release stress and draw into your life the things and people you most want to have around you. Sit in a place where you know you will be undisturbed. Focus on your breathing, and bring into your mind a picture of how you would like things to be. If you want to create a new job, for example, see

Organizer Sheet 106

Stress Management Action Plan

Use this Organizer before your stress gets out of control.

The symptoms of stress that are causing me real concern (look back to Organizer Sheet 104): _____

_____

_____

_____

_____

The key factors in my life that are causing me real stress (look back to Organizer Sheet 105): _____

_____

_____

_____

_____

The specific things I can do to begin managing these symptoms:

☐ Develop non-work-related interests.
☐ Restore mental and physical balance through massage or some other kind of alternative therapy.
☐ Take up some kind of exercise program.
☐ Practice focused breathing, power sounds, mindful walking, visualization, or affirmations.
☐ Start to really communicate my thoughts and feelings.
☐ Something else (explain): _____

_____

_____

_____

in your mind's eye the building where you would most like to work. Imagine your office—the color scheme, the furniture, the prints and photographs on the walls. Visualize the kind of work you would love to do and imagine yourself there, doing what you want to do the most. Fill in as many details as possible so that picture is rich in color and texture.

When you are satisfied that you have all the details exactly the way you want them, let the image float out of your mind. Open your eyes and be aware of the space in which you're sitting. Creating your inner reality is the first step to creating the outer reality that you choose for yourself.

- *Affirming yourself.* Negative thinking can be a major source of stress when you allow the occasional critical comment to snowball into a constant stream of silent, mental nagging and fault-finding.

You can reduce stress if you stop reproaching yourself and start affirming yourself. Replace negative self-thinking with positive and approving comments. Write down how you want to be, and then repeat those statements to yourself as often as you can throughout the day. "I release all the symptoms of stress from my life; I am calm and peaceful; I sleep soundly and wake refreshed."

When you use affirming statements, you are reprogramming your subconscious. You are deleting the old scripts you learned as a child and replacing negative beliefs about yourself with new beliefs about the kind of person you are and the kind of person you will choose to be in the future.

- *Communicating.* People who are able to talk about their feelings, concerns, hopes, and dreams are generally happier and less stressed than those people who keep these things bottled up. Generally, women are better at sharing their emotions. Men, generally, tend to prefer to discuss sports or work or politics rather than how they feel.

Find someone you can trust and talk to that person. Say what's worrying you, what you fear most, and what you most want. The actual process of talking through your fears can help put things into perspective. You'll realize that often you are concerned about things that only *might* happen. In fact, ninety-five percent of the things we worry about never happen.

307

▪ *Valuing yourself.* Recognize that you and your worth as a person are not related to the work you do. You are not your work. Release the idea that you have to be perfect and that everything you do has to be just right.

Once you accept that perfection is not part of the human condition, you can get on with doing and being the best that you can. If you can learn to like yourself more, then you'll relax more. As you relax, your stress-related symptoms will begin to settle, and your body will gratefully accept the opportunity to move from the fight or flight response mode to a calmer and more tranquil state of being.

Stress Management Action Checklist

☐ Look at your life (at home and at work) as objectively as possible, and identify those situations and people that most often produce an automatic fight or flight reaction.

☐ Wherever possible, minimize your contact with those stress-inducing situations and people.

☐ Develop interests that are not in any way related to your paid work; cultivate these interests so you can reconnect with the happy person you have inside yourself.

☐ Use exercise, massage, or some other physical activity or therapy to allow your body to release stress-related hormones and toxins.

☐ Use meditation, visualization, and affirmations to allow your mind to circumvent repeated negative self-thinking. Turn negative thoughts off, slow down, chill out, and stop worrying.

☐ Acknowledge that it is unrealistic to try to achieve perfection. Accept that you are great just as you are.

Teamwork

Great teams aren't created overnight. Terrific team spirit doesn't just happen. Teams usually begin as a disparate group of people, drawn together by common circumstances: They just happen to work in the same department, or they've been asked to work together to achieve a specific goal. A team, then, starts as a group of different people with different ideas, experience, personalities, beliefs, attitudes, views, values, ways of operating, and types and levels of intelligence.

In many cases, this group of individuals will continue to operate individually, doing their jobs as they see fit, focusing their attention on getting through each day, making it to the weekend, and holding out for the summer vacation. Sometimes, though, something magical happens, and the individuals blend together into a team. If you've ever been part of a real team, you'll know how good it feels to be able to operate in a safe, dynamic, supportive, exciting, and creative environment.

Turning a Group Into a Team

It's often said that the difference between a group and a team is that a team shares a common goal. In fact, the real difference is that the people on a team not only share a common goal, they also share a deep commitment to achieving their goal and a healthy respect for the contribution each individual makes to the team's common success. Everyone on the team wants to do it; everyone is willing to give it their best shot; and everyone recognizes that everyone else will also use all their energy and all their skills to make it happen. That is teamwork.

Taking an assortment of people and changing them from a group into a team takes time, patience, and focus. But, if you do it, you—and everyone on the team—will become more productive, be more successful, and have much more fun.

Understanding the Team-Building Process

Any time you gather a group of people and ask them to join together to achieve a common goal, the group will work through a particular process. At first everyone will be fairly cool, guarded, and watchful. People won't be inclined to disclose too much about themselves (not the really important information, anyway). They'll hold back their honest opinions and their best and brightest ideas.

At this stage, people are checking each other out. They are wondering where the others are coming from, whether they will fit in with the group, and how they can stay out of trouble, gain some kind of advantage, drive the process the way they want it to go, or do as little as possible.

The next stage of the team-building process is when things start to happen. People have taken a measure of one another and decided, more or less, whom they can get along with and whom they don't have time for. They've also decided whose ideas are best and, invariably, reach the conclusion that their own way of thinking is the most sensible, logical, creative, innovative, or whatever. The outgoing, upbeat personalities begin to relax into their more usual style, and they start to push in the direction they want the group to move. The quieter people become even quieter, sometimes to the point where they withdraw completely from the proceedings, even though they're still sitting at the table. Disputes and disagreements break out. Factions form. Gossip and rumor take hold, and everyone, generally, begins to wish that they were somewhere else, doing something completely different.

The third stage of the process is when people begin to calm down a little. Although there still may be some undercurrents of hostility, generally people make some effort to get along. Routines are established; people settle into their roles; it appears as though people are working as a team. It's important to recognize that, at this stage, you've still got a group, and many groups never move on from here.

The final stage in the process is when these individuals combine their skills, energy, commitment, vision, and experience and begin to function together as a team. This metamorphosis often happens either as the result of some kind of external pressure (e.g., "If we don't get this right, we'll be out of a job!"), an unexpected crisis (e.g., "The building's on fire, and we've got to save whatever we can"), or an enhanced common goal (e.g., "Okay, the Olympic Games are coming up, and we've got to win for our country"). It can also happen because of the way in which the team leader manages this crucial final stage of the team-building process.

Building Your Team

Step 1: Know What to Expect

Key question: At the beginning, how do I keep my perspective, my sense of humor, and my sanity?

During stage one, when people are warily circling around one another, don't get alarmed and don't assume that things won't improve. During stage two, when it feels as if you are stuck in the middle of a disaster movie, don't lose your sense of humor and do steady your nerves. Even in your darkest hour, believe that things will improve. During stage three, when people return to normal kinds of behavior and seem to be getting along much better, don't heave a sigh of relief and hope things stay just the way they are. This is when you start the real job of building your team.

Step 2: Understand What Motivates People to Behave the Way They Do

Key question: How can I build self-confidence and self-esteem in my people?

All people, no matter who they are or what job they do, have certain needs. Everyone needs to feel secure. This includes knowing that they'll keep their job, continue to get a paycheck every month, and be able to make the mortgage payments.

People also need to feel confident. They need to know what they're supposed to be doing and that they can do it and do it well.

People need to feel as though their contributions are important, and their views, opinions, and ideas are respected and valued. And, finally, they need to feel as though new opportunities will be made available to them and that, even though it may be a slow journey, they are on the road to a better job and a brighter future.

Understanding what motivates people will help you, as a team leader, to respond to problems that occur because of team dynamics. Usually, problems in teams occur because:

- *One or more people on the team start to feel insecure.* They get worried about what lies ahead. They start to wonder if someone else on the team is going to outshine them and how this will affect their own future within the organization. The team leader's role is to share information equally with everyone. Treat everyone equally, and never use threats of job loss to try to improve performance.

- *One or more people on the team start to lose confidence.* They begin to assume (usually incorrectly) that everyone except them knows what they're doing. The team leader's role is to notice when people need coaching, mentoring, or training, and then to offer the right kind of support at the right time. Effective team leaders make sure that everyone knows what to do and how to do it.

- *One or more people on the team begin to feel left out.* They notice that it is always others who get positive feedback, encouraging comments, and helpful one-on-one coaching. It may seem to them that their ideas and suggestions are dismissed out of hand. The team leader's role is to support and encourage everyone equally, pay equal attention to everyone's ideas and suggestions, and treat everyone with equal respect and consideration.

- *One or more people on the team begin to feel as though they're not getting anywhere, and they're not going anywhere.* The team leader's role is to tell and show everyone that there are equal opportunities available to all. If one person on the team achieves success, then it should be celebrated as a team success and something to which everyone has contributed.

Use Organizer Sheet 107, Motivation, to take an objective look at what motivates you and what is most likely to be the prime motivator for each person on your team.

Step 3: Understand Personality Types

Key question: Am I doing or saying anything that could be misinterpreted or misunderstood?

Your personality is shaped by environment (e.g., where and how you're raised), conditioning (e.g., the kinds of comments you hear about yourself while you're growing up), lifestyle (e.g., whether you have a comfortable and happy childhood or experience struggles from day one), and the particular experiences life throws at you while you're growing up.

Some people on your team will be independent, creative, imaginative, and unorthodox. Some may be sociable, adventurous, optimistic, and outgoing. Others may be cautious or analytical, pushy or neurotic, unemotional or overemotional. The permutations are endless. The key point to remember is that everyone can make a significant contribution to the success of the team, provided that you allow people to contribute according to their own special skills and strengths.

Step 4: Model the Behavior You Want to See

Key question: How can I be the kind of team leader I would like to follow?

The key to successful teamwork is for you, as the team leader, to constantly and consistently model the behaviors and attitudes that you want to see within the team. It's unrealistic for a team leader to have one or two special relationships on the team and then expect everyone to pull together. In the same way, if the team leader shares information with just part of the team, then it shouldn't be a surprise if the uninformed begin to feel fearful and suspicious.

Motivation

Use this Organizer at the start of the team-building process for yourself and the other individuals on your team.

What motivates me?

Money	Priority 1, 2, 3, 4, 5, 6 *(circle one)*
Status	Priority 1, 2, 3, 4, 5, 6 *(circle one)*
Security	Priority 1, 2, 3, 4, 5, 6 *(circle one)*
Recognition	Priority 1, 2, 3, 4, 5, 6 *(circle one)*
Approval	Priority 1, 2, 3, 4, 5, 6 *(circle one)*
Career advancement	Priority 1, 2, 3, 4, 5, 6 *(circle one)*

Name: _____

What motivates this individual?

Money	Priority 1, 2, 3, 4, 5, 6 *(circle one)*
Status	Priority 1, 2, 3, 4, 5, 6 *(circle one)*
Security	Priority 1, 2, 3, 4, 5, 6 *(circle one)*
Recognition	Priority 1, 2, 3, 4, 5, 6 *(circle one)*
Approval	Priority 1, 2, 3, 4, 5, 6 *(circle one)*
Career advancement	Priority 1, 2, 3, 4, 5, 6 *(circle one)*

Name: _____

What motivates this individual?

Money	Priority 1, 2, 3, 4, 5, 6 *(circle one)*
Status	Priority 1, 2, 3, 4, 5, 6 *(circle one)*
Security	Priority 1, 2, 3, 4, 5, 6 *(circle one)*
Recognition	Priority 1, 2, 3, 4, 5, 6 *(circle one)*
Approval	Priority 1, 2, 3, 4, 5, 6 *(circle one)*
Career advancement	Priority 1, 2, 3, 4, 5, 6 *(circle one)*

Name: _____

What motivates this individual?

Money	Priority 1, 2, 3, 4, 5, 6 *(circle one)*
Status	Priority 1, 2, 3, 4, 5, 6 *(circle one)*
Security	Priority 1, 2, 3, 4, 5, 6 *(circle one)*
Recognition	Priority 1, 2, 3, 4, 5, 6 *(circle one)*
Approval	Priority 1, 2, 3, 4, 5, 6 *(circle one)*
Career advancement	Priority 1, 2, 3, 4, 5, 6 *(circle one)*

Respect each individual and the unique contribution each individual makes to the team effort. Delegate sensitively so that people get to do the work they can handle and to use their strengths, skills, and experience. Communicate openly and equally with everyone on the team; if you cannot share information with everyone, then don't share it at all. Recognize that all people have the right to their own ideas and opinions. You don't have to agree with them, but you do need to recognize that their opinions are valid for the individuals who hold them. Offer the same level of praise and encouragement to everyone.

Use Organizer Sheet 108, Team-Building Process, to clarify behaviors you need to model when the team is at stage one (checking out one another), stage two (getting involved with one another), stage three (settling in), and stage four (working together).

Even if you do not like everyone equally, or approve of everyone equally, or feel that everyone is working equally hard, the only way you are going to turn this disparate group of people into a real team is to treat everyone equally. If you can do that, then you will begin to see amazing and measurable changes.

Teamwork Action Checklist

- ☐ Don't expect too much, too soon. Everyone is going to be too busy to work. They'll be watching one another and watching you.
- ☐ As team members get familiar with one another, expect the sparks to fly. There are bound to be disagreements and disruptions, and there may be some jostling for position to see who can get closest to you.
- ☐ When the team begins to settle in and settle down, don't imagine that your work is over. It's just beginning.
- ☐ Consistently and constantly model the behaviors and the attitudes that you want to have permeate throughout the team.
- ☐ Build an atmosphere of mutual support, encouragement, communication, and approval. Encourage people to have fun. Laughter brings people together, and it's a great stress buster.
- ☐ Treat everyone equally, with equal respect, and never forget to say thank you.
- ☐ Celebrate individual successes as a team success too, because everyone has contributed, in one way or another.

315

Team-Building Process

Use this Organizer at the start of the team-building process.

☐ My team is currently at stage 1: They are checking out one another. They are cool, cautious, not too involved, and watching what happens.

☐ My team is currently at stage 2: They are getting involved. Some people are upfront and in-your-face; some are withdrawing from the proceedings. Gossip, rumor, and disagreements are everyday occurrences.

☐ My team is currently at stage 3: They are settling in and settling down.

☐ My team is currently at stage 4: They are working together energetically, cooperatively, and enthusiastically as a team.

The behaviors I need to model to move the team along:

_____

_____

_____

_____

Teleworking

Teleworking (sometimes called telecommuting) helps companies to be more productive because employees who work at home or from home for some of the week are generally more effective. Once people are released from the regular burden of commuting into work and home again, they are free to focus on the important aspects of their job, such as meeting deadlines, building quality into everything they do, and managing multiple tasks and priorities.

Many employers are happy to allow their people to work at home because the organization reaps the benefits of reduced overheads, increased productivity and profitability, and retention of valued and key players. Many people love to work at home because they can cut out the commuting time; work in a peaceful, undisturbed environment free from office politics; wear what they like; and have their job performance judged on the work and the results they produce.

If you are thinking of introducing teleworking into your organization, then you'll need to plan ahead and focus on some key issues—notably, which jobs, which people, which equipment, and which schedule, are best suited to the teleworking arrangement.

Which Jobs Are Suitable?

Many salespeople, as a matter of course, work from home. They use their office at home as their base from which they can travel to see clients, and they return home to manage their paperwork.

Increasingly, consultants of all kinds—writers, editors, designers, software programmers, and anyone whose job requires limited face-to-face contact with customers—are happy to work at home for part, if not all, of the working week.

Although many managers, from time to time, take a day or so at home to find the peace and quiet they need to finish a report or some other major task, by and large, most managers need to be in the office, where the action is.

Which People Are Best Suited to Teleworking?

Basically anyone who is effective in their job at the office will be just as (if not more) effective when they work at home—provided, of course, they want this arrangement. For some people, the notion of working alone, wearing casual clothes, and freeing themselves from the pressures of commuting represents bliss. Other people actually need interaction with their colleagues and would feel isolated and sidelined if they were working alone most of the time.

When making arrangements for teleworking, choose the people who are motivated to do well, who manage their time and their workloads, who enjoy solving their own problems and making their own decisions, and who generally meet their deadlines and targets with a minimum of fuss.

If you are concerned about employees' ability to work at home full-time, try the arrangement out with them for one or two days a month. If that works and they're happy and meeting their targets, then you can increase the amount of time they spend at home. Use Organizer Sheet 109, Who's Right for Teleworking?, to assess who should telework.

Which Equipment Do Teleworkers Need?

Anyone working at home on a regular basis is going to need a separate room, desk, locking filing cabinet, computer, printer, modem, fax, telephone line, and answering machine. A dedicated telephone line for a fax and computer modem for accessing e-mail and the Internet are recommended. Teleworkers must be able to get in touch with the office as and when they need to,

Who's Right for Teleworking?

Use this Organizer (one for each candidate) before you select the people who will take part in the teleworking program.

Name: _____

Job title: _____

Time management skills
- ☐ Excellent
- ☐ Good
- ☐ Okay
- ☐ Not good

Ability to meet agreed-on performance goals
- ☐ Excellent
- ☐ Good
- ☐ Okay
- ☐ Not good

Motivation to succeed
- ☐ Excellent
- ☐ Good
- ☐ Okay
- ☐ Not good

Ability to work unsupervised
- ☐ Excellent
- ☐ Good
- ☐ Okay
- ☐ Not good

Additional comments:

_____

_____

_____

_____

and their coworkers and managers need to know that, during working hours, they are available and can be contacted swiftly and easily.

Communication for teleworkers needn't be a problem because they can use one-on-one telephone calls, conference calls, e-mail, and fax to keep in touch and keep their finger on the pulse of what's happening in the office. Generally, when an organization asks someone to work at home, the organization accepts responsibility for providing the PC and all the other tools of the trade. In some instances, as when an organization is responding to a request that someone be allowed to work at home, the employee may be expected to provide all the equipment needed to do the job and stay in touch. The approach you take with regard to the supply of equipment is going to depend, to a large extent, on your organization and your budget.

Which Teleworking Schedule Works Best?

You may want to suggest that someone start working at home for two or three days each week or, if you prefer, one week out of three. You and the worker can test the water and see how things go. If all is well, you can then discuss and agree on a different schedule—for example, four days at home and one day each week in the office, or three weeks at home and one week in the office.

There's no right or wrong schedule for teleworking. It is best to work out an arrangement that suits the individual and the job.

It is important, though, that teleworkers still attend team meetings (even if it is only one or two days each month) so that they and their coworkers know that they are a valued and important part of the team. Organizer Sheet 110, Teleworking Schedules, will help you to select a work-at-home schedule that suits individuals (and your organization) best.

One more recommendation: Make sure that everyone in the business knows that teleworking is a type of work schedule, not a privilege. To prevent problems with other staff members, try to come up with other flexible work arrangements so that everyone in the organization feels there are options and alternatives available to them, too.

Organizer Sheet 110

Teleworking Schedules

Use this Organizer (one for each teleworker) before the program starts.

Name: _____

Working-at-home schedule:

☐ 4 days in the office and 1 day at home

☐ 3 days in the office and 2 days at home

☐ 2 days in the office and 3 days at home

☐ 1 day in the office and 4 days at home

☐ Some other schedule:

_____

_____

_____

Introducing Teleworking Into Your Organization

Select Your Strategy

Key question: Why do we want to introduce teleworking?

Decide whether you are going to introduce teleworking across the board in the company, as an option in a specific function or department only, or as an option only to people who do specific jobs.

Select Your People

Key question: Who will do their best work at home?

Decide whether you are going to choose people for teleworking, or whether the work-at-home schedule is on a voluntary basis. Either way, you can expect a few problems.

If you choose who can telework, then some people who would like to work at home will not be offered the option, and this could cause ill feelings. If employees are allowed to choose this work arrangement, then it is highly likely that some people you would consider unsuitable will volunteer.

You may want to draw up a list of specific criteria and, for example, make teleworking available only to people who have been with the organization for over a year, or who live within a certain radius of the office or (conversely) outside a certain radius of the office.

Select the Equipment

Key question: Who's going to need what, and how much will it cost?

Ensure that everyone has the right equipment and the space they need. If you are buying the equipment, make sure that all new equipment for home use is compatible with the equipment you already have in the office.

Allocate Hot Desks at the Office

Key question: How can we make sure that everyone still feels part of the team?

Your teleworkers will need some kind of work space on the days when they are working in the office. You'll need to organize desks, chairs, PCs, telephones, and storage in dedicated areas for teleworkers. Don't ever lose sight of the fact that these people are part of the organization and valued members of the team. Make sure that your teleworkers have the same opportunities for training and career development as the people who work in the office full-time.

Organize Monitoring and Mentoring Systems

Key question: How do I keep on top of performance?

You'll need to measure your teleworkers' performance against results. For each person, you'll need to define and agree on SWEET—sensible, written, easy to understand, easy to measure, task-oriented—performance goals (see Appraisal).

Monitor performance on a regular basis. If teleworkers are not meeting their agreed-on performance goals, then you have to take the same line that you would take if those people were not meeting their goals in the office. Before teleworking actually gets under way, use Organizer Sheet 111, Teleworking Monitoring, to clarify the monitoring systems that will work best for you and your people.

Some people will take to teleworking like ducks to water. For other people, the first few weeks may be strange and a little difficult. Set up a mentoring program (see Coaching and Mentoring Partnerships) so that they have a champion in the office whom they can turn to for advice and support, if and when they need it.

Establish a Communication Framework

Key question: How do we keep in touch?

If workers aren't at their desk in the office, it's easy to forget to pass on relevant but relatively unimportant information. But it is exactly that kind of information that gives people the sense that they belong within an organization.

Make sure that you set up some kind of communication framework—maybe a newsletter, facts sheet, or an informal monthly gathering—so that teleworkers have regular access to all the relevant information they need. Perhaps more than any other group of employees, teleworkers need to be reassured that they are part of the team, important to the team, and valued by the team. If you feel that it would help, you may want to increase the number of appraisal interviews to, say, two appraisals each year or even an informal appraisal every three months.

Teleworking Monitoring

Use this Organizer before the teleworking program starts.

I intend to monitor the teleworking program with:

Formal Monitoring Systems:
- ☐ Appraisal every six months
- ☐ Appraisal every three months
- ☐ Appraisal every month

Informal Monitoring Systems:
- ☐ Informal telephone calls between the teleworker and the worker's line manager every day

Informal one-on-one meetings:
- ☐ Every week ☐ Every month

Informal team meetings:
- ☐ Every week ☐ Every two weeks ☐ Every month

Some Other Monitoring System:

_____

_____

_____

_____

_____

_____

_____

_____

_____

_____

Teleworking Action Checklist

☐ Decide which jobs qualify for teleworking and which people will be best suited to this way of working.

☐ Try teleworking yourself for a week or so because the experience will help you to understand some of the real benefits and problems your people may encounter.

☐ Decide how you are going to schedule the number of days at home and the number of days at work for each person.

☐ Make sure that everyone has the equipment they need, and the right kind of home insurance for that equipment.

☐ Establish SWEET performance goals with each individual, and create a system so that you can measure actual performance against those targets.

☐ Set up a good communication framework, hot desks, and regular team meetings so that your teleworkers don't feel isolated or forgotten.

☐ Remember that teleworkers are entitled to a life outside of work. So don't telephone them at home in the evening or on the weekend unless it's a major emergency. Wait until the next day, just as you would if they were working in the office.

Time Management

Effective time management is about planning your day, week, and month; taking control of your paperwork; and preventing other people from wasting your time. If you are constantly running from one appointment to another and your desk is invariably drowning under a sea of paper, and if you find that your workload seems to be increasing and your productivity seems to be decreasing, then it's time to get proactive.

If you are prepared to give some serious thought to the three key activities—planning, taking control of your paperwork, and preventing other people from wasting your time—then you can turn your life around, reduce your stress levels, and increase your productivity.

Key Activity 1: Planning

Key question: How do I fit everything I have to do into the time I have available?

Time is a finite resource. There are twenty-four hours in each day and seven days in each week. No matter how hard you try, you can't change this fact. Instead, you need to plan carefully so you can make the best possible use of the time that is available to you. The best way to do this is to begin with the big picture—the months—and then work down to the detail—the days, hour by hour.

Chunk Your Time

Each week you'll have established tasks and meetings that you have to make time for. These will be items such as team, board, and client meetings; planning, review, and troubleshooting sessions; appraisals; interviews; and special projects.

Block in established, regular meetings that you can't control.

In many instances, you'll have to accept that other people—key account clients, your boss, your CEO, your board—are going to call the shots for these meetings. They'll ask you to be in a certain place at a certain time, and, invariably, these arrangements will be scheduled to suit their needs rather than yours. Part of your working week will be scheduled in response to other people's requirements, and there isn't much that you can do about it. Some of these meetings will be regular weekly or monthly events (e.g., every second Monday budget review; every Tuesday afternoon key account number one; every Thursday morning key account number two; and so on).

Using whatever time management system you prefer—a Day Timer, perhaps, or a Filofax—begin by investing in a set of month-at-a-glance inserts that let you see your schedule for an entire month laid out over two pages. Alternatively, if you prefer, use copies of Organizer Sheet 112, Time Management for Regular Meetings, to block in, using a red pen, any established, regular meetings over which you have very little control.

Block in established, regular meetings and activities that you can control.

Next you need to think about those regular meetings and interviews where you are in a better position to select a time and place that suit your needs. Still working with your month-at-a-glance inserts, block out chunks of time—full days and half-days—that you will use to schedule established meetings and activities such as team meetings, appraisals, or interviews.

Block in personal project time.

Too many managers make the mistake of planning for meetings and routine activities but forget about their personal projects. A personal project can be any activity that requires your personal attention and has long-term implications. For example, you may

Time Management for Regular Meetings

Activity	Week 1	Week 2	Week 3	Week 4
	Monday am Monday pm	Monday am Monday pm	Monday am Monday pm	Monday am Monday pm
	Tuesday am Tuesday pm	Tuesday am Tuesday pm	Tuesday am Tuesday pm	Tuesday am Tuesday pm
	Wednesday am Wednesday pm	Wednesday am Wednesday pm	Wednesday am Wednesday pm	Wednesday am Wednesday pm
	Thursday am Thursday pm	Thursday am Thursday pm	Thursday am Thursday pm	Thursday am Thursday pm
	Friday am Friday pm	Friday am Friday pm	Friday am Friday pm	Friday am Friday pm

be responsible for generating ideas for next year's marketing campaign; writing the copy for a recruitment ad; writing a proposal to generate new work. If you don't plan to make time for your personal projects, then you'll find yourself doing this kind of work at home in the evenings or on the weekends.

Select half-day chunks and, using a red pen, block them into your month-at-a-glance inserts. Or use a copy of Organizer Sheet 113, Time Management for Personal Projects, to:

- Write in the names of the personal projects for which you alone are responsible and that contribute to your success. These projects may involve planning, creating, reviewing, monitoring, or decision making.

Time Management for Personal Projects

Use this Organizer (one for each personal project) before you start work on the project.

Personal Project: _____

Priority:
- ☐ Urgent and Important
- ☐ Important but not urgent
- ☐ Urgent but not important
- ☐ Neither urgent nor important

Amount of time I need to allocate to this project:
- ☐ I need to work on it every day.
- ☐ I need to work on it every week. Which day? _____
- ☐ I need to work on it every month. When? _____

I intend to complete this personal project by: _____

- Decide how much time you need to allocate to each project on a daily, weekly, or monthly basis so that you can be sure you will reach your goals.

You'll now be able to see how the month ahead is shaping up and how much time you have available for making telephone calls, answering letters and e-mail, checking reports, monitoring sales figures, networking, and all the other things you have to do. Figure 4 is a sample monthly calendar with meeting and personal project time blocked out.

Once you can see the pattern of the month ahead, then you can start planning your daily schedule for the free days that you have available. Two important timesaving tips are:

1. When planning your schedule, give serious thought to how you can chunk activities together at nearby locations so that you can minimize traveling time

Figure 4. Blocking Out Time Periods in the Month

Sun	Mon	Tue	Wed	Thu	Fri	Sat
1	2 9:00 to 1:00 Johnson and Paul	3	4 8:30 to 12:30 Team meeting	5 8:00 to noon Personal projects	6 9:00 to 7:00 pm Chicago Latimers	7
8	9 10:00 to 2 Board meeting	10 8:00 to noon Personal projects	11 8:30 to 12:30 Team meeting	12 9:00 to 5:00 pm Chicago Latimers	13	14
15	16 Appraisals ALL DAY	17 8:45 to 1:00 pm Kay	18 8:30 to 12:30 Team meeting	19	20	21
22	23 9:00 to 4:00 pm Latimers— Here	24 8:00 to noon Personal projects	25 8:30 to 12:30 Team meeting	26 2:00 to 7:00 Planning meeting	27 8:00 to noon Personal projects	28
29	30					

2. Allocate chunks of time to similar activities. It's more time-effective to spend a whole morning twice a week on catching up with your mail than it is to look at your mail for an hour every day.

Prepare a Daily To-Do List

The advantage of having an up-to-date to-do list is that you can see at a glance everything that you have to do. Also, if it's written down, you won't forget. Then, when you can draw a line through something, you get a real sense of achievement and satisfaction.

To create a to-do list that actually works, you need three items: a master list, a to-do list, and a diary.

Your master list should preferably be kept in a spiral-bound notepad, small enough to fit into a purse or jacket pocket. Each day, as appointments, ideas, and promises occur to you, you write every single item down on your master list.

At the end of the day, you check off each item on your to-do list that has been completed. Transfer the items on your master list that still have to be done either onto your to-do list for the next day or, if you plan to schedule things for the future, into your diary. Cross each item off your master list when it is transferred to your to-do list. Figure 5 is a sample of how to manage your master and to-do lists.

The keys to success are to remember to write everything down, check off each item when it's completed, and transfer all future items into your diary. If you do these three things, then you'll see, at a glance, what needs to be done and what has been achieved.

Key Activity 2: Taking Control of Your Paperwork

Key question: Do I see to it, scrap it, or send it on?

When you pick up a piece of paper, do your best to make a decision about whether to see to it, scrap it, or send it on.

See to It

Much of your paperwork will need your personal attention; you have to make a decision about whether to say yes, no, or perhaps to the issue at hand. A good timesaving tip is to prepare several standard letters. For example, to reply to requests for a meeting, you can have on hand letters with several different responses (e.g., "Yes, let's meet on the . . ." or "No, not just now, but get back to me in the fall," and so on). You can number each standard response letter, and then either note on the incoming mail

Figure 5. Time Management Lists

Master List	Today's To-Do List	Tomorrow's To-Do List	Diary
TUESDAY Call Sophie✘ September 20 10:30 meeting with J. Horowitz✘ Collect dry cleaning✘ Order flowers✘ Review budgets✘ Call Jose✘	Call Sophie✔ Collect dry cleaning Order flowers✔ Review budgets Call Jose	Collect dry cleaning Review budgets Call Jose	September 20 10:30 meeting with J. Horowitz

the number of the letter you want your secretary to send or simply print out a standard response from your PC. Organizer Sheet 114, Paperwork Standard Responses, will help you keep track of which standard replies to use in different situations.

If you need to discuss a piece of paperwork with someone else, resist the temptation to put the item into an "I'll see to it later" pile. Later sometimes never comes, and, within a fairly short time, an innocent document can have turned into the paper equivalent of a ticking time bomb.

In advance, write up or have printed a whole pad of Post-it Notes with a simple message such as, "Please look at this and get back to me tomorrow with your response." Attach the notes to the document that needs input from someone else, and then dispatch it.

Scrap It

If you have any doubts about whether to keep something for future reference or "just in case" you may need it, always ask yourself the key question: "If I lost this piece of paper now, what difference would it make?" If the answer is none, then scrap it.

If there are documents you think you really need to keep, try scanning them onto your computer hard disk. That way you can store the information on your PC, but you can lose the paper.

Organizer Sheet 114

Paperwork Standard Responses

Use this Organizer before you write your standard replies.

Yes, I'll be there.
☐ letter L1 ☐ memo M1

Sorry, I can't make it.
☐ letter L2 ☐ memo M2

Please get back to me. I need to speak with you.
☐ letter L3 ☐ memo M3

What's happening?
☐ letter L4 ☐ memo M4

Please pay your account.
☐ letter L5

Can you do this for me?
☐ letter L6 ☐ memo M6

We urgently need to meet.
☐ letter L7 ☐ memo M7

Send It On

Be prepared to delegate. (See Delegating.) Again, the key question is, "If I handle this, am I making the best use of my valuable time?" If the answer is no, then send it on to someone else to deal with. Keep a list of every item you've delegated in this way, and check through your list once a week to confirm that you have verified the status of the item. You can use Organizer Sheet 115, Delegated Paperwork, to keep track of documents you've sent on to other people.

If you ruthlessly apply the see to it, scrap it, or send it on system, you'll find that you will save a considerable amount of time and reduce the amount of paper on your desk.

Delegated Paperwork

Use this Organizer whenever you delegate paperwork.

Item of paperwork I've delegated: _____

_____

Person to whom I've delegated this item: _____

The results I'm looking for: _____

_____

Agreed date by when this item will be handled: _____

Get Your Priorities Right

It's human nature to want to do the easy and enjoyable work first and leave the boring, monotonous, or tricky tasks until there's time or we feel up to tackling it. As all managers know, if you leave something to stew for long enough, it'll burst into flames and burn your fingers.

You must prioritize everything you do, and you must even build in chunks of time for the things you don't want to (yet have to) do. Everything you do can fit into four categories:

- *Urgent and important.* Urgent means there's a time-sensitive issue involved. If something has to be completed by tomorrow or by the end of the week, then it is urgent. Important means that goals are involved—either your organization's goals, your team's goals, or your personal goals. Closing a million-dollar deal by the end of the week is both urgent and important. So is finalizing the budget by next Tuesday or holding a press meeting tomorrow to announce a scientific breakthrough.
- *Urgent.* Urgent means there's a time-sensitive issue involved, but although the deadline is fast approaching, the task itself

isn't critical. Finalizing the color scheme for your office may have to be done by the end of the week, but in the larger scheme of things, this isn't too important.

- *Important.* Important means that although you have plenty of time to finish it, the task is related in some way to important goals. Reorganizing your salespeople's commission structure for the meeting next November is important, but not urgent. Choosing a new PR company in time for Christmas is also important, but it may not yet be urgent.
- *Do I really have to do this?* When you have this reaction to work you have to do, it's time to seriously think about whether these jobs can be delegated. If, for whatever reason, you can't delegate, then you have to hunker down and get on with it. Tricky or boring jobs don't go away. The best way to tackle them is by chipping away at them. If you write two pages a day, a ten-page report will be finished in a week. If you check three batches of figures each week, you'll be finished in a month.

If you prioritize everything on your master list and prioritize all your paperwork, you'll find yourself doing the right thing at the right time and keeping on top of the jobs that are often left until it's too late.

Key Activity 3: Preventing Other People From Wasting Your Time

Key question: Who wastes my time, and how can I stop them?

If you've made a commitment to yourself to get serious about how you manage your time, you'll be shooting yourself in the foot if you allow other people to waste your valuable time. If you let them, other people will waste your time by, among other things:

- Interrupting you in your office for no good reason
- Delegating their problems upward to you when you have delegated work down to them
- Getting you involved in conversations that go round in circles

- Asking for your advice when they have no intention of acting on it
- Arriving late for meetings and then staying late—and causing you to be late for your next meeting

Put an end to unexpected visitors by advertising the days and times when you have an open door and are available for impromptu meetings. Make sure that, on all other occasions, either your secretary guards your door or your door remains shut. People will soon get the message and will stop calling on you for no good reason. If someone does get through to you in your office, stand up from your desk and don't invite them to sit down. Explain that you are working to a deadline and can give them five minutes only.

Keep telephone calls short and to the point by clarifying your objectives and your core statement before you make or take the call. (See Communication.) Do the business and then politely but firmly close the conversation. Remember that every minute of time that someone else is wasting for you, you could be doing something productive that would move you closer to achieving your goals.

Time Management Action Checklist

- ☐ Start with the big picture and block in, on your month-at-a-glance sheets:
  1. Regular meetings you can't control
  2. Regular meetings and activities you can control
  3. Time for working on your personal projects
- ☐ Every day, throughout the day, write everything you have to do into your master list.
- ☐ At the end of each day, transfer all new items from your master list into either your to-do list for tomorrow or your diary. Check off each item as it is transferred.
- ☐ Every time a piece of paper lands on your desk or drifts into your hand, ask yourself whether you should:
  1. See to it?
  2. Scrap it?
  3. Send it on?
- ☐ Advertise the fact that you are not totally available, all of the time.
- ☐ Plan your work and stick to your plan.
- ☐ Value your time and don't allow other people to waste it.

Training

Even if you don't expect to be delivering training yourself, it's important that you understand how people learn and that you can recognize the skills needed to deliver training wisely and well. Knowing what to look for will help you to assess and evaluate how well your training department or outside consultancy is delivering training to your people.

People learn new skills and attitudes through the four-stage process of what has now come to be known as Kolb's Learning Cycle (D. Kolb, *Experiential Learning,* Prentice-Hall, 1983). This learning cycle involves (1) doing something or finding out about it, (2) thinking about what has been done or found out, (3) drawing certain conclusions, and (4) experimenting with new ways of doing something.

For example, you want to learn how to program your new and highly sophisticated central heating unit. You read the instruction manual and (you hope) punch all the right buttons and click all the right switches. (This is stage 1: doing something or finding out about it.) That night, you arrive home to a cold house. The central heating isn't working! So you look at the unit again, re-read the instructions, drink a cup of coffee, and wonder how on earth you are going to fix the problem. (This is stage 2: thinking about what has been done.) With a sudden flash of insight, you realize that you should have pressed the red button, then changed the dial and then activated the set switch—in that order. (This is stage 3: drawing certain conclusions.) With a sigh, you reset the appliance using this new sequence (stage 4: experimenting with new ways of doing something), and you go to bed, tired and dispirited.

One of two things will happen: Either the heating will come

on when you want it to, which means you've learned how to program the unit, or the heating won't come on. In the latter case, either you have to repeat the process all over again, trying out new approaches until the heating finally works or—worst-case scenario—you give up, never having learned, and ask someone to come and do it for you.

Understanding the way that learning occurs will help you to see that learners need certain key opportunities and experiences to help move them from a "don't know, can't do" position to a "do know, can do" position. In essence, anyone learning a new skill or attitude needs:

- Relevant training input
- Time to absorb the new information and practice the new skills
- Expert feedback on performance and the opportunity to discuss new ideas
- Freedom to try new things to see if they'll work

Creating a Training Strategy

The Learning Process

A meaningful training session will take learners through the four key stages of Kolb's Learning Cycle.

Stage 1: Doing it or finding out about it.

Just about everyone who works has, at one time or another, sat through a training event that was as relevant and as exciting as watching coffee get cold. From your point of view, as a manager, if you want your people to take on new skills and information, the training has to be informative, interesting, involving, and, perhaps most important of all, relevant to their jobs and their personal performance goals. What they learn in class has to be useful and practical for them at work. It has to make their job easier or help them to do their job better or help them to progress along their career path.

Trainers worth their salt will make sure that the content of the course is relevant and meaningful to the people who are attending. And, when designing relevant training, the first step is to define the learning goals.

A learning goal is a simple statement that describes what you want the learners to be able to do or know at the end of the training session. At the end of a training session on, say, selling techniques, learners should be able to accomplish a specific action. For example:

- Demonstrate effective listening skills.
- Use a range of open, closed, and probing questions.
- Explain an idea or concept using a time, place, or loop sequence.
- Prepare a brief report that describes the benefits of using clear communication with clients.

A key point to remember is that meaningful and measurable learning objectives should always start with an active verb, such as *list, describe, make, explain,* and *prepare.* Avoid words such as *understand* and *know* because it is difficult (if not impossible) to measure whether or not someone actually understands or knows something.

The number of learning goals you'll need for your course will depend on the topic, the amount of time you have available for training, and the level of the course. For example, senior managers may need to be able to do and know ten new things after the training (ten learning goals); junior people may need to be able to do and know four new things after the training (four learning goals).

Use Organizer Sheet 116, Learning Goals, when preparing measurable learning goals so that everyone can see what it is you want people to learn and be able to do at the end of the training course.

When you are clear about what you want someone to do or learn, then you can start designing the content of the course. For example, you want members of your staff to be able to demonstrate effective listening skills. If that's the learning objective, you must tell and show them what these skills are. You must explain why effective listening skills are important so they don't just use these

Organizer Sheet 116

Learning Goals

Use this Organizer at the start of the training design process when preparing the learning goals.

At the end of the course, participants should be able to:

Build: _____

Create: _____

Define: _____

Demonstrate: _____

Describe: _____

Design: _____

Explain: _____

Explore: _____

Identify: _____

List: _____

Make: _____

Prepare: _____

Use: _____

skills, but they know why they're using them and why they're important.

Organizer Sheet 117, Training Content and Delivery, will help you to design a training course that has the right mix of trainer input and learner activities.

Stage 2: Allowing time to absorb the new information and practice the new skills.

People don't just learn by watching and listening, they mostly learn by doing. Effective training gives people a chance to actually try out new skills with each other, in the training classroom. It's only through practical activities and exercises that people can find out for themselves what's involved. In class they have a chance to practice in a safe environment where failure is permitted and, hopefully, they can improve.

Stage 3: Providing expert feedback and giving people time to discuss what's been learned so far.

Everyone needs to know how they're doing. "Have I got it right? Am I successful?" These are key questions people need answers to—especially when they find themselves in a learning situation.

Everyone—from the CEO of the company downward—feels at a disadvantage when learning something new, precisely because it is new. In fact, the more competent and highly skilled people are in their regular, day-to-day work, the more likely they are to feel stressed and on edge when they are in a learning situation. This is because they're doing something new that they may not, at least in the beginning, be very good at. This situation is probably in direct contrast to their usual work performance and is likely to make them uncomfortable.

For everyone, feedback is important during the learning process. Trainers and facilitators have to be able to say, tactfully and clearly, what someone is doing right and what someone needs to change. People also need encouragement and recognition of their efforts. They need to hear things such as, "Yes, that's good, you're

Training Content and Delivery

Use this Organizer (one for each learning goal) when designing the course.

Learning Goal

At the end of the course, the participants should be able to: _____

_____

_____

_____

To achieve this learning goal, the participants need to be given the following information by the trainer (facts, figures, and ideas): _____

_____

_____

_____

To achieve this learning goal, the participants need to have the following opportunities to think about the information they've been given or to try out new skills through practical exercise(s):
☐ Group discussion ☐ Brainstorm exercise ☐ Working in pairs
☐ Working in trios   ☐ Working in groups of three or four people
☐ Working in teams

Ideas for practical exercises: _____

_____

_____

_____

_____

_____

_____

getting there." They don't need to hear, "You have to be able to do better than that!"

People also need to be able to ask questions because this is a good way for them to confirm that they really understand. They need to discuss their ideas and also hear what other people have learned. That way each person's learning, ideas, and insights can be shared throughout the group, so that everyone benefits.

Stage 4: Providing the opportunity to try new things.

Theory is fine, but real learning takes place when people get to use a hands-on approach. You can explain to someone how to give a business presentation, but if you really want to focus someone's mind on the process, don't ask them to talk about how they would make a presentation, ask them to actually stand up in front of a group of people and deliver. Such training exercises are hands-on, relevant, and challenging, and they provide wonderful learning opportunities. Use Organizer Sheet 118, Training Course Schedule, to plan every minute of your training day.

Good training offers something for everyone—discussion; brainstorming; and hands-on, high-energy, fun activities involving pairs, trios, groups, and teams. Participants should leave a course feeling energized and motivated to put the learning into practice at work.

Training Delivery Skills

A good trainer or facilitator empowers people and helps them to learn, while a poor trainer or facilitator does quite the opposite. So what's the difference?

Good trainers know their topic.

Key question: Do I know enough or do I need to learn more?

Good trainers and facilitators have an armory of knowledge and competencies that they bring to each training session and use, professionally and skillfully, to enable people to learn, develop, and

Training Course Schedule

Use this Organizer (one for each training day) when you are designing the program.

Date: _____

9:00 to 9:30   Topic: _____
☐ Trainer input   ☐ Discussion   ☐ Activity   ☐ Break   ☐
Details: _____

9:30 to 10:00   Topic: _____
☐ Trainer input   ☐ Discussion   ☐ Activity   ☐ Break   ☐
Details: _____

10:00 to 10:30   Topic: _____
☐ Trainer input   ☐ Discussion   ☐ Activity   ☐ Break   ☐
Details: _____

10:30 to 11:00   Topic: _____
☐ Trainer input   ☐ Discussion   ☐ Activity   ☐ Break   ☐
Details: _____

11:00 to 11:30   Topic: _____
☐ Trainer input   ☐ Discussion   ☐ Activity   ☐ Break   ☐
Details: _____

11:30 to 12:00   Topic: _____
☐ Trainer input   ☐ Discussion   ☐ Activity   ☐ Break   ☐
Details: _____

12:00 to 12:30   Topic: _____
☐ Trainer input   ☐ Discussion   ☐ Activity   ☐ Break   ☐
Details: _____

12:30 to 1:00   Topic: _____
☐ Trainer input   ☐ Discussion   ☐ Activity   ☐ Break   ☐
Details: _____

1:00 to 1:30   Topic: _____
☐ Trainer input   ☐ Discussion   ☐ Activity   ☐ Break   ☐
Details: _____

1:30 to 2:00   Topic: _____
☐ Trainer input   ☐ Discussion   ☐ Activity   ☐ Break   ☐
Details: _____

2:00 to 2:30   Topic: _____
☐ Trainer input   ☐ Discussion   ☐ Activity   ☐ Break   ☐
Details: _____

2:30 to 3:00   Topic: _____
☐ Trainer input   ☐ Discussion   ☐ Activity   ☐ Break   ☐
Details: _____

3:00 to 3:30   Topic: _____
☐ Trainer input   ☐ Discussion   ☐ Activity   ☐ Break   ☐
Details: _____

3:30 to 4:00   Topic: _____
☐ Trainer input   ☐ Discussion   ☐ Activity   ☐ Break   ☐
Details: _____

4:00 to 4:30   Topic: _____
☐ Trainer input   ☐ Discussion   ☐ Activity   ☐ Break   ☐
Details: _____

4:30 to 5:00   Topic: _____
☐ Trainer input   ☐ Discussion   ☐ Activity   ☐ Break   ☐
Details: _____

5:00 to 5:30   Topic: _____
☐ Trainer input   ☐ Discussion   ☐ Activity   ☐ Break   ☐
Details: _____

5:30 to 6:00   Topic: _____
☐ Trainer input   ☐ Discussion   ☐ Activity   ☐ Break   ☐
Details: _____

6:00 to 6:30   Topic: _____
☐ Trainer input   ☐ Discussion   ☐ Activity   ☐ Break   ☐
Details: _____

grow. People who are serious about training delivery make sure they have an in-depth knowledge of their topic. They know what they are talking about, and they are able to demonstrate that they can put the principles into practice. Good trainers walk the talk. For example, someone giving a leadership course should be able to demonstrate and model leadership skills while conducting the training.

Good trainers prepare in advance.

Key question: Have I planned every minute of the training session?

They know what they're going to do and how they're going to do it. The whole training session is carefully mapped out, and they always have additional activities or input ready, just in case they're needed. Course material (e.g., transparencies, flip charts, course notes) is sharply presented and easy to understand and follow. Good trainers know how to use electronic equipment (e.g., projectors, video cameras, and audiocassette recorders).

Use Organizer Sheet 119, Training Resources, to create a checklist of the resources you'll need for your training course.

Good trainers like their job.

Key question: Do I enjoy passing on skills and knowledge?

They are confident and enthusiastic, and they have great interpersonal skills. They explain clearly, listen well, ask the right questions, offer honest and thorough answers, provide constructive feedback, and include and encourage all the participants. They understand that people don't usually get it right the first time around, so they are unfailingly patient and courteous, keep their temper, and retain their sense of humor at all times, with everyone.

Organizer Sheet 119

Training Resources

Use this Organizer before you run the course.

For the training session on _____, when I expect there will
be _____ participants, I'll need to prepare and provide:

☐ Overhead projector	How many? _____
☐ Overhead screen	How many? _____
☐ Whiteboard	How many? _____
☐ Flip chart	How many? _____
☐ Flip chart easel	How many? _____
☐ Video camera	How many? _____
☐ Audiocassette recorder	How many? _____
☐ Videocassette recorder	How many? _____
☐ TV	How many? _____
☐ Laptop computer	How many? _____
☐ Name badges	How many? _____
☐ Felt marker pens	How many? _____
☐ Ballpoint pens	How many? _____
☐ Pencils	How many? _____
☐ Notepads	How many? _____
☐ Folders for course notes	How many? _____
☐ Packs of adhesive tape	How many? _____
☐ Drawing pins	How many? _____
☐ Paper clips	How many? _____
☐ Scissors	How many? _____
☐ Anything else?	What and how many? _____

☐ Handouts/course notes   How many? _____

Covering which topics? _____

_____

_____

_____

☐ **Overhead projector transparencies**   How many? _____

Covering which topics? _____

_____

_____

_____

☐ **Anything else?**   **What and how many?** _____

_____

_____

_____

Good trainers evaluate.

Key question: How can I measure whether or not they've learned?

At the end of each course, good trainers ask the participants to complete an evaluation questionnaire. This gives participants the opportunity to tell the trainer to what extent they found the training useful and enjoyable. Evaluation questionnaires also allow participants to make suggestions regarding if the course is to run again with a different group. Ask your participants, at the end of the course, to complete a copy of Organizer Sheet 120, Training Course Evaluation, because it will give you direct and immediate participant feedback on the training. Organizer Sheet 121, Trainer Assessment, can be completed on the spot if you need to observe and evaluate a trainer or facilitator during the training delivery session.

Training Course Evaluation

Use this Organizer (one for each participant) at the end of the training course.

Course title: _____

Date of the course: _____

Course objectives: _____

Course Content
☐ I found the course very informative and helpful.
☐ I found the course useful.
☐ I found some parts of the course useful, but some areas were not covered in sufficient depth. Specifically: _____

Additional comments on course content: _____

_____

Training Delivery
☐ I found the training delivery clear and interesting.
☐ I found the training delivery reasonably clear and easy to follow.
☐ I found the training delivery less than interesting and not easy to follow. Specifically: _____

Additional comments on training delivery: _____

_____

Training Schedule
☐ I found the schedule worked for me. The pace was good, and the mix of trainer input and practical activities was just right.
☐ I found the schedule contained too much trainer input and not enough practical activities.
☐ For me, there were too many activities and not enough trainer input.
☐ Overall, I was disappointed with the schedule. Specifically: ____

_____

Additional comments on the training schedule: _____

_____

Training Resources
☐ I found the visuals clear and easy to read. The handouts and information sheets look interesting, and I'll refer to them after the course.
☐ I had trouble reading and understanding the visuals.
☐ The handouts and information sheets look complex and hard to understand. I probably won't look at them again after the course.
☐ I was very disappointed with the visuals and the course information sheets. Specifically: _____

Additional comments on the training resources: _____

_____

Trainer Delivery
☐ I found the trainer enthusiastic and motivated, knowledgeable, and able to deliver information easily and confidently.
   Overall: ☐ Excellent   ☐ Very good
☐ I found the trainer able to deliver the training clearly and confidently.
   Overall: ☐ Good   ☐ Satisfactory
☐ I feel the trainer needs to improve interpersonal and communication skills.
   Overall: ☐ Disappointing
Specifically: _____

_____

Additional comments on trainer delivery: _____

_____

I would recommend this course to my colleagues because: _____

_____

I would not recommend this course to my colleagues because: ___

_____

I would like to see the following changes to the course: _____

_____

Trainer Assessment

Use this Organizer during the course, when assessing a trainer's job performance.

Interpersonal and Communication Skills

Ability to put people at their ease:
☐ Excellent ☐ Good ☐ Reasonable ☐ Poor

Ability to present information and provide clear and logical explanations:
☐ Excellent ☐ Good ☐ Reasonable ☐ Poor

Ability to ask the right kinds of questions:
☐ Excellent ☐ Good ☐ Reasonable ☐ Poor

Ability to inspire confidence:
☐ Excellent ☐ Good ☐ Reasonable ☐ Poor

Ability to generate interest and enthusiasm in the topic:
☐ Excellent ☐ Good ☐ Reasonable ☐ Poor

Ability to involve everyone in the learning process:
☐ Excellent ☐ Good ☐ Reasonable ☐ Poor

Ability to remain calm, patient, and good-humored:
☐ Excellent ☐ Good ☐ Reasonable ☐ Poor

Training Design Skills

Information input:
☐ Very interesting and relevant ☐ Interesting and relevant
☐ Not interesting and not relevant
Specific comments: _____

_____

Choice of exercises and activities:
☐ Very appropriate and relevant ☐ Appropriate and relevant
☐ Not appropriate and not relevant
Specific comments: _____

_____

Overall course design:
☐ Very appropriate and relevant ☐ Appropriate and relevant
☐ Not appropriate and not relevant
Specific comments: _____

_____

Use of Equipment and Resources

Ability to use visual and audio equipment:
☐ Excellent ☐ Good ☐ Reasonable ☐ Poor

Ability to prepare interesting, meaningful, attractive, and informative visuals:
☐ Excellent ☐ Good ☐ Reasonable ☐ Poor

Ability to prepare clear, logical, well-structured, and informative handouts:
☐ Excellent ☐ Good ☐ Reasonable ☐ Poor

Overall Design and Presentation Skills

☐ The course was well designed and clearly presented. Participants should be able to find a practical use for much of the course content.
☐ The course was not very well designed or clearly presented. Participants are likely to feel that much of the information and many of the activities were neither interesting nor particularly relevant.
☐ The course was badly designed and presented. Participants are likely to feel that their time has been wasted.

Specific comments:

_____

_____

_____

_____

_____

Training Action Checklist

☐ Decide what it is you want your people to be able to do or know after the training is completed.

☐ Write your learning goals, making sure that each learning goal starts with an action verb. For example: *explain, describe, create, prepare, produce, design.*

☐ In order for participants to achieve the learning objectives, you must decide:
   1. What to tell the participants (trainer's input)
   2. What the participants need to try out for themselves (activities and exercises)

☐ Prepare the visuals and course notes. Keep the information clear and concise. If there's too much to read, people will ignore the notes once the course is over.

☐ Work out your course schedule. Aim for variety and interest. Avoid too much lecturing or "chalk and talk." Get people involved in doing things. Allow time for food and comfort breaks.

☐ During the training, provide praise, encouragement, and constant feedback on performance.

☐ Keep your temper and your patience with all participants— regardless of the circumstances!

Troubleshooting and Crisis Management

Any manager who believes "that kind of thing couldn't happen here" is seriously mistaken, if not totally deluded. Unexpected crises and disasters occur all the time in business. The unwary manager can be zapped by the elements (e.g., fires, floods, hurricanes, typhoons, and earthquakes), by people (e.g., insider dealing, computer sabotage, fraud, industrial espionage, sleaze), and by politics (e.g., the national economy, legislation, terrorist groups), to name just a few.

In some organizations, those that haven't prepared in advance, a crisis of any kind can spark off a frenzied response. Managers can be seen keeping their heads down and refusing to communicate; or they speak to the media and say the wrong thing; or two managers offer conflicting opinions within a half-hour of each other. The people involved and their organizations lose credibility and stakeholder confidence.

The solution is to anticipate and prepare in advance. That way everyone in the business can be reading from the same page of the book. Managers will be presenting a united front, and, in most cases, public confidence can be maintained to a reasonable degree.

Creating a Strategy for Troubleshooting and Crisis Management

Gather Your Team

Key question: Who can handle risk assessment and damage limitation?

Draw together a team of people with a variety of skills and qualities that will enable them to respond quickly and effectively if faced with a crisis situation. You need people with authority and presence who know your organization and the sector in which it operates. Within the team, you need a range of different abilities—good organizational and communication skills; the ability to quickly secure funding and resources; a wide network of contacts within your sector and, preferably, within the media too. You need people on the team who are skilled problem solvers and who can make tough decisions. Everyone must be able to work together as a team.

Try to take the team somewhere special for a long weekend or a short week. Not only will this be a great team-building exercise, it will also give you the time you need to do some preparatory work.

Carry Out a Risk Assessment

Key question: What could go wrong?

Your first task, as a team, is to generate a specific list of worst-case scenarios. Your list will depend, to some extent, on the nature of your business. For example, if you process chemicals, you may want to consider the risk of environmental pollution; if you run a hospital, you may want to consider the risk of the staff contaminating patients with the AIDS virus. Use Organizer Sheet 122, Troubleshooting and Crisis Management Risk Assessment, to think through the possible risks your organization could face in the future.

355

Troubleshooting and Crisis Management
Risk Assessment

Use this Organizer before disaster strikes.

Product failure likely to cause danger or distress to our customers:
☐ Highly likely   ☐ Possible   ☐ Remote possibility
Our systems for checking and preventing this occurrence are:
☐ Excellent   ☐ Good   ☐ Fair   ☐ Must be improved

Service disruption likely to cause danger or distress to our customers:
☐ Highly likely   ☐ Possible   ☐ Remote possibility
Our systems for checking and preventing this occurrence are:
☐ Excellent   ☐ Good   ☐ Fair   ☐ Must be improved

Environmental issues likely to cause damage to the environment (e.g., explosion, chemical or toxic leak, oil spill, water contamination):
☐ Highly likely   ☐ Possible   ☐ Remote possibility
Our systems for checking and preventing this occurrence are:
☐ Excellent   ☐ Good   ☐ Fair   ☐ Must be improved

Industrial sabotage (e.g., installation of computer virus; theft of ideas, research, or product plans; leakage of sensitive information to competitors or the media):
☐ Highly likely   ☐ Possible   ☐ Remote possibility
Our systems for checking and preventing this occurrence are:
☐ Excellent   ☐ Good   ☐ Fair   ☐ Must be improved

Insider dealing, fraud, or embezzlement:
☐ Highly likely   ☐ Possible   ☐ Remote possibility
Our systems for checking and preventing this occurrence are:
☐ Excellent   ☐ Good   ☐ Fair   ☐ Must be improved

International or political issues:
☐ Highly likely ☐ Possible ☐ Remote possibility
Our systems for checking and preventing this occurrence are:
☐ Excellent ☐ Good ☐ Fair ☐ Must be improved

Indiscretions in business or personal dealings by people at senior level in the organization:
☐ Highly likely ☐ Possible ☐ Remote possibility
Our systems for checking and preventing this occurrence are:
☐ Excellent ☐ Good ☐ Fair ☐ Must be improved

Health and safety issues:
☐ Highly likely ☐ Possible ☐ Remote possibility
Our systems for checking and preventing this occurrence are:
☐ Excellent ☐ Good ☐ Fair ☐ Must be improved

Financial issues:
☐ Highly likely ☐ Possible ☐ Remote possibility
Our systems for checking and preventing this occurrence are:
☐ Excellent ☐ Good ☐ Fair ☐ Must be improved

Labor relations issues:
☐ Highly likely ☐ Possible ☐ Remote possibility
Our systems for checking and preventing this occurrence are:
☐ Excellent ☐ Good ☐ Fair ☐ Must be improved

Even though some of the suggestions the team generates may cause your hair to stand on end, dismiss nothing. Any worst-case scenario is a possibility, and if it's happened to someone else, it could also happen to you.

Once you and your team have generated some ideas, you can begin to divide the possibilities into different categories—for example, under headings such as natural disasters, acts of terrorism, human error.

Even though most of the items on your list will never happen, you need to be realistic. For each potential crisis, the team needs to generate ideas about:

- What we can do now to prevent this situation from ever happening
- What we can do in the future if, despite our best efforts, it does happen

Plan for the Future and Expect the Worst

What can we do now?

Key question: Can we take any preventative action?

Clearly, there isn't much you can do to prevent natural disasters, but there's much that can be done to prevent potential crises like fraud or insider dealing or environmental pollution. Now is the time to look at the processes and procedures already in place within your organization and to start thinking about positive action that can be taken to prevent such crises from occurring in the future.

What can we do in the future?

Key question: How will we respond?

No matter how smart or forward-thinking you might be, things happen. Major problems can result if your organization hits the headlines in a big way and you are totally unprepared. If, however, you have an outline plan plus a team of people who know and understand their role in a crisis situation, there's a good chance that you and your organization will be able to ride out the storm.

For each potential crisis you've identified, you need to create a plan of action so that, if this scenario actually happens, you know what to do and what to say. Bear in mind that your aim at all times is damage control.

You also need to delegate specific roles and responsibilities to each team member—in-house communication, external communication, staff welfare, security, administration, finance, and resources. Use Organizer Sheet 123, Team Roles and Responsibilities, to identify the key players you need to have on your risk assessment and crisis management team.

It's important that your plans be as flexible as possible because you may have to cope with details that you could never have imagined, even in your wildest dreams.

Try a Run-Through

Key question: Will what we have in mind work in practice?

With the team, run through one of the plans you've created. Identify the snags and glitches and any gray areas where people are having trouble working together or carrying out their agreed-upon roles. You need to iron out the potential difficulties now, not later, when it's for real.

Keep the Team Together

Key question: How do I maintain interest and momentum?

It's important that the team retains its sense of identity, so draw everyone in for regular meetings. A key activity when you meet is to analyze how other organizations have handled their crises. If you use other people's dramas and disasters as a learning tool for your organization, you'll quickly know which strategies to avoid and which strategies get results. Learning from other people's mistakes helps you to manage your own crises (if and when they occur) coolly, calmly, and with the utmost professionalism. Organizer Sheet 124, Scenario Planning, will help you to identify likely scenarios and to determine what your preferred message ought to be for presentation to the outside world. (See Public Relations.)

Team Roles and Responsibilities

Use this Organizer before you finalize the team.

Front Person: Network and communicate with the media and other external organizations. Disseminate our preferred message to the outside world.
Best person for this role: ——————————————————————.

In-House Spokesperson: Communicate internally and disseminate our preferred message to everyone within the organization.
Best person for this role: ——————————————————————.

Facilitator and Organizer: Make practical arrangements. Secure resources and funding. Organize people and generally get things done.
Best person for this role: ——————————————————————.

Creative Genius: Find solutions to insoluble problems and create workable plans. Do the impossible.
Best person for this role: ——————————————————————.

Controller: Set up and monitor finances, systems, and procedures. Make sure that everything goes according to plan.
Best person for this role: ——————————————————————.

Cheerleader: Supporter, motivator, and pathfinder able to network and use important connections.
Best person for this role: ——————————————————————.

Scenario Planning

Use this Organizer before your crisis management plans are finalized.

Natural Disaster
Priority tasks: _____

_____

_____

Financial Disaster
Priority tasks: _____

_____

_____

Product or Service Failure Disaster
Priority tasks: _____

_____

_____

Indiscretions in Personal or Business Dealings Disaster
Priority tasks: _____

_____

_____

Health and Safety Disaster
Priority tasks: _____

_____

_____

Troubleshooting and Crisis Management Action Checklist

- ☐ Gather together a team of experienced, coolheaded people who have the authority to make things happen.
- ☐ Carry out a risk assessment; look for the loopholes in systems and procedures and try to anticipate everything—from those things that you may reasonably expect to go wrong to those things that seem to verge on the impossible.
- ☐ For each item on your risk assessment list, prepare an outline plan of how you and your team would respond if this likely risk turned into a reality. Rehearse your plans so that everyone on the team can run through their roles and responsibilities and you can identify any flaws.
- ☐ Do whatever it takes to ensure that, in a crisis, everyone in the organization presents a united front in public.
- ☐ Watch how other people in other organizations deal with disasters, and learn from their mistakes.
- ☐ Take nothing for granted, and don't ever assume you've thought of everything.
- ☐ Keep the team together, motivated, and up-to-date.

Index

365